TEXT AND PERFORMANCE IN CONTEMPORARY BRITISH THEATRE

Text and Performance in Contemporary British Theatre interrogates the paradoxical nature of theatre texts, which have been understood both as separate literary objects in their own right and as material for performance.

Drawing on analysis of contemporary practitioners who are working creatively with text, the book re-examines the relationship between text and performance within the specific context of British theatre. The chapters discuss a wide range of theatre-makers creating work in the United Kingdom from the 1990s onwards, from playwrights like Tim Crouch and Jasmine Lee-Jones to companies including Action Hero and RashDash. In doing so, the book addresses issues such as theatrical authorship, artistic intention, and the apparent incompleteness of plays as both written and performed phenomena. *Text and Performance in Contemporary British Theatre* also explores the implications of changing technologies of page and stage, analysing the impact of recent developments in theatre-making, editing, and publishing on the status of the theatre text.

Written for scholars, students, and practitioners alike, *Text and Performance in Contemporary British Theatre* provides an original perspective on one of the most enduring problems to occupy theatre practice and scholarship.

Dr Catherine Love is a theatre academic and arts journalist. She is currently an Honorary Research Fellow at the University of Manchester. She has previously published journal articles and book chapters on the work of theatre-makers including Katie Mitchell, Michael Pinchbeck, Simon Stephens, and Elevator Repair Service, and she is the author of *Tim Crouch's An Oak Tree*. She also reviews theatre across the North of England for the *Guardian*.

TEXT AND PERFORMANCE IN CONTEMPORARY BRITISH THEATRE

Catherine Love

LONDON AND NEW YORK

Designed cover image: Hispanolistic/Getty Images

First published 2023
by Routledge
4 Park Square, Milton Park, Abingdon, Oxon OX14 4RN

and by Routledge
605 Third Avenue, New York, NY 10158

Routledge is an imprint of the Taylor & Francis Group, an informa business

© 2023 Catherine Love

The right of Catherine Love to be identified as author of this work has been asserted in accordance with sections 77 and 78 of the Copyright, Designs and Patents Act 1988.

All rights reserved. No part of this book may be reprinted or reproduced or utilised in any form or by any electronic, mechanical, or other means, now known or hereafter invented, including photocopying and recording, or in any information storage or retrieval system, without permission in writing from the publishers.

Trademark notice: Product or corporate names may be trademarks or registered trademarks, and are used only for identification and explanation without intent to infringe.

British Library Cataloguing-in-Publication Data
A catalogue record for this book is available from the British Library

ISBN: 978-0-367-64891-6 (hbk)
ISBN: 978-0-367-64864-0 (pbk)
ISBN: 978-1-003-12681-2 (ebk)

DOI: 10.4324/9781003126812

Typeset in Bembo
by MPS Limited, Dehradun

CONTENTS

Acknowledgements   *vii*

Introduction   1
   Contemporary experiments with text 3
   Postdramatic theatre and text 8
   (Re)theorising text and performance 11
   Situating this study 14
   The shape of the book 20

1   The problem of the theatre text   22
   Text as problem 23
   A brief history of text and performance 29
   Playwriting and performance in the post-war period 36
   'Text-based' versus 'non-text-based' 42
   Conclusion 49

2   Dramaturgical innovations and evasions of authority: authorship and intention   53
   The death – and rebirth – of the author 54
   Staging the writer 62
   Making the text visible 69
   Playwrights abdicating authority 74
   Playing with unstageability 77
   Conclusion 83

3 Contemporary approaches to classic texts: supplementation and iterability 86
   Staging classic texts 87
   Reinventing the canon 92
   The author's return and the absent 'work' 98
   After Chekhov 106
   Conclusion 110

4 On the page: changing technologies of editing and publication 114
   Print and performance 116
   Texts as material 122
   Innovating on the page 128
   Design or documentation? 137
   Plays in the digital space 142
   Conclusion 147

Bibliography *152*
Index *169*

ACKNOWLEDGEMENTS

The ideas in this book have been on a long journey, with many people who have helped along the way.

The very first seeds of this project were planted during my postgraduate studies. I will be forever grateful to the brilliant academics in the Department of Drama at Queen Mary, who inspired a curiosity and enthusiasm for the field during my MA that has stayed with me in the years since. Huge thanks to my PhD supervisor Dan Rebellato, whose feedback has pushed and strengthened my thinking at every step, and to my advisors Elaine McGirr and David Overend. I also want to thank the rest of the team at Royal Holloway who supported me throughout my doctoral studies, as well as my PhD examiners, Liz Tomlin and Duška Radosavljević, whose insightful thoughts on my thesis helped to propel these ideas into new territory.

Thank you to all the theatre-makers who have inspired the analysis in these pages, many of whom have been generous with their time and thoughts over the years. I'm also grateful to the publications that have offered me a platform to write about this work and to all the other critics and bloggers who have expanded my mind and made me a better writer. Thanks, as well, to Michael Pinchbeck, who invited me to share some of my ideas about text and performance in a chapter in *Acts of Dramaturgy* (2020).

I want to thank everyone who has helped to make this book a reality. Thanks to Jenny Hughes and Maggie Gale, whose rigorous feedback was invaluable in shaping the book proposal. Thank you to Ben Piggott and all the team at Routledge for their support at every stage of this process. And thank you to the reviewers of the proposal and the draft manuscript, whose input has helped me to sharpen my ideas.

There are many other people who have influenced and supported this work – too many to name individually. Thanks to everyone who offered feedback on work-in-progress at various conferences. I'm especially grateful to the community at TaPRA, which has nourished my thinking over the years. And a big thank you to wonderful current and former colleagues and students at the University of Manchester and the University of York, who continue to push and inspire me.

Finally, thank you to the friends and family who have been there all the way, marking the milestones, sympathising with the struggles, and accompanying me on my many evenings at the theatre. The last and biggest thanks of all go to my husband Mark, for the unfailing love, belief, and support that has kept this project – and me – afloat.

INTRODUCTION

At the Almeida Theatre in London, there's much excitement about a new version of *The Oresteia*. Before seeing it for myself, I keep hearing about how radically director and adaptor Robert Icke has rewritten this classic. It's one of three high-profile productions of *The Oresteia* in 2015, alongside Rory Mullarkey's new translation at Shakespeare's Globe and a revival of Ted Hughes' version directed by Blanche McIntyre at HOME in Manchester. All three productions are versions of versions, each far removed from the ancient dramatic trilogy composed by Aeschylus, performed for an Athenian audience who 'had no basis for conceptualizing the text as something separable from performance' (Wiles 2000: 167), and preserved over the centuries via many different scribes, editors, and scholars. In this context, it seems obvious that there can be no such thing as a 'faithful' *Oresteia*. And yet reviews of Icke's version of this cycle of plays frequently stress its departure from Aeschylus' original.[1] His production is quickly absorbed into a familiar rhetoric of 'radical' versions of the classics, which are ultimately measured – whether admiringly or damningly – in terms of the perceived distance between the seemingly stable and historical dramatic work and the updated performance. Never mind that any English-language production of Greek tragedy is always using a translated script; productions like Icke's are still frequently seen through the lens of fidelity to or transgression of the classic text.

In Made in China's show *Tonight I'm Gonna Be the New Me*, performed in London later that same year, there's an altogether different tension between text and performance. On stage, Jess Latowicki performs for us, while her fellow company member and real-life partner Tim Cowbury scripts her from the shadows. Or, at least, this is what appears to be going on. The reality is much more complicated, as the show constantly questions who has authorship and agency in this performance. That also extends to the audience. At one point, Latowicki asks a spectator 'do you ever get the feeling that someone is putting words in your

DOI: 10.4324/9781003126812-1

mouth?' and quickly instructs them 'say yes' before they have an opportunity to answer.[2] As theatre-maker and writer Andy Field puts it, Made in China's work does not 'so much synthesize text and performance as set them at war with one another' (2020: 65). This confrontation between text and performance is at the root of the company's existence, born as it was out of a meeting at Goldsmiths, University of London between one student on a playwriting course (Cowbury) and another studying performance (Latowicki). Their shows often prod at the power of author and text, while simultaneously undercutting this power with an emphasis on the unpredictability of live performance.

On the surface, these two shows have little in common beyond the fact that I saw them both within the space of a few months in 2015. But what they reveal in different ways is the continued difficulty that haunts attempts to conceptualise the relationship between text and performance. The popular discourse surrounding Icke's *Oresteia* and other contemporary versions of the classics illustrates a belief in the text as something solid and enduring, even when it has been passed down in countless different forms over hundreds or even thousands of years. The text is viewed as the reliable document, as opposed to the fickle ephemerality of performance. A show like *Tonight I'm Gonna Be the New Me*, meanwhile, is characteristic of a generation of theatre-makers questioning the centrality of text and problematising the supposedly clean divide between ways of working centred around page and stage. Similarly to other contemporary companies including Action Hero, RashDash, and Sh!t Theatre, Made in China works with written text as one material among many in its process, eschewing the models of both the pre-written, solo-authored play, and the collectively devised performance. Both the company's resistance to a perceived hierarchy of text over performance and the continued uncertainty that pervades the relationship between script and staging filter through in the form and content of its work. Its shows typically dramatise concerns around authorship and power, whether through the 'scripting' of Latowicki in *Tonight I'm Gonna Be the New Me* or through the all-powerful voiceover that put competing performers through their paces in the company's earlier show *Gym Party* (2013).

These are just two moments of many I might have chosen from my experiences as an audience member in the second decade of the 21st century. During these years, in which I was frequently watching and writing about theatre across the United Kingdom in my roles as a reviewer and a scholar, I was regularly struck by the tricky dynamic between text and performance. Many British theatre-makers, institutions, and critics were at this time engaged in a specious battle between so-called 'text-based' and 'non-text-based' theatre, with the script occupying a central place in fraught distinctions between different theatre-making practices. Directorial experiments that I often found thrilling were regularly criticised by mainstream reviewers for disregarding the letter of the playtext and elevating the director to the maligned position of 'auteur'. Yet all the while, increasing numbers of theatre-makers were teasing away at the role of text and authorship in their shows, staging fascinating power struggles between author and performer (who were sometimes one and the same person), or writing texts that challenged popular understandings of what a play could be. This was also a time of collaborations across the trenches, with more and more projects situating themselves in the no man's land between the 'text-based' and 'non-text-based' camps. There are various, interconnected reasons for these antagonisms and experiments, including structures of funding, development, training, and criticism. But at their root, I suggest, is a persistent and profound uneasiness about the nature and role of the theatre text.

This book explores that uneasiness, with the aim of re-examining the relationship between text and performance. As I will discuss, dominant understandings of text and performance in mainstream British theatre have tended to see the script as the authoritative instigating force for theatrical production. I contend that this underestimates both texts and performances and simplifies the complex relationship that they share. I am interested in teasing out the nuances of this relationship and exploring the many questions that it raises. To what extent can a text ever determine performance? What can and cannot be specified on the page? What is the role of authorial intention in theatre-making processes? How far can a production 'depart from the text' while still being considered a version of that play? How do constantly evolving stage conventions relate to the changing technologies of the printed (and, more recently, digital) page?

In considering these questions and others, *Text and Performance in Contemporary British Theatre* documents and analyses creative work with text among British theatre companies and writers over the last three decades. It explores some of the many lives of the text in contemporary British theatre, from revivals of Shakespeare to devised performances to dramaturgically innovative new plays, drawing on the perspectives and practices of a range of theatre-makers and critics. Building upon the important work of other scholars, my analysis challenges many of the assumptions about text that have historically shaped British theatre practices, institutions, and discourses. I consider the peculiar duality of the playtext and contextualise this within changing conditions of production and publication, as well as accounting for the function of text in theatre-making processes that do not begin with words on the page. This project responds to both a proliferation of performance practices that are experimenting with text(s) and a growing critical interest in the relationship between text and performance during the period under investigation, which I outline below. The book extends this work by offering a sustained engagement with the relationship between text and performance in the specific context of contemporary British theatre-making practices.

Contemporary experiments with text

As I go on to discuss in greater detail in Chapter 1, British theatre at the turn of the 21st century was often characterised according to the presence or absence of a solo-authored, pre-written playtext. At this time, industry rhetoric tended to divide theatre-makers into one of two categories: 'text-based' and 'non-text-based'. The reality, however, is much more complicated. Over the three decades that form the focus of this book, the relationship between text and performance has itself been a site of frequent experimentation. Writers and other theatre-makers have collaborated in a number of different ways; playwrights have used various tactics to undermine their assumed authority within their own texts; directors have tested how far it is possible to intervene creatively in a play; immersive and interactive theatre-makers have extended elements of authorship to audience-participants; and playwrights, theatre companies and solo performers alike have played with the layout of the published playtext. Numerous examples of such experiments, and others, will be explored in later chapters of the book. In this context of creative innovation and investigation, many theatrical orthodoxies – including the sharp separation of text from performance and the implicit hierarchy of the former over the latter – have come under pressure.

Existing scholarship, meanwhile, has both perpetuated and contested the division of British theatre-making practices on the basis of their perceived relationship to text. Mirroring the schism in the industry, many early 21st-century analyses of contemporary British theatre fall into one of two camps: studies of playwrights and plays, such as Vicky Angelaki's edited collection *Contemporary British Theatre: Breaking New Ground* (2013), the Methuen Drama *Modern British Playwriting* series (2012–2013), and Martin Middeke, Peter Paul Schnierer, and Aleks Sierz's *The Methuen Guide to Contemporary British Playwrights* (2011); and studies of devising and ensemble practices, prominent examples including *Devising Performance: A Critical History* (2006) by Deirdre Heddon and Jane Milling, *Making Contemporary Theatre* (2010) by Jen Harvie and Andy Lavender, *Devising in Process* (2010) by Alex Mermikides and Jackie Smart, and *Making a Performance: Devising Histories and Contemporary Practices* (2007) by Emma Govan, Helen Nicholson, and Katie Normington. While several of these books acknowledge the porosity between so-called 'text-based' and 'non-text-based' practices, they nonetheless direct critical attention towards one category or the other, thus reinforcing the notion of a binarised British theatre sector.

Alongside these studies, though, there have been a number of challenges to the 'text-based'/'non-text-based' divide in contemporary British theatre. Among the most influential of these is Duška Radosavljević's use of the term 'theatre-making' in her book of the same name. This term, which Radosavljević defines as 'a deprofessionalized, collaborative activity that takes an active and integrated intellectual and embodied approach to the notion of theatre authorship (whether or not it is based on text)' (2013a: ix), helpfully dissolves any idea of hierarchy between text and performance or any division between 'text-based' and 'non-text-based' practices. Throughout her book, the broad umbrella term of 'theatre-making' is applied to developments in several seemingly distinct theatrical processes – the staging of classic texts, devising and adaptation, new writing, verbatim theatre, and what Radosavljević dubs 'relational works' – in order to demonstrate an increasing dispersal of theatrical authorship in the 21st century. For Radosavljević, 'theatre-making anticipates an all-inclusive collaborative process' (23) which challenges previous divisions of theatrical labour and also includes the audience as co-creators.

Theatre-Making is one of the few existing volumes that brings together the work of playwrights and of theatre-makers working with text in a range of different ways, with an eclecticism of case studies that this book seeks to emulate. I also share Radosavljević's desire to move beyond binaries of text-based versus devised theatre and theatre versus performance, and I often use the helpful vocabulary of 'theatre-making' and 'theatre-makers' as inclusive, catch-all terms. But whereas Radosavljević offers a fascinating and expansive consideration of different European and Anglo-American theatrical genealogies, breaking down old divisions between East and West, I am interested in taking a more detailed look at British theatre culture and its specific attitudes towards text and performance. Moreover, while Radosavljević's book similarly re-examines the relationship between text and performance, she suggests that there has been a 'major overhaul' (90) of this relationship in the 21st century, largely driven by ensemble ways of working. Although I agree that this period has seen a lively and intensified concern with texts and performances, I am arguing that recent developments are underpinned by a set of misconceptions about the theatre text that stretch back much further, and that contemporary experiments have exposed rather than radically transformed the ways in which texts and performances interact.

The binarised theatre landscape to which Radosavljević and I are both responding is compellingly outlined by Jacqueline Bolton in her PhD thesis *Demarcating Dramaturgy*. While Bolton's principal focus is the role of the dramaturg in English and German theatre cultures, she also persuasively identifies what she calls a 'two cultures' divide in English theatre between 'text-based' and 'non-text-based' practices, which can be seen across arts subsidy, cultural policy, and the development of new work. My work touches on, and in some cases develops, these areas of investigation. In Chapter 1, for example, I examine in more detail some of the ways in which Arts Council funding has contributed to a dichotomised approach to different theatre-making practices. *Text and Performance in Contemporary British Theatre* also builds upon Bolton's arguments for 'more inclusive notions of "text"' and 'more nuanced approaches to authorship' (2011: 91), which I agree are necessary to move past a reductive 'text-based'/'non-text-based' binary. Bolton proposes dramaturgy as a 'bridge' between text and performance that might illuminate connections between the 'two cultures' of English – and, I would suggest more broadly, British – theatre-making. While I find this suggestion promising, my focus is not on any one role or set of practices within the theatre-making process. Instead, my investigation continues to pursue Bolton's and Radosavljević's interrogations of theatrical authorship through an extended engagement with ideas of authoring and intention in Chapter 2. I also advance the idea of a more inclusive definition of the theatre text within the under-explored contexts of editing and publishing in Chapter 4.

One of the factors that Bolton identifies as underpinning the division of 'text-based' from 'non-text-based' work is the critical discourse of poststructuralism. The poststructuralist shift of authority away from the author (which I explore further in Chapter 2) has often been taken rather literally and used to reject the playwright as author-god, while critiques of representation have been directed at the mimetic fictional worlds of dramatic texts. Liz Tomlin has interrogated this line of thinking in *Acts and Apparitions*, in which she rejects a binary between the 'radical, oppositional narrative of deconstruction' typically associated with 'non-text-based' practices and the 'reactionary, traditional narrative of logocentrism' that has been applied to the dramatic playtext (2013: 8). Tomlin breaks down this simplistic alignment of form and ideology by rigorously revisiting the post-structuralist theory on which it is based, arguing that *no* theatre can fully escape the bind of representation. She proposes instead that 'the poststructuralist challenge to logocentrism might best be identified in practice that explores ways of exposing and acknowledging its own representational structures and narratives' (76) – regardless of whether that practice involves a pre-written playtext. I similarly believe that it is important to move beyond this division, which serves to obscure both the genuine potential for ideological critique contained within individual pieces of theatre and the actual ways in which text and performance interrelate in any given work. Working from this foundation, my concern is less with the political analysis of performance that interests Tomlin – though there are moments in the book where I briefly address the political implications of particular pieces – and more with other ways in which understandings of the relationship between text and performance might be expanded and nuanced.

In addition to the works discussed above, there is a growing body of literature that offers an expanded view of the writer's role within theatre-making practices. Sarah Sigal's *Writing in Collaborative Theatre-Making* (2017), for example, investigates the previously under-explored role of the writer and the text in collaborative processes, recognising how playwriting has functioned within practices too often misleadingly labelled 'non-text-based'. Relatedly, Mark Smith's PhD thesis *Processes and Rhetorics of Writing in Contemporary British Devising* (2013) examines the intersection of writing and devising in the practices of Frantic Assembly and Forced Entertainment, while Helen Freshwater (2007) brings similar critical attention to bear on text, authorship, and authority in the work of Complicite. The intention to bring theatre texts into dialogue with devising and physical theatre practices likewise informs Dymphna Callery's *The Active Text* (2015), which offers a practical handbook for applying physical theatre techniques to playtexts. Processes of creating text for performance that extend beyond conventional playwriting frameworks, meanwhile, have been explored at length by John Freeman in *New Performance/New Writing* (2007; 2016), which examines practices such as immersive theatre, body art, autoethnography and applied drama – though Freeman continues to distinguish these practices in contrast to dramatic plays, thereby retaining aspects of the 'text-based'/'non-text-based' binary in a different guise. Furthermore, the critical discussion that has developed around theatre-makers such as Tim Crouch – whose work I discuss in Chapters 2 and 4 – has complicated any distinction between playwrights and devisers.[3] Crouch's shows exist as published playtexts that bear his name as the author, yet these pieces are created in close collaboration with other theatre-makers and usually feature Crouch as performer and co-director, as well as frequently leaving gaps for audience involvement. All these interventions usefully complicate the idea that playwriting and devising practices are cleanly divorced from one another, beginning to build a more complex picture of the various ways in which British theatre-makers work with text. The following chapters extend this work and build more connections between practices that have often been examined separately, bringing collaborative experiments with text into dialogue with innovations in solo-authored playtexts.

Finally, in response to some of the experiments with text discussed above, there have been important attempts to widen and nuance the conversation about text and performance within academic and professional institutions. Two efforts worth mentioning here are Cathy Turner's 'Writing Space' research project and Stephen Bottoms' 'Performing Literatures' conference and special journal edition. 'Writing Space' intended to 'nurture theatre and performance writing across an expanded field' (Turner 2008: 1) by bringing together practitioners from a range of different artistic backgrounds – including playwriting, live art, and physical theatre – to self-reflexively consider their writing practices outside the usual structures of writer development. This project offered a model for developing texts and writers without the assumption of a solo-authored dramatic playtext as the central outcome of the writing process and the authoritative instigating document for performance, with implications for both development processes within the theatre industry and approaches to training in the academy. Meanwhile, 'Performing Literatures' responded to the disciplinary separation of theatre and performance from literature and the simultaneous persistence of text in various theatre-making practices, inviting a reconsideration of the role of text in relation to performance. As Bottoms reflects in his introduction to the journal edition that emerged from the conference (2009a), the responses to his call for papers were skewed away from playtexts, suggesting an anti-text bias within the discipline (to which I return in Chapter 1). Both the conference and the resulting journal articles propose a rethink of how theatre scholars define texts and understand their relationship to performance – an ongoing project in which this book is firmly situated.

Responding to these various contexts, *Text and Performance in Contemporary British Theatre* further explores the porous boundaries between creative practices that have previously been siloed by both critics and theatre institutions. The book brings together various examples of British theatre-making from over the last three decades that have playfully expanded understandings of the theatre text, regardless of whether these experiments have been instigated by playwrights, directors, performance artists, or collectives. I build upon important work that has analysed and begun to break down the 'text-based'/'non-text-based' binary, focusing specifically on the particularities of the contemporary British theatre landscape. My analysis answers calls from other scholars for renewed understandings of the theatre text and theatrical authorship, extending this into previously neglected areas such as the physical object of the printed playtext and its routes to publication.

Postdramatic theatre and text

Since the early 21st century, many of the experiments mentioned above have been analysed under the rubric of postdramatic theatre. Discussing the sorts of dramaturgically innovative plays that I explore in later chapters, David Barnett asserts that since the 1990s 'texts written for the theatre have been displaying qualities that have made their association with "drama" increasingly difficult to sustain' (2008: 14), an observation that is also made by Karen Jürs-Munby (2006) and Małgorzata Sugiera (2004). These apparent challenges to dramatic principles across a wide range of contemporary theatre-making have led such scholars to align this work with what Hans-Thies Lehmann has dubbed postdramatic theatre: a theatre after or beyond drama. While I have some scepticism about the postdramatic as a category, which I expand upon below, Lehmann's framework has proved hugely influential and occupies an important place in contemporary critical discourse around text and performance. Tomlin (2013), for example, observes how Lehmann's widely known terminology has resulted in a tendency to define theatre practice as either dramatic or postdramatic, mapping onto the existing binary between 'text-based' and 'non-text-based', while Bottoms (2009a) notes the significance of Lehmann as a frame of reference for many of the papers given at the 'Performing Literatures' conference. Here, then, I want to address this intellectual context and situate my own critical interventions in relation to it.

In *Postdramatic Theatre*, Lehmann makes the case that a range of late-20th-century Western theatre has moved beyond the dramatic paradigm and is therefore better described as 'postdramatic'. Dramatic theatre, according to Lehmann, is defined by its reference to a whole, coherent world; dramatic theatre 'proclaims wholeness as the model of the real' (2006: 22). In postdramatic theatre, by contrast, this wholeness is abandoned in favour instead of multiple, clashing theatrical signs, to which spectators are free to react in idiosyncratic ways. Before going on to unpack some of Lehmann's ideas, it's important to note that his observations of what he refers to as the 'new theatre' of the late 20th century are based upon his specific perspective as a German theatregoer. Most of his examples are drawn from central European theatre practice, alongside a few prominent North American theatre-makers whose work has toured internationally, such as Robert Wilson, and fleeting mentions of a handful of British practitioners. Therefore, although the term 'postdramatic theatre' has gone on to have considerable currency in the British context, it's worth questioning how far Lehmann's theory speaks to theatre culture in the United Kingdom specifically. A similar note of caution has been sounded by Peter M. Boenisch, who argues that the 'ossified antagonism of supposedly innovative experiments with bodies and images on the one hand, and text-based theatre on the other' (2010: 162) is unique to British theatre and that Lehmann's definition of the postdramatic cannot simply be aligned with one side of this binary. This should be borne in mind throughout the following discussion.

Nonetheless, I would suggest that the distinction between dramatic and postdramatic theatre is troubled by text, towards which Lehmann has a somewhat ambivalent attitude. As Edith Cassiers, Timmy De Laet, and Luk Van den Dries note, 'text seems to constitute the turning point where dramatic and postdramatic theatre are at once most closely related and most different' (2019: 33). Lehmann sees dramatic theatre as 'subordinated to the primacy of the text' (2006: 21), whereas staged text is 'merely a component' (46) in postdramatic theatre, in which emphasis is placed on 'disruption' or 'conflict' between page and stage. For Lehmann, 'the step to postdramatic theatre is taken only when the theatrical means beyond language are positioned equally alongside the text and are *systematically thinkable* without it' (55, my emphasis). This provides a useful framework for conceiving of the text as just one among many theatrical elements, in contrast to a text-led orthodoxy which sees the written play as authoritative over all other aspects of the production. However, by insisting upon a theatre in which 'theatrical means beyond language' are 'systematically thinkable' without the text, Lehmann denies the palimpsestuous supplementarity of performance. Postdramatic theatre, according to Lehmann, 'wants the stage to be a beginning and a point of departure, not a site of transcription/copying' (32). This, though, ignores the essentially double nature of theatrical performance. As I discuss in Chapter 1, both plays and performances are at once complete and incomplete, continually gesturing towards one another – an ontological paradox that has proved problematic for many generations of thinkers.

To further complicate matters, the text has not entirely receded into the background of Lehmann's 'panorama of postdramatic theatre', but appears in the form of the new, 'no longer dramatic' text, or as the traditional dramatic text which is '*de-dramatized*' in its theatrical presentation. Lehmann stresses that his careful choice of the term 'theatre' – rather than, say, performance – signals a 'continuing association and exchange between theatre and text', but that in postdramatic theatre the text is no longer 'master' of the theatrical event (2006: 17). One of the more useful aspects of Lehmann's intervention is this challenge to the perceived authority of the playtext, which Lehmann relocates as just one of the manifold components of live performance. This might seem to imply that *any* text may be staged in either a dramatic or a postdramatic way; it is what theatre-makers *do* with the text that determines its status in performance. However, the notion of the 'no longer dramatic' text suggests that the postdramatic impulse can be found not just in performance, but also in the written material of some plays. In her introduction to the English translation, Karen Jürs-Munby reinforces the idea that certain playwrights produce radically incomplete texts that move beyond the dramatic paradigm, suggesting that 'a "turn to performance" can be observed' in the work of writers such as Elfriede Jelinek, Martin Crimp, and Sarah Kane, whose plays involve the audience as 'active co-writers of the (performance) text' by eliminating elements such as dramatic plot, conventional character, and speech prefixes (2006: 6). Likewise, Barnett identifies a 'no longer dramatic' text that 'suggests itself as a relativized element for performance from the outset and points to its own indeterminacy and status as uninterpreted material' (2008: 16), aligning these texts with the characteristics of postdramatic theatre. Barnett's key argument is that playwrights such as Crimp and Kane actively disrupt meaning from within their texts, thus refusing a cohesive dramatic model and 'leav[ing] all possible readings open' (21). He concludes that 'postdramatic texts configure themselves in such a way that they openly invite creative approaches', but that this invitation '*is not and cannot be binding*' (23, my emphasis). This would seem to dissolve the differences previously identified between texts, none of which can be binding in their invitation to interpreters and all of which are open to multiple readings. It is not that the playtexts examined by Barnett and others are not doing something interesting and experimental on the page – indeed, I give considerable attention to such experiments in later chapters – but these texts, like any other texts, cannot determine their realisation as either 'dramatic' or 'postdramatic' performances. This is at the root of my problem with the category of the postdramatic when applied to theatre texts.

One reason why the postdramatic or 'no longer dramatic' text has been the focus of many responses to *Postdramatic Theatre*, particularly in a British context, is that this has been understood as a way of continuing to ally certain theatrical texts with radical experimentation. In her persuasive breakdown of this development, Tomlin suggests that what has happened as a result is 'an ever-widening of the postdramatic boundaries to ensure that all potentially radical work can be encompassed within its ever-broadening remit, and a corresponding narrowing of the boundaries of the dramatic' (2013: 52). While understandable on the part of artists and scholars keen to stake out their claim to experimentalism, there's a danger that such categories become distractions from the actual work of ideological interrogation in which such art purports to be engaged. There is something useful in thinking about how certain texts or performances might move beyond drama, when drama is defined as a specific representational model with its foundations in Aristotelian aesthetics. What is less productive is either a simplistic conflation of drama and text that deepens the divide between so-called 'text-based' and 'non-text-based' theatre-making, or an ambivalent approach to texts that leads to an ideological project of dividing 'radical' postdramatic texts from 'regressive' dramatic ones, without necessarily reflecting how truly radical (or not) these texts are.

As well as suggesting the possibility of 'no longer dramatic' texts, Lehmann insists that postdramatic theatre-making includes 'directors who may stage traditional dramatic texts but do so by employing theatrical means in such a way that a *de-dramatization* occurs' (2006: 74, original emphasis). This de-dramatization renders the dramatic plot of the text secondary to the other theatrical elements of its staging. Many of the examples that Lehmann discusses throughout his book could be classified under this heading of 'de-dramatization', as they take classic playtexts (often Shakespeare plays or Greek tragedies) as their point of departure. There are connections that can be drawn between these practices and the seemingly 'radical' revivals of classics by British directors that I discuss in Chapter 3 – many of which are influenced by the practitioners whom Lehmann cites. However, the possibility of such de-dramatization would seem to make the distinction between 'dramatic' and 'postdramatic' texts essentially meaningless in the context of their performance. Again, it seems to be the theatrical treatment of the text that matters. Lehmann himself even acknowledges that some works which remain dramatic might share many features with postdramatic theatre, concluding that 'it is only the constellation of elements that decides whether a stylistic moment is to be read in the context of a dramatic or a postdramatic aesthetics' (25). This makes defining any individual piece of theatre – or indeed any text – as either dramatic or postdramatic a somewhat subjective and ambivalent endeavour.

While I think there is real value in Lehmann's work, as I have identified, my analysis in *Text and Performance in Contemporary British Theatre* deliberately sidesteps the postdramatic as a category. Like Tomlin, I am keen to avoid another binary that all too easily slots into the well-worn grooves of the 'text-based'/'non-text-based' divide. This book is written in an intellectual context that has been irrevocably shaped by the concept of postdramatic theatre in a way that I do not wish to deny. My investigation, however, moves in a different direction. Rather than exploring the experiments of the theatre-makers discussed in this book in terms of their relationship to the dramatic, I am more interested in how they navigate assumptions and conventions to do with the theatre text and its role in relation to performance.

(Re)theorising text and performance

This book is certainly not the first scholarly text to scrutinise the relationship between text and performance. As I expand upon in the first part of Chapter 1, many theorists have sought to define this relationship, with varying results. My approach challenges and re-examines some of this existing theory, as well as drawing from, synthesising and developing other theoretical frameworks that I argue offer a more nuanced and productive basis for understanding the complex exchange between texts and performances. In this section, I offer a brief introduction to some of the most important efforts to retheorise the relationship between text and performance, establishing the key influences for my own thinking. These thinkers will be returned to in later chapters as I flesh out my approach to the analysis of texts and performances.

In a North American context, W. B. Worthen has considered the perplexing position of the playtext across a number of different studies. More than perhaps any other theatre scholar, he has grappled with the doubleness of plays as both literature and performance. Often, these investigations have used the distinctive cultural position of Shakespeare's plays as a vehicle for interrogating ideas of authorship and authority, in ways that I build upon in my consideration of classic playtexts in Chapter 3. In these studies, Worthen has mounted vital challenges to the notion of fidelity to Shakespeare's work and has probed the relationship between text, performance, and meaning (1997, 2003, 2011, 2014), with implications for all dramatic literature. This approach reaches its apotheosis in *Drama: Between Poetry and Performance* (2010), which – as the title suggests – situates plays at the threshold where literature meets performance. This book looks at 'the drama's two lives' (xii), proposing a way of reading plays that is alive to their status as both printed literature and material for embodied performance. Worthen stresses 'the interplay between the text and conventions and practices of reading we bring to it' (xv) and invites readers to be attentive to the ways in which plays 'imagine the conditions of their use' (ibid.), while simultaneously being clear that plays cannot definitively govern their theatrical enactment. My own analysis takes inspiration from this mode of reading, as will be seen in later chapters. For Worthen, though, there is something particular about the playtext as a form of writing; other types of text for performance do not hold the same interest for him. This separation of the play from other performance writing is something that I question throughout this book, both through observations of the porosity of different forms of practice and through analysis of the relationships between different kinds of texts and performances. Worthen is also, notably, one of the only theatre scholars to have given serious attention to the modern play as a printed object in *Print and the Poetics of Modern Drama* (2005). This book considers the rarely asked question of how the materiality of a dramatic text informs its reading and its potential for performance, establishing lines of investigation that I pursue further in Chapter 4.

When discussing the relationship between text and performance, Worthen often persuasively describes theatrical enactment as something that exceeds the material on the page. However, this view has been compellingly contested by Julia Jarcho in *Writing and the Modern Stage: Theater Beyond Drama*. Her title deliberately echoes Lehmann's move past the dramatic paradigm, but whereas Lehmann primarily explores a theatre beyond drama in *performance*, Jarcho identifies a mode of modern *playwriting* that resists the dramatic and is, she argues, 'a disruptive theatrical force in its own right' (2017: xiii). The experimental texts in which Jarcho is interested, by writers such as Samuel Beckett, Gertrude Stein, and Suzan-Lori Parks, disrupt the often-cherished liveness of performance and 'turn the theater into a place where the determining force of *how things are, here and now* can be confronted and shaken' (ibid., original emphasis). Moreover, it is '*as writing* that they make theater lodge a complaint against the here-and-now' (xiv, original emphasis); the resistance of this writing to absorption by performance is what constitutes its radical potential, in Jarcho's view. Her thesis draws heavily on Theodor Adorno's argument about the importance of non-identity in works of art, focusing on how a range of modern playwrights have used the text to undermine the here-and-nowness of performance. One of the issues that Adorno takes with performance is that it is not 'autonomous from its genesis' (2013 [1970]: 136); as a live, ephemeral art form, its existence and its moment of origin are one and the same. A performance is inseparable in time and space from its own creation. This is why Adorno favours text over performance and why, following Adorno, Jarcho advocates a 'turn *toward* the literary' (2017: x, original emphasis), proposing a way to 'value the script as a form apart' (14). However, I wonder if performance's relationship with text complicates Adorno's argument. In some sense, performance *is* separate from its genesis, if part of that genesis arises from the text as a separate artistic entity. This is the case regardless of whether the text itself actively resists performance in the ways that Jarcho identifies. In suggesting this, though, it's important not to slip back into a theoretical position that situates the text as the blueprint for performance – a common metaphor that I question at various points in the following chapters. The text does not dictate or constrict performance, but it does act as one point of departure. There are, nonetheless, useful resonances between Jarcho's perspective on the resistant text and some of the arguments I make later in this book about the slippage and non-identity between text and performance. Like Jarcho, I deny that any performance can ever 'complete' the text or offer a definitive rendering of it. In response to Jarcho's challenge to the notion that performance will always exceed what is found on the page, meanwhile, I propose that plays and performances are incommensurable, with each in a sense exceeding the other.

Dan Rebellato has similarly drawn on Adorno's ideas about the non-identity of art in his essay 'Exit the Author', which is a key reference point in Chapter 2. Beginning with the observation that 21st-century playwrights are increasingly 'absenting themselves from their plays' (2013: 11), Rebellato explores the idea that authorship has become 'a key area of theatrical experimentation' (ibid.). He resists the suggestion that what can be witnessed in these plays is a straightforward rejection of authorial intention. Revisiting the influential arguments of Roland Barthes, Michel Foucault, and Jacques Derrida, he argues persuasively that these poststructuralist thinkers are not completely denying or doing away with authorial intention in the reading of texts, but are instead 'redefining the author's role' (22) – a nuancing of the influential 'death of the author' discourse to which I return in Chapter 2. For Rebellato, this lays the groundwork for an argument about how '[t]he assertion of authorship multiplies and destabilizes the experience of the play in performance' (27), thus aligning the plays in question with Adorno's principle of non-identity in art. These texts are 'politically more questioning and radical, in Adorno's terms, because they insist that the world can be other than it is' (ibid.). While I'm intrigued by Rebellato's and Jarcho's use of Adorno's framework as a means of assessing the radical potential of dramaturgically innovative plays – albeit with some reservations, as discussed above – this kind of political analysis is not the focus of my investigation. Instead, Rebellato's intervention is helpful in its paving of the way for a reconsideration of the role of intention in the interpretation and staging of plays, which I pursue in Chapter 2. Importantly, moreover, Rebellato identifies a number of experiments with text and authorship that I examine further in this book: the undermining of the playwright figure within their own plays, the dramaturgical openness of plays that do not define details such as place and character, and the absence of authorial commentary in much contemporary playwriting.

As Rebellato's essay illustrates, any project that interrogates the text today does so in the wake of poststructuralism. Poststructuralist theorists challenged many of the traditions and assumptions of Western philosophy, unsettling seemingly stable notions of meaning and truth. As already seen in discussions of the 'text-based'/ 'non-text-based' binary, poststructuralism has had a profound impact on questions of text and authorship, in ways that I will explore in more detail in Chapter 2. Like Rebellato, I return to Barthes' and Foucault's arguments about authorship and situate these in relation to contemporary experiments with the theatrical text. But my most sustained engagement with poststructuralist thinking is through the work of Derrida. Rather than reversing the hierarchy of the binaries underpinning Western culture, such as speech and writing, Derrida's typical deconstructive manoeuvre demonstrates that each side of the binary bears the trace of the other within it. This trace is, for Derrida, constitutive of language. Derrida refutes the belief that writing is a corruption of pure, originary speech, arguing that the 'supplement' (in this instance, writing) that produces the sense of real or pure presence reveals that such real or pure presence does not exist. There is nothing, in other words, beyond supplementation. For Derrida, furthermore, linguistic meaning depends both on difference (the definitions of words are determined through reference to other words) and on deferral (the idea that the signifier both supplements and supplants the pure concept to which it is supposed to refer, which is forever deferred) – the two words captured and intermingled in the French pun *différance*, the term invented by Derrida to describe the process of making meaning through language (1976). This view of language disrupted Western philosophical and linguistic traditions based on what Derrida calls 'the metaphysics of presence' by denying the possibility of any pure concept or authority to which we can appeal to decide meanings.

I find elements of Derrida's theory of language – and particularly his discussion of the supplement – useful for conceptualising the complex relationship between text and performance. Like Marvin Carlson (1985), I believe that the idea of supplementation offers a more precise and nuanced explanation of the complex relationship between text and performance than models that see performance as illustrating, translating, or fulfilling the play on the page. In Chapter 3, I expand on this framework, which I use as a way of unpicking the common idea that an individual performance of a play – especially a classic play – is just an ephemeral version of an enduring, stable (and, implicitly, textual) 'work'. Here I also refer to Derrida's work on the iterability of language, which has similarly been applied to playtexts by Rebellato (2013). It's important to add, though, that my analysis in this book is not straightforwardly aligned with poststructuralist thinking. In common with Tomlin's approach, I am applying and re-examining elements of Derrida's theory while rejecting the ways in which Derridean poststructuralism has been used in the service of upholding a reductive binary between dramatic and postdramatic or 'text-based' and 'non-text-based' theatre. Reaching across the divide between analytic and continental philosophy, I draw on key concepts from Derrida's theory of language while also occasionally borrowing from analytic thinking and attempting to pursue that tradition's clarity of argument.

Situating this study

Building upon the literature discussed above, there are several key ways in which *Text and Performance in Contemporary British Theatre* intervenes in existing discourses and suggests future lines of enquiry. Moving beyond the perceived binary between so-called 'text-based' and 'non-text-based' theatre, I investigate some of the factors underpinning this dichotomy in a specifically British context. I examine the relationship between text and performance in a way that recognises the peculiar ontology of the playtext, while also accommodating the many other texts used in contemporary British theatre-making and blurring any supposedly definitive boundaries between these various texts and practices. Throughout the book, I support my theoretical discussions with a wide selection of examples, bringing together approaches that have previously tended to be examined in isolation and offering original analyses of a range of contemporary theatre-making practices. The book also makes new forays into a number of areas that deserve further exploration, including the complicated connections between arts subsidy and attitudes towards the theatre text; the complex and contested attribution of theatrical authorship; the relationship between the dramatic canon and new interventions in classic texts; the role of text in documenting performance; the use of innovative formatting on the page as a means of experimenting with theatrical text; and the many possible implications of digital creation, publication, and documentation for shared understandings of plays and performances.

This book focuses on contemporary British theatre, but I do not pretend that this is an easily bounded category. The contemporary, as used in this book, encompasses the three decades from 1990 to 2020, which I identify as a period of particularly rich experimentation with theatre texts by British practitioners and a time of intense debate about the relationship between text and performance. While much of the theatre that I discuss throughout the book was made in the 21st century, key developments in the 1990s – including the emergence of physical theatre into the mainstream, the textual innovations of playwrights like Martin Crimp and Sarah Kane, and the increasing visibility of devising practices – laid much of the groundwork for what was to follow, which is why I include this decade in my investigation. This was also the decade in which fault lines between different practices began to assume the distinct form of a dichotomy between so-called 'text-based' and 'non-text-based' theatre, as I explore in Chapter 1. While the book is primarily concerned with the contemporary, it also extends beyond this specific period, examining some of the historical contexts that underpin current attitudes towards text and performance and looking ahead to possible future developments. Like any study that looks to the immediate past, I am conscious that my findings run the risk of being quickly overtaken by events – as has happened on more than one occasion during the writing of this book. My aim, though, is that this analysis will create productive avenues for further enquiry.

What is meant by 'British' theatre-making during this time, meanwhile, is undeniably complex, as indeed is the very notion of Britishness. As Jen Harvie acknowledges in *Staging the UK*, her study of the relationships between performance and the nation's understanding of itself, British identities are 'multiple, mutually contingent, and mutually embedded – simultaneously holding in tension multiple determinants' (2005: 7). I also agree with Harvie that 'the UK' is 'not a stable, universally and timelessly agreed entity; rather, it and its meanings are constantly conceived in different ways' (3), which are performed and re-performed.[4] It's important to remain conscious of this multiplicity and mutability when delineating the area that I am calling 'British theatre'. All the practices, discourses, and institutional structures that I discuss in this book are located within a wider globalised theatrical context, as well as in the specifically British set of conditions that I go on to explore. Especially in the context of rapid technological development and ever-increasing connectivity, all theatre is being made, shown and received – to greater and lesser extents – on an international platform. Art and artists frequently travel across national borders, and theatre-makers working in one country will often have international influences. In this context, 'British theatre' is a flawed but necessary shorthand for work made and shown in the United Kingdom. I use it to refer mostly to British-born artists, though I also analyse theatre made by individuals who were born and/or raised elsewhere but are now resident in the United Kingdom and make most of their work in this context, such as Nigerian poet and playwright Inua Ellams and Canadian writer-performer Deborah Pearson. I will also occasionally mention theatre companies who work across different national contexts, such as Dead Centre, which is based between Dublin and London.

In doing so, I am wary of simply assimilating theatre-makers with hybrid national identities to a 'British' tradition, in the way that many critics have done with Irish playwrights such as George Bernard Shaw, Oscar Wilde, and Samuel Beckett. As Harvie notes, this

> sadly mimics the imperial history of Britain's relationship with Ireland and suggests that discourses on British theatre are prepared to accommodate other traditions if they are perceived as not only enhancing but also unthreatening because subordinate and colonial. (2005: 116)

Harvie also points out how the category of British theatre often 'assumes the more authoritative status of calling itself "British" when it refers more accurately to English theatre' (146). I want to avoid reproducing this sort of imperial logic while at the same time acknowledging the complex and hybrid nature of 'Britishness'. My intention in using 'British' in the flexible way that I do in this book is to address a specific theatre-making context, within which both theatre-makers who define themselves as British and practitioners who identify with other nationalities or combinations of nationalities are making work. This approach, I hope, reflects the complexity and diversity of British theatre culture, while remaining aware of its limitations and exclusions. It's also important to note the historical specificity of 'British' as a category that does not apply prior to the Acts of Union 1707, which should be borne in mind throughout my discussions of the history of theatre texts.

The examples that I focus on throughout the book are inevitably influenced by my own theatregoing, which has been concentrated in and around the cities in which I have lived over the last 15 years: Southampton, London, Manchester, and York. Readers will notice that these are all English cities and therefore this analysis is potentially open to accusations of being England-centric. While I have made efforts to include theatre-makers who originate from or are working in a wide range of geographical locations across the United Kingdom, the book reflects both the limitations of my own geography and the continued England- and, more specifically, London-centric patterns of the British theatre sector. One way of illustrating these patterns is through looking at the distribution of government subsidy. An investigation of arts funding distribution across England, Scotland, and Wales in 2016 found that Arts Council England's grant-in-aid funding averaged out at £8.20 per capita in 2015/16, which was roughly comparable with Creative Scotland's £8.72 per capita in 2014/15 (no figure is provided for 2015/16) and Arts Council Wales' higher figure of £10.84 for 2014/15. However, London has received dramatically higher per capita funding than the other regions of England; the most recent per capita figure cited in the report, for 2012/13, was £20.32 (Dempsey 2016). Drilling down to theatre specifically, the British Theatre Consortium's (BTC) *British Theatre Repertoire 2014* report revealed that England had the largest share of theatrical productions across the United Kingdom at 87%, while Scotland, Wales, and Northern Ireland accounted for 6%, 5%, and 2%, respectively. Within England, meanwhile, London had the greatest proportion of productions (22%), and due to its number of long-running shows in the West End it claimed the vast majority of theatre attendances at 62% (BTC 2016). The London-centric nature of the British theatre sector is also exacerbated by the concentration of critical attention in the capital, with comparatively little major national media coverage of theatre in other regions of England or in Scotland, Wales or Northern Ireland.

While the book addresses British theatre as a whole, it's worth acknowledging some key differences between the specific performance cultures of the British nations and their approaches to the theatre text. There is, as Trish Reid points out, an 'absence of a continuous distinguished playwriting tradition in Scotland' (2012: 40). As Ian Brown (2011) addresses, there are many, complex reasons behind this absence – or, as some have argued, perceived absence. Whatever the cause, though, the crucial point is that 'the role of Scottish playwriting had different roots and different kinds of prominence from English theatre-writing' (Brown 2011: 2). Meanwhile, thanks to 20th-century companies and theatre-makers such as Glasgow Unity and John McGrath, who built on popular performance forms that stretch back much further, there is an important tradition of politicised populism in Scottish theatre. This has been consolidated by the founding of the building-less National Theatre of Scotland (NTS) in 2006, whose internationally successful production of *Black Watch* (2006) followed in the tradition of McGrath's *The Cheviot, the Stag and the Black, Black Oil* (1973) with 7:84 Scotland. *Black Watch*'s director John Tiffany has suggested that '[f]uelled by variety, visual art, music and a deep love of storytelling, Scotland's artists have created a form of theatre that is as significant and vital as its written drama' (quoted in Reid 2012: 16). Due to a complex web of interconnected factors, storytelling and popular forms have been as influential for the development of Scottish theatre as its dramatists, if not more so.

Among Scotland's most prominent contemporary playwrights, meanwhile, the likes of David Greig and Anthony Neilson are known for their embrace of collaborative and experimental ways of working, throwing into question some of the text-led orthodoxies that dominate south of the border.[5] It's also striking how quickly NTS has established itself in the Scottish theatre landscape, with a significant emphasis on experimental, site-specific and community projects over main-stage production processes centred around text and writer.

When National Theatre Wales (NTW) was established in 2009, its model was largely inspired by that developed by NTS. It too is a national theatre without walls, and much of its work to date has been site-specific and community focused. Prior to the founding of NTW, Wales had a more piecemeal theatre network than either Scotland or England, with a strong amateur tradition but relatively few professional theatre venues. Several of the better-known theatre companies to have been based in Wales, meanwhile, were from what might be considered a 'non-text-based' or physical theatre background: Brith Gof, Pearson Brookes, Frantic Assembly (which formed in Swansea before later relocating to London) and Volcano Theatre, to name just a few.[6] Welsh theatre has been described as 'expansive, interdisciplinary and experimental', with much of its homegrown work 'blur[ring] the distinctions between theatre, live art and dance' (Geliot and Gomez 2016). Furthermore, alternative theatre in Wales has been actively supported since the 1970s through institutions such as Chapter Arts Centre, Moving Being, and the Centre for Performance Research (previously Cardiff Laboratory Theatre), as well as having an academic counterpart in the Performance Studies department founded at Aberystwyth University by Brith Gof's Mike Pearson in the late 1990s. Since its inception, NTW has commissioned and partnered with many of the artists nurtured through such channels, reflecting a stylistically diverse theatre culture. Alongside this, the Welsh theatre and performance landscape also includes a significant strand of Welsh-language theatre.

Theatre in Northern Ireland, meanwhile, has arguably been shaped more by political and religious forces than by artistic ones. Civil unrest during the Troubles forced many theatres to close for extended periods, while 'theatrical performance regularly found itself at odds with the self-perception of Ulster Protestant identity' (McDowall 2013: 327), thus hindering the development of a local theatre culture. Ophelia Byrne characterises Northern Irish theatre as 'a theatre struggling to articulate an artistic and political line presenting its society's "own way of things"' (Byrne 2016), a description that implies how the nation's theatre has grappled with attempts to define itself in relation to its Irish and British neighbours. Even prior to the partitioning of Ireland in 1921, Mark Phelan suggests that the Irish National Theatre Society displayed an 'unwillingness to cross [the] proto-partitionist border' (2004: 597), hence excluding the North from its imagining of a national theatre culture. With the exception of the Ulster Literary Theatre (1902–1934), furthermore, Northern Irish playwrights were largely neglected by the theatre establishment in their own country until the 1970s. All of this meant that there was not a national playwriting tradition to anything like the same degree as in England. When greater commitment to Northern Irish playwrights did emerge, there was a reductive expectation that they must engage with the Troubles, which have continued to dominate notions of Northern Irish theatre even in what might be termed a 'post-conflict' landscape (Phelan 2016). In the 21st century, meanwhile, the Arts Council of Northern Ireland stresses the importance of the country's independent theatre sector, which encompasses a wide range of practices, often outside of traditional theatre settings.

In some ways, then, the attitudes towards text and performance that this book is addressing are more prominent in England than in the other nations that make up the United Kingdom. Yet the porous borders and frequent exchanges between England and its immediate neighbours make hard distinctions between the theatre cultures of these four nations difficult to sustain. For better or worse, moreover, there is a continued artistic and critical investment in the idea of *British* theatre as a cohesive entity with an associated set of conventions, values and aesthetics, which demands to be interrogated as a whole. Part of my argument is that British theatre has been hampered by a false understanding of the relationship between text and performance, which is entangled with national cultural myths around the uniquely literary nature of British drama. As Harvie notes, 'the apparent truth of British theatre as fundamentally literary is reiterated so frequently and often uncritically that it is reinforced and naturalised' (2005: 114–115). This yoking of British theatre and the literary, or of Britishness and playwriting, is exemplified by books such as Aleks Sierz's *Rewriting the Nation* (2011) and Michael Billington's *State of the Nation* (2007). This nation-specific myth-making, therefore, is part of what I am challenging.

However, the arguments set out in this book may also resonate across other Western theatre contexts that share many of the same cultural lineages and which continue to exist in a relationship of creative interchange with British theatre practice. Furthermore, the experiments with text and performance that I discuss are in dialogue with similar experiments beyond the United Kingdom by companies, writers, and directors including the Wooster Group, Elfriede Jelinek, Elevator Repair Service, Benedict Andrews, Branden Jacobs-Jenkins, Ivo van Hove, Roland Schimmelpfennig, Jackie Sibblies Drury, Simon Stone, Suzan-Lori Parks, Ontroerend Goed, and The TEAM. This list is far from exhaustive and names just a few of the European, North American, and Australian artists who have inspired my thinking about the countless possibilities of text and performance, alongside the examples explored in the chapters that follow. Before moving on, it's also worth briefly addressing the complex position of British theatre in relation to continental Europe. As catalogued by Harvie (2005), there has been a long-standing relationship of both closeness and distance between Britain and the rest of Europe. Looking back further, Rebellato (1999) suggests that the new playwriting of the 1950s was pointedly defined against Europe as its 'other', an intermittent trend that has continued into the 21st century. Since the UK public voted narrowly in favour of leaving the European Union in June 2016, this historically troubled relationship has become even more fraught. At the same time, British theatre-makers have continued to seek inspiration from continental Europe, with knowledge and creativity flowing back and forth across the Channel.

The shape of the book

One of the central aims of this book is to contribute to the collective understanding of contemporary British theatre in a way that simultaneously widens and complicates conceptions of the theatre text. Rather than exploring a small selection of in-depth case studies, I discuss a range of different theatre-makers, including some whose work has been frequently referenced in discussions of text and performance and others who have received relatively little critical attention to date. The intention here is to provide an eclectic snapshot of British theatre-making between 1990 and 2020 and to illustrate the far-reaching implications of my interventions. My analysis, while often focusing on specific plays and productions, is also based on an understanding of these practices as existing within a complex matrix of social, economic, political, and cultural conditions. I examine the understandings of text and performance that sit beneath institutional structures within the British theatre industry, as well as investigating some of the ways in which these structures have themselves perpetuated a flawed perception of the relationship between page and stage.

In Chapter 1, I expand on the central problem with which this book is concerned. I offer a brief overview of the many attempts to get to grips with the relationship between text and performance, interrogating the underlying questions, concerns, and assumptions that thread through these accounts. My main point here is that the paradoxical doubleness of the theatre text poses a long-standing theoretical problem that requires further exploration. In this chapter I also discuss the historical specificity of the hierarchical understanding of text and performance within British theatre and the division of so-called 'text-based' and 'non-text-based' work, arguing that a shift beginning in the 1950s and 1960s has driven a wedge between different theatre-making practices. Ultimately, I suggest that this divide is underpinned by a misunderstanding of the relationship between text and performance, and that it is therefore necessary to rethink this relationship.

In Chapter 2, I begin this process of rethinking by challenging the popular notion of performance 'serving' the writer's intention as expressed in the text. I consider the tricky idea of authorship, which has a contested history in the context of British theatre practice. Within mainstream play-led producing structures, the playwright is still often understood as the primary author of the theatrical event, whose vision directs the rest of the creative team. Meanwhile, ever since Barthes sounded the death knell of the author in 1967, other theatre-makers have been attempting to subvert and evade the theocratic authorship identified by post-structuralists. The chapter focuses on the work of writers and theatre-makers who have attempted to question or disrupt authorship in their work using various theatrical strategies. Through an examination of these practices, I reposition the concept of authorial intention in relation to plays and performances, arguing that artistic intentions are indeterminate, multiple and embedded in creative processes.

Having re-examined theatrical authorship in Chapter 2, in Chapter 3 I explore the implications that this has for the dramatic canon. I look at a range of contemporary approaches to classic texts, considering the emergence of a trend for so-called 'bold' or 'radical' revivals, as well as analysing contemporary deconstructions of classic plays. These reimaginings of texts that have traditionally been seen as blueprints for performance have begun to deconstruct the perceived power of play and playwright, although they have sometimes been confronted with a critical backlash – the premises of which I also interrogate. I deconstruct perceived hierarchies of text over performance and vice versa by proposing that both playtexts and performances are supplements (in a Derridean sense) for an absent, ideal 'work', to which they refer and defer. I also apply Derrida's theory of iterability when exploring the relationships of playtexts to different contexts, with a focus on how theatre-makers have remade canonical texts for changed social and political realities.

Finally, in Chapter 4 I look at the life of drama on the page, considering how the distinct textual identities of plays can influence perceptions of their possibilities in performance. After a brief look back across the history of the play as a physical artefact, I consider how publishing conventions have changed in recent years to reflect the heterogeneity of contemporary theatre texts, exploring innovations in form and layout. This chapter also considers the role of text as documentation and explores the implications of a shift towards digital publishing and performance archiving. The digital environment multiplies the possibilities for how readers encounter written texts, in ways that might well disrupt the perceived authority of the play and make it easier to conceptualise theatre texts as the multiple, mutable things that they are. At the close of the book, I look forward, with the hope that the problem of the theatre text, while not exactly solved, might at least be approached with greater nuance, curiosity and complexity.

Notes

1 Kate Bassett, for example, discusses 'how radically yet intelligently this rewrite departs from the original structure of Aeschylus's Ancient Greek trilogy' (2015: 867), while Lloyd Evans hyperbolically suggests that Icke's version 'takes us as far from the original as possible' (2015: 868).
2 I have written about this performance at greater length in the blog post '*Tonight I'm Gonna Be the New Me*, or Who's in charge of this story?' (Love 2015c).
3 Examples of this critical literature on Crouch's work include Stephen Bottoms (2009b), David Lane (2010), Emilie Morin (2011), and Duška Radosavljević (2013a), as well as my own book on *An Oak Tree* (Love 2017).
4 This argument is heavily influenced by Benedict Anderson's concept of nations as imagined communities (2006).
5 Greig was one of the founding members of the experimental theatre company Suspect Culture (1993–2009), while Neilson typically develops his plays during the rehearsal process in collaboration with actors. It should be noted, though, that both Greig and Neilson have worked widely in England, demonstrating that it is far from straightforward to separate the theatre cultures of these neighbours.
6 Many of the members of these companies were not born and bred in Wales, again illustrating the porosity of British theatre cultures across the four nations.

1
THE PROBLEM OF THE THEATRE TEXT

Each section of *Song from Far Away* (2015) begins with a date and the same two words: 'Dear Pauli'. The text is constructed as a series of letters, each written by Willem to his younger brother, who has just died suddenly and unexpectedly. These letters narrate the days immediately following Pauli's death, as Willem travels from New York back to his native Amsterdam for the funeral. On the page, there is nothing but these letters, occasionally interspersed with lyrical sections of text in italics. Only in the final couple of pages does it become clear that these sections are the lyrics to a song, the musical notation of which is placed at the end of the text. This is the only intrinsic hint that *Song from Far Away* might have some relationship to performance. Structurally, it's more reminiscent of a short story or a novella than a play. There are no stage directions, no indicated speakers, no references to the theatrical context for which this play was written. And yet, it remains a text for performance. Despite its distinctly literary appearance, the piece is a product of theatrical collaboration. This is immediately signalled in the attribution of the text, which is jointly credited to playwright Simon Stephens and songwriter Mark Eitzel, who is responsible for the piece of music that is woven throughout. Not only this, but the play was written specifically for Dutch actor Eelco Smits, who performed the monologue in Ivo van Hove's premiere production.[1]

As some reviews of van Hove's production observed, it was not an especially theatrical performance.[2] Smits was alone on stage throughout in Jan Versweyveld's deliberately bland set: a cream-coloured box with two large windows looking out onto blackness, with barely any furniture or props. Aside from subtle shifts in lighting and the effect of snow falling outside the windows – and of course Eitzel's music – Smits delivered the words of the text with very little adornment. Critic Matt Trueman even suggested that the show was pointedly anti-theatrical:

If theatre is a here and now art-form – all presence and shared space – then *Song from Far Away* is a self-sabotaging show. It does everything it can to get away from us and, the more it succeeds in that, the more it fails as theatre. (2015)

Yet even this seemingly sparse production, with its focus on the short-story-like script, contained many elements that bore no direct relationship to the text. The location, for a start, is not suggested anywhere in the playtext. Willem describes the spaces he passes through, but there is never any indication of where he is speaking from – or, indeed, that he's speaking at all, given the formal device of the letters and the absence of any speech prefixes. The most striking decision of van Hove's production, meanwhile, was to have Smits perform naked for much of the show, a choice that emphasised the emotional vulnerability of the character as written but that did not arise from any explicit indications in the text.

In this example, some of the contradictions of the theatre text become apparent. A script like *Song from Far Away* is indisputably a text for performance, yet there are no formal features common to this and other playtexts that consistently mark them as objects of the theatre. Van Hove's production, meanwhile, was perceived as a relatively transparent staging of Stephens' words and Eitzel's music, but it still had to supply many details that were absent from the playtext. In this first chapter, I expand upon such contradictions, outlining the problem of the theatre text in the context of contemporary British theatre. I look at how and why playtexts have been considered problematic, identifying many of the concerns that the rest of the book addresses. The chapter also offers a brief historical survey, examining some of the ways in which dominant attitudes towards text and performance in Britain (and beyond) have changed over time, and arguing that a confluence of factors in the 1950s and 1960s created a schism – between text and performance, and between 'text-based' and 'non-text-based' theatre practices – with consequences that are still being felt today. Below, I lay the groundwork for later chapters, establishing just what it is that makes the theatre text so tricky.

Text as problem

As illustrated by my opening example, theatre texts are peculiar and troublesome items. Within Western theatrical and scholarly traditions, they have been understood both as literary objects in their own right, studied and interpreted in the same way as novels or poems, and simultaneously as material for performance, with the external space of the theatre inscribed in their structure. As will be seen throughout this book, there can be a tendency to think of the text as a stable dramatic work containing the unchanging essence of the play, which is merely decanted into different productions. But this assumption is immediately challenged by the ways in which these texts transform through the processes of reading, rehearsal, and performance. W. B. Worthen identifies the strange duality of the theatre text when he writes that '[o]n the one hand the text of the play appears as a single fabric, to have a specific shape, size, and texture, a kind of organic wholeness', but on the other hand, 'in performance the text becomes material for use, used and used up' (2010: xiii). This has created a persistent difficulty in theorising the theatre text in its different forms; because of its dual identity, the play presents itself as something of a paradox, an object at once complete and incomplete.

The problematic nature of the theatre text is an issue for scholars of both performance and literature, with playtexts existing somewhat uneasily within each discipline, belonging fully to neither one nor the other. Benjamin Bennett, who has written at length about the problem posed by dramatic texts, attempts to claim plays for literature by arguing that the 'profound *disruptive* effect' (1990: 1, original emphasis) of drama is structurally constitutive of literature as a field. For him, the problem of theatre – or, in his words, 'the theater itself as a problem' (2) – is a crucial and generative challenge within literature. While Bennett is coming at this subject from a literary rather than a theatrical perspective, and therefore much of his argument has limited relevance for my focus here, he does helpfully diagnose the problem posed by playtexts:

> there is nothing whatever that is rhetorically or formally unique about a dramatic text; there is no characteristic or set of characteristics, or complex of 'family resemblances,' by which we would recognize a dramatic text as something different from a narrative text, *if we did not know about the institution of the theater*, if the theater, as an institution, were not already there to be 'meant' as the text's vehicle. (ibid., original emphasis)

This lack of distinctive characteristics is especially evident in a play like *Song from Far Away*, which apart from its explicit framing as a text for performance is indistinguishable from a short story on the page. As Bennett points out, it's thus impossible to make sense of drama in purely literary terms; it depends for its identity on the external reality of the theatre. Drama is, confusingly, 'neither clearly literary nor clearly distinguishable from the literary' (Bennett 1990: 11).

This struggle to accommodate playtexts as both literary objects and material for performance crops up repeatedly in the writing of critics, scholars, and commentators. A handful of examples begins to illustrate the issue. In the early 19th century, for instance, Charles Lamb famously claimed that the 'Lear of Shakespeare cannot be acted' (1811: 136), insisting that only on the page could one fully appreciate Shakespearean drama. When these plays are performed, he contends, 'we have only materialized and brought down a fine vision to the standard of flesh and blood' (126). Likewise, Lamb's contemporary Samuel Taylor Coleridge suggested that Shakespeare had his 'proper place in the heart and in the closet', rather than on the stage (Puchner 2002: 14). These are just two voices among many thinkers who have tried to situate Shakespeare within the literary camp, downplaying the theatricality of his plays.[3] On the other hand, Northrop Frye argues that '[f]or all the loving care that is rightfully expended on the printed texts of Shakespeare's plays, they are still radically acting scripts' (2020 [1957]: 247). In direct response to Lamb and Coleridge, meanwhile, Jonas Barish asserts that what they 'signally fail to convey is a sense of the *indispensability* of performance, the fact that the script *must* be incarnated by live actors, or it remains forever impalpable and wraithlike' (1981: 331, original emphasis). While the *concept* of performance is certainly indispensable for drama, Barish's formulation here suggests that the play only finds its completion when performed; he struggles with the 'wraithlike' quality of the script as words on a page.

Similar problems have plagued theatre practitioners. A century after Lamb, the director Edward Gordon Craig was similarly arguing that Shakespeare's plays belonged in print because these texts are complete and therefore not in need of theatrical supplementation:

> When no further addition can be made so as to better a work of art, it can be spoken of as 'finished' – it is complete. *Hamlet* was finished – was complete – when Shakespeare wrote the last word of his blank verse, and for us to add to it by gesture, scene, costume or dance, is to hint that it is incomplete and needs these additions. (1957 [1911]: 143)

According to Craig, a true text for performance is 'incomplete anywhere except on the boards of a theatre' and would be 'unsatisfying, artless, when read or merely heard' (144). Echoes of this argument can be detected in the later writings of avant-garde theatre-makers who resisted the dramatic text – including Antonin Artaud's famous rejection of 'masterpieces'. Artaud insisted that 'it is urgent, for the theatre, to become aware once and for all of what distinguishes it from written literature', emphasising 'transient' performance over 'fixed' texts (quoted in Drain 1995: 267). The supposed fixity of dramatic texts was also attacked or questioned by Futurists like F. T. Marinetti, Dada artists who embraced randomness and spontaneity, and other theatre-makers who prioritised the visual over the verbal, including Craig as well as designers such as Adolphe Appia. For many of these artists, pre-written plays – and especially canonical plays – represented complete literary artworks that belonged in the library or the museum, not on the stage (although, in practice, many of them did not entirely leave texts behind). Whether asserting the literary artistry of plays that therefore demand to be read and studied rather than staged, or deliberately eschewing dramatic texts that are seen as 'finished' and thus not open to the creative interventions of performance, several generations of artists, academics, and commentators have insisted upon the completeness of playtexts.

Yet however 'finished' or 'complete' a play might appear on the page, in performance there are always elements that go beyond the written content of the script, as seen with *Song from Far Away*. These elements have an ambivalent relationship with the text. In one sense, it is performance – or at least its possibility – which defines a theatre text *as* a theatre text. Were there not these elements beyond its control, there would be nothing to distinguish drama from any other literary category. Even texts that are often considered to be unstageable depend for their identity upon the theoretical *possibility* or *concept* of performance and all the unpredictability this entails. At the same time, however, the bodies and objects on stage partly depend on something external to which they refer: the text. In the theatre, Bennett argues, we understand that an object on stage 'represents not merely "an" object, but the object meant by the text' (2005: 210), while at the same time that object is 'emphatically material' (211) in its immediate presence before us. In this way, the undeniable materiality of the stage – its resistance, in Bennett's words, 'to being fully textualized' (179) – confounds any attempt to render the meanings of page and stage self-identical. As Simon Shepherd and Peter Womack put it, 'the doubleness [of plays] is irreducible' (1996: viii).

It is this doubleness that has troubled many theatre-makers, writers, and critics. There is, to borrow Barish's phrase, an 'ontological queasiness' attached to the theatre text, which is similar and connected to the queasiness that Barish sees underpinning the pervasive anti-theatrical prejudice (1981: 3). Throughout theatre's history, as Barish documents, theatricality has had stubbornly pejorative associations, with the stage often provoking mistrust among philosophers, moralists, and law-makers. The tricky relationship between text and performance has often been part and parcel of this prejudice. Barish summarises the view of many over the centuries who have objected to theatre on moral grounds:

> It is the playing, then, the physical presence of live actors performing the scene before one's eyes, that constitutes the danger. Plays, when sufficiently edifying, are acceptable if they are not played. (325)

As he notes, the attempt to separate the acceptable and seemingly stable dramatic text from its dangerously unpredictable and seductive live performance is 'a recurrent illusion of the antitheatrical prejudice in all ages' (324). Building on Barish's work, Martin Puchner suggests that at times this anti-theatrical effort to sever text from performance has even played a 'constitutive role' in the art form (2002: 1), specifically in the case of modernist theatre and the 'closet play': a curious genre of drama written with the explicit intention of *not* being staged.

These difficulties have persisted into the 21st century, gaining new dimensions following the establishment of Performance Studies as an academic discipline. Originating under Richard Schechner at New York University in 1980, Performance Studies has eschewed a focus on canonical dramatic works in favour of what Schechner calls the 'broad spectrum', which includes 'entertainments, arts, rituals, politics, economics, and person-to-person interactions' (1992: 9). While the take-up of 'Performance Studies' as a disciplinary label in the United Kingdom has been somewhat uneven, this new research paradigm has had a significant impact on British theatre scholarship, arguably serving to marginalise the study of the dramatic text and certainly reinforcing the opposition between text and performance in much research, as has been observed by Jacqueline Bolton (2011) and Stephen Bottoms (2009a). Bottoms' editorial for the 'Performing Literatures' edition of *Performance Research* offers a revealing snapshot of theatre scholarship in the 2000s. As I noted in the Introduction, this journal edition stems from a conference of the same name which invited scholars to reassess relationships between theatre, performance, and literature. Bottoms notes that 'of the sixty or so paper proposals that I received, less than half a dozen of them chose the discussion of particular play-texts (or their performance) as their central focus' (2009a: 2), adding that this tallies with his experience as a peer-reviewer for the 2008 Research Assessment Exercise (RAE). He concludes that a focus on the live performance event has 'resulted in a situation whereby a largely reflexive disinterest in dramatic literature and theatre history has become the new orthodoxy' (ibid.).[4] While the journal edition itself nuances and complicates this orthodoxy, the initial response to Bottoms' call for papers, as well as the range of research submitted for the RAE, suggests that many contemporary performance scholars have responded to the problem of the text by avoiding it altogether.

Some, meanwhile, have attempted to circumnavigate the problem of written drama's indeterminate relation to performance by arguing – similarly to the avant-garde practitioners discussed above – that plays are complete and can only be transformed into theatre through a process of breaking open. Puchner, for example, observes the phenomenon of 'fully autonomous pieces of writing that seem to have left the requirements of the stage behind, and yet they were written with the intention of performance', and argues that 'these plays require a new theory of the dramatic text and its relation to performance' (Puchner 2011: 293). He outlines 'three conceptions of dramatic literature and its theatrical performance': the play as 'a set of instructions given by a writer to actors' (ibid.); the script as 'an incomplete artwork' (295); and the dramatic text as complete and performance as a process of 'transformation and adaptation' (ibid.). For Puchner, the models of both text as instructions and text as incomplete artwork fail to account for the autonomy of the play as a piece of literature. In the former, 'the dramatic text, despite its powerful position, could not achieve a literary integrity of its own' (ibid.). When viewed as incomplete, meanwhile, the 'dramatic text can be appreciated as literature, although it depends on another art form, performance, for its completion' (ibid.). Puchner instead favours the model of the text as complete, because '[w]e do not have to ascertain what the text fixes and what it does not fix [...], for in this third model the text is complete, without gaps, and must be adapted in its entirety' (296). This process also has the advantage of placing emphasis on the adaptors rather than on the playwright, loosening the authority that is often attributed to the writer. Puchner adds that this theory of adaptation applies to *all* texts that might be transformed for the stage (novels, for instance, as well as plays), which he sees as another point in its favour. This, though, minimises distinctions between plays and other literary texts, any of which might be adapted for the stage. Puchner's theory thus denies the ontological strangeness of the playtext, sidestepping its reliance on the external context of the stage.

In addition to the challenges of conceptualising the playtext as both literary object and element of performance, the growing number of texts for performance not written in advance of rehearsals by individual playwrights has produced a further problem. How is one to define these texts? In response, several scholars and theatre-makers have distinguished between playtexts and what has been variously referred to as writing for theatre, writing for performance, texts for performance or performance writing. This category has been used to encompass various theatre texts produced outside the conventional model of the pre-written script, such as texts created through group devising processes, scripts for autobiographical solo performance, collectively written texts, and texts that have been developed by writers working in the rehearsal room (rather than being largely finished before the rehearsal process begins). John Freeman summarises the characteristics typically associated with what he labels 'performance writing', asserting that it 'tends towards the transgressive, the fluid and the questioning' (2016: 49–50) and 'is located within a landscape where only uncertainty reigns' (50). Such texts, he adds, 'are rarely regarded as literary and are seldom seen as stand-alone objects' (ibid.). Yet I would argue that these various texts – however labelled – share with solo-authored playtexts a paradoxical completeness and incompleteness. What David Overend, for instance, has described as a 'relational performance text' (2011), referring to site-specific theatre texts that are open to unpredictable encounters with audiences, would be better understood as a playtext that contains a relatively great degree of indeterminacy. As Overend himself notes, his concept of the relational performance text depends upon established boundaries and 'a negotiation between "script" (as the predetermined, written, fixed structure of the performance), and "divergences" or "detours" (as relational and process-based)' (2011: 45). In this respect, it's no different from more conventional-looking playtexts, which can never supply all the details of their performance. Similarly, Freeman's definition of 'performance writing' as 'provisional, contextual and unfinished' (2007: 21) could as easily describe the 'dramatic writing' to which he opposes it.

However, Ben Payne has helpfully suggested that the attraction of phrases like 'performance writing' and 'writing for theatre' is that this terminology 'appears to allow writing to directly engage with other performing art forms, free from the historical and ideological associations of "plays" and "playwrights"' (1998: 28). Struggle as they might to maintain a definitive separation from the solo-authored, pre-written playtext (as I explore further in Chapter 4), terms like 'writing for theatre', 'writing for performance', and 'relational performance text' are perhaps best understood as attempts to break with both the literary connotations of written drama and with some of the misunderstandings of the relationship between text and performance discussed throughout this book. While in theory all texts are at once complete and incomplete, it's worth acknowledging the dominance of an attitude towards dramatic writing in Britain which sees it as a comprehensive set of instructions for performance or as a self-contained literary work. It is against such an attitude that these alternatives are positioning themselves. While I dispute his definition of 'performance writing' as something fundamentally distinct from other forms of text used in performance, Freeman does offer the useful insight that any divide between theatre and performance 'is apparent in attitude rather than form or content' (2016: 48). As he elaborates, '[t]here are two points of view: one locates the written script as the mainstay and basis for the performance, while the other regards the performance as an autonomous event' (ibid.). The fact that the former view has been dominant in British theatre culture over the last century or so – as I discuss below – provokes the latter perspective into a position of opposition. Thus, there has been a need to distinguish experimental texts from playtexts that replicate the conventions of the dominant model and to mount a case for these texts while they have occupied the fringes of British culture.

As illustrated by the range of voices cited in this section, the problem of the playtext has been observed in numerous contexts beyond Britain, especially in other Anglophone cultures. This might thus be thought of as a concern that extends across Western theatrical and literary traditions – and indeed I will continue to occasionally refer to examples from North America and continental Europe. However, as established in the Introduction, I'm suggesting that this problem has some distinct characteristics in its British manifestation. Within this context, it's worth asking how our present anxieties around the theatre text came about. The dichotomy between text and performance in British theatre is, I suggest, historically and culturally specific. At least a partial understanding of how the currently dominant conception of the theatre text developed might therefore cast additional light on some of the difficulties discussed above.

A brief history of text and performance

While current approaches to and assumptions about the theatre text can seem firmly entrenched, the central position of play and playwright in British theatre culture is a historically specific phenomenon. In their history of English drama, for example, Shepherd and Womack note that the role of the playwright has been far from constant over time, varying from 'a kind of craftsman, producing dialogue to the actors' specifications' to 'an artist, and actors as the servants of his [sic] controlling conception' (1996: vii). Payne even goes so far as to argue that 'the privileged position of the writer and of the text here is little more than a blip in the history of theatre and a concept entirely peculiar to British performance practice' (1998: 25). Although this book is primarily concerned with practices and discourses from the 1990s onwards, it's important to recognise the historical contingency of contemporary understandings of text and performance and to contextualise the emergence of orthodoxies that might seem permanent in the present. The main focus of my historical discussion in this chapter is on what I identify as a significant shift beginning in the 1950s and 1960s, when a convergence of factors instigated the division of theatre-making practices based on their perceived relationship with text. First, though, I want to take a brief look at some significant earlier developments in the relationship between text and performance and its changing perceptions over time. Here I draw on the accounts of a range of other scholars, highlighting notable areas of overlap and disagreement. In doing so, I remain alert to the ways in which British theatre historiography itself might have, as Jen Harvie argues, 'described – and so produced – its object as uniquely British [...] through a narrative which constructs British drama and theatre as uniquely and consistently literary' (2005: 113). The following is not an attempt to offer a continuous or conclusive historical narrative, but rather to note some of the key flashpoints and debates in a way that can help to inform present concerns.

While historical accounts vary, it's fairly uncontroversial to state that the gradual, discontinuous shift towards conceiving of the playtext as an authoritative set of instructions for performance has its beginnings in the development of print culture in Europe from the late 15th century. Although the developing relationship between performance and printed text has been differently interpreted by various historians, there's little doubt that the increasing dissemination of print had an influence on theatrical activities, whatever the precise timing and nature of that influence. In her study of shifting constructions of authorship, Silvija Jestrovic notes that print culture 'brought a sharper distinction between text and more immediate performative forms in the sense in which both their structure and authorship began to stabilize' (2020: 57). According to Jestrovic, this 'resulted in the separation between the embodied and the textual, marking a turning point in the process of fixing the author' (58). Interestingly, the first section of Shepherd and Womack's (1996) chapter on medieval drama is titled 'The Birth of the Author', positioning 16th-century Reformation playwright John Bale as one of the first dramatic authors. However, they also suggest that in the early modern period an emerging authorial conception of theatre as arising from solo-authored texts co-existed with a social understanding of theatre as an art form that was created collaboratively. Some, such as Julie Stone Peters, have argued that print was already playing a crucial role in the formation of drama as an art at this time. She locates print 'at the heart of the Renaissance theatrical revival', insisting that '[i]t is not mere coincidence that theatre and printing emerged as central forms of cultural communication during the same period' (2000: 1) and arguing that the two forms mutually influenced one another. In Chapter 4, I return to this history of the play as printed book and how its material form might both index and instigate changing understandings of the text's relation to performance.

During the early modern period, then, plays were beginning to become established as printed documents, sometimes with authors attached. But the nature of authorship and the status of playtexts at this time is disputed. It's important to note that many plays remained unpublished and, as Luke McDonagh (2021) points out in his examination of dramatic copyright, playwrights often had limited ownership over what they wrote. Plays were commonly understood as belonging to acting companies, who would often develop and revise scripts in the course of rehearsal and performance. These plays could then be printed and circulated as commodities without the permission – or even the attribution – of their writers. Several scholars have therefore suggested that theatrical creativity at this time is best understood as collaborative and polyvocal, involving cooperation between playwrights – who often worked together on the writing of plays – and among the various theatre workers involved in staging the scripts (Masten 1997; Cox and

Kastan 1997; Vickers 2007; Stern 2009; McDonagh 2021). Some studies of early modern collaboration have focused on specific partnerships between writers in ways that acknowledge the importance of cooperation while still looking for the distinctive marks of individual playwrights, as Heather Hirschfield (2001) discusses in her survey of theories about early modern authorship. Meanwhile others, such as Jeffrey Knapp (2005), have argued that single authorship was in fact the dominant paradigm in English Renaissance theatre and that the uncertainty surrounding the authoring of early modern texts has been overstated. Though I do not seek to draw any decisive conclusions from these different accounts, the nature of the debate itself is suggestive of the complexity and state of flux that seems to characterise early modern understandings of authorship, text, and performance. This complexity is stressed by Janet Clare (2012), who sees the emergence of the author in this period as slow and discontinuous. As discussed by Grace Ioppolo (2006), there's also much evidence that writers themselves frequently revised their scripts for performance, further complicating modern ideas about the complete and authoritative playtext while supporting the notion of a close, ongoing relationship between playwrights and their plays. As Ioppolo puts it, 'authorship could be a continual process, not a determinate action' (2006: 1). Moreover, in addition to printed plays, 'the circulation of texts in manuscript form was common and constituted a non-printed and often preferable and authoritative form of "publication" during this period' (Ioppolo 2006: 9). Within this context, theatre texts had a complicated identity, existing as playwrights' manuscripts, transcribed copies, working documents of the theatre, individual parts for actors, and printed books that might be published in multiple editions with the involvement of various other parties – a multiplicity that I discuss further in Chapter 4.

There's evidence to suggest that a relatively fluid conception of page and stage continued into the following decades and centuries. Worthen uses the prominent – and, in his view, paradigmatic – example of Shakespeare to outline how the relationship between text and performance was understood in the 17th and 18th centuries. He claims that the perceived authenticity and success of Shakespearean performances had to do not with the degree to which they were seen to reproduce the text, but 'with how the stage articulated its Shakespeare with the theatrical tastes of its audience' (1997: 28). This resulted in performances that frequently cut characters, altered key plot points and even changed endings (most famously in Nahum Tate's much-performed 1681 version of *King Lear*, in which Lear and Cordelia both live), with theatre-makers seemingly not seeing any inconsistency or irreverence in this approach. Something similar appears to have been true of Shakespeare's textual identity, which continued to shift along with the shifting tastes of society, even as the playwright was being elevated to a privileged authorial position. For example, Jacky Bratton suggests that Alexander Pope's 1711 edition of the plays 'laid claim to Shakespeare as an author, and established a text of his work by wholesale excisions and extensive emendation, fitting the plays into the polite and gentlemanly diction of modern poetry' (2003: 85). If one follows Bratton's line of argument, then the establishment of Shakespeare as an authorial figure is ironically achieved through the substantial editing of texts which, as an indirect consequence of this intervention, would later be seen as revered, authoritative documents. Shepherd and Womack also track the evolution of Shakespeare's plays through the various editions that appeared in the early 18th century, which executed 'an ongoing remake of the Shakespearean text in the image of its editors' culture' (1996: 89). It was only later that changing cultural understandings of authorship 'produced an anxiety about textual authenticity' (ibid.), with drastically rewritten versions of Shakespeare's plays continuing to appear regularly on British stages right up to the early 19th century. On the other hand, as McDonagh notes, between the late 17th and early 18th centuries playwrights were beginning to gain greater legal and professional recognition. By the passing of the Statute of Anne – the first British copyright legislation – in 1710, 'the dramatist had grown in esteem and authorial attribution of plays in print and in stage playbills had become the norm' (2021: 64). This arguably laid the groundwork for later notions of authorial ownership and control.

Although interpretations of the period's developments vary, many theatre historians agree that there was a significant transformation of the playwright's role and status over the course of the 19th century. During this century, playwriting was increasingly professionalised and developments in copyright law and publishing began to offer greater protection and literary clout to the play as the writer's property. These developments can be seen, in turn, to further divorce text from performance; according to Barish, the attempt to separate drama from theatre 'reaches epidemic proportions in the 19th century' (1981: 326). Tracing the playwright's arc towards professionalism and artistry, John Russell Stephens stresses the importance of copyright protection, artistic freedom, and proper remuneration, asserting that it is 'when the playwright ceases to be a servant and becomes master of his [sic] own play that his true professionalism emerges' (1992: xiii). This hierarchical notion of the playwright becoming 'master' of their creation is echoed throughout Stephens' book, reflecting modern attitudes towards theatrical authorship which were structured during the period Stephens is writing about. Shepherd and Womack (1996) reiterate Stephens' narrative of the increasing professionalisation of the playwright over the course of the 19th century, connecting this to the growing seriousness and respectability of dramatic authorship. In these and other accounts, emphasis is placed on an interconnecting series of shifting material factors that determined the status of text and playwright in this period: copyright law, censorship, theatre licensing, the dominant role of the actor-manager, and commercial pressures.[5]

As can be seen in Stephens' emphasis, these developments are often depicted as a gradual, progressive enabling of the playwright's art. In her overview of 19th-century performance and theatre historiography, Jane Moody notes the tendency of theatre historians to track 'the rise of a leisured, genteel social institution and the gradual emergence into professional respectability of both the actor and the playwright' (2000: 113).[6] Reinforcing this assessment of the ways in which 19th-century drama has typically been framed, Nina Auerbach offers a summary of common attitudes towards Victorian theatre, which share a tacit literary bias:

Collaborative, messy, and lost, the theatre is generally, and wrongly, dismissed as sub-canonical, at least until the 1890s, when the self-conscious literacy of Wilde and Shaw elevated it to the verbal sophistication that would become Edwardian drama. (2004: 3)

This evolutionary view of 19th-century British theatre is supported by the opinions of critics of the time such as William Archer, who in 1882 had 'a somewhat gloomy view of the present state of the drama' (1882: 1) and asserted that 'the English drama does not exist as literature' (3), before later celebrating what he saw as the revival of serious playwriting at the turn of the century. Archer had an acknowledged predisposition towards literary drama, explaining his desire to 'see in England a body of playwrights, however small, whose works are not only acted, but printed and *read*' (4, original emphasis). These views, which became dominant among the intellectual elite at the end of the 19th century, have continued to filter down through subsequent versions of events.

Taking a more critical view of the development of the text/performance hierarchy and the literary bias of British theatre historiography, Bratton identifies the 1830s as the decade in which the groundwork for modern attitudes was laid. Bratton breaks down the assumption that 'the study of the theatre is always at the service of the written drama' (2003: 6), making a significant intervention in theatre historiography. Situating changes in theatrical production within a wider project to establish a new middle-class hegemony, she draws a parallel between the Reform Acts of 1832, which tempered political unrest by enfranchising only a limited bourgeois class, and simultaneous reforms in the theatre that shored up the power of a middle-class intellectual elite. Led by Edward Bulwer Lytton, a group of reformers campaigned for changes to the theatre licensing system and improved remuneration for playwrights, leaning heavily on rhetoric about the decline of drama and the absence of great writers – variations of which have been repeated by later commentators. The 1832 report of the Select Committee led by Bulwer Lytton recommended that 'the Author of a Play should possess the same legal rights, and enjoy the same legal protection, as the Author of any other literary production' (quoted in Stephens 1992: 90), attempting to frame playwriting in literary terms. Dewey Ganzel's view that 'only when the legal status of the dramatist was changed could literary quality emerge' (1961: 384) exemplifies the widespread opinion that these reforms were necessary for the elevation of drama as a serious, *literary* form. Whereas Stephens' account largely repeats this inherited wisdom by foregrounding Bulwer Lytton's complaints about the injustice of the existing system, Bratton critically interrogates the way in which Bulwer Lytton and his allies reframed British theatre history to support their cause, with long-lasting implications. In the debate about theatrical reform, Bratton argues that theatre history was shaped in such a way that it favoured 'the high moral and spiritual status of the artist' (2003: 77), appropriated Shakespeare as 'a natural, untutored genius' (85), and asserted a commitment to 'criteria of authenticity and textual purity' (88). The legacy of these ideas lives on today. The campaigning of

Bulwer Lytton and his colleagues resulted in the 1833 Dramatic Copyright Act, which was a significant step towards enshrining the rights of playwrights as the authors of their work, although legal complexities and ambiguities remained.[7] The establishment of the Dramatic Authors' Society in the same decade and the 1843 Act for Regulating Theatres can be seen as further strides towards professionalisation. Indeed, Home Secretary Sir James Graham asserted that the 1843 Act was supported by the government with 'the intention to improve the dramatic art' (quoted in Thomas, Carlton and Etienne 2007: 61), indicating that theatrical reform was largely motivated by a desire to improve and promote dramatic literature.

Following these reforms, the late 19th century saw an effort 'to foreground plays as (almost novelistic) literary products' (Luckhurst 2006: 6). Playwrights like George Bernard Shaw and Arthur Wing Pinero sought to establish themselves as serious literary writers, publishing their plays in formats that conformed to the expectations of readers more accustomed to novels.[8] When considering this development, though, it's worth also acknowledging the impact of theatrical censorship and regulation, both during this period and either side of it. It was partly as a result of censorship that these playwrights wrote for an audience of readers: many of Shaw's plays, for example, were unable to be performed publicly under the censorship regime in Britain at the time due to their subject matter. Shepherd and Womack explain that there has long been a close relationship between state regulation and authorship, even suggesting that the one may be (at least partially) responsible for the other. As they note, any licensing authority needs a script of some kind in order to decide whether a performance can be permitted to go ahead and thus 'entails dramatic authorship both as a condition and as a consequence'; in this regulatory model, the primacy of the playtext is reinforced 'by making the text into a sort of promise which the performers are legally bound to keep' (1996: 3–4). The regulation and censorship of theatre stretches back to before the first English playhouses, with the position of Master of the Revels created during the reign of Henry VIII. Two centuries later, with the passing of the 1737 Licensing Act, theatrical censorship became enshrined in British statute law and responsibility for its enforcement was handed to the Lord Chamberlain.

Before its successful abolition in 1968, there were several attempts to reform or repeal theatre censorship, typically spearheaded by playwrights and often justified with an appeal to the notion of serious, literary drama. In his evidence to the 1909 Joint Select Committee on Censorship and Licensing, for example, Archer stated that the effect of censorship was 'to depress and to mutilate and actually to keep out of existence serious plays' (quoted in Thomas, Carlon and Etienne 2007: 94). In the Joint Select Committee's report, meanwhile, there's a reproduction of the anti-theatrical text bias. The Committee concluded that '[i]deas or situations which on a printed page may work little mischief, when represented through the human personality of actors may have a more deleterious effect' (quoted in Freshwater 2002: 54). The same argument was advanced 40 years later, when the then Lord Chamberlain Lord Clarendon insisted that there is a considerable difference between reading, in private, certain types of books, and of sitting amongst strangers of both sexes and of all ages and watching a play [...] for the emotional and psychological effect of a stage play is recognised as being much greater than any other form of art. (quoted in Thomas, Carlton and Etienne 2007: 148)

On the other side of the debate, arguments against censorship often stressed the need for parity between the approach to drama and to other written forms such as novels and journalism, which did not face the same kind of censorship. The fact that censorship was, for so many years, deemed to be necessary for theatre in a way that was not necessary for other mediums once again suggests an underlying uneasiness with the unpredictability, liveness and co-presence of performance, as has been explored at greater length by Helen Freshwater (2002).

At the same time as the idea of the serious dramatic author was in ascendance, there was 'a curious historical phenomenon: the emergence of the theater as art coincided with the emergence of the dramatic text as literature' (Puchner 2011: 293). By the turn of the 20th century, plays – or, at least, some plays – had secured a place for themselves as literary objects. Running parallel to this development, a growing number of practitioners were making the case for theatre as an art in its own right – as opposed to either theatre as pure entertainment or drama as an outpost of literature. The rise of the director, exemplified by a figure like Edward Gordon Craig, signalled a new interest in theatre as a sensory as well as a verbal art form. While visual spectacle was already a central aspect of popular 19th-century forms such as melodrama, practitioners like Craig and Appia – inspired by Richard Wagner's concept of the *Gesamtkunstwerk* (total work of art) – were staking out a place for it within the realm of high art. This was often paired with a rejection or demotion of the dramatic text. In the early 20th century, Puchner observes a consequent polarisation between a modernist anti-theatricalism and an avant-garde theatricalism. Both positions involve a fraught relationship with the dramatic text. For those in the modernist anti-theatrical camp, live performance was suspect because of the unpredictability of human bodies as signifiers to convey the text; for many avant-garde theatre-makers, meanwhile, the text was a source of tyranny that must be toppled to free the forces of theatricality. On the one hand, the interest in the book as a container for drama was taken to a new extreme in the closet plays of modernist writers such as Gertrude Stein and Stéphane Mallarmé. On the other hand, the emergence of the historical avant-gardes across Europe and North America marked a significant challenge to the now established dominance of the dramatic text, and can be seen as a precursor to more recent antagonisms between text and performance. As Elinor Fuchs explains, 'many theaters came to regard the author's script as an element of political oppression in the theatrical process, demanding submission to external authority' (1996: 70). Surveying this avant-garde rebellion against plays, I'm inclined to agree with Puchner that these artists unwittingly 'overshot their target': 'instead of rebelling, as they should have, against one particular conception of the dramatic text, namely, the conception of the text-as-instructions, they articulated their rebellion against the dramatic text *tout court*' (2011: 294). In retrospect, it's somewhat regrettable that avant-garde theatre-makers tended to (at least in theory) reject *all* dramatic texts, thus creating an opposition between text and performance that has persisted in various guises. While the centres of avant-garde theatre-making were largely in continental Europe, not Britain, these experiments were absorbed into the cultural lineage and creative imagination of subsequent practitioners who sought, in various ways, to reject the theatrical mainstream.

The theatre text, then, has variously been thought of as a set of working theatrical documents, as something multiple and malleable, as disposable entertainment, as the literary work of the serious dramatic author, and as an authority to be resisted. Contested accounts and contradictory evidence suggest that the relationship between theatrical performances and their multiple texts was relatively fluid in the early modern period and into the 17th and 18th centuries. The roots of current British understandings of text, performance, and dramatic authorship can be located somewhere in the 19th century, although interpretations of the shift in the playwright's status in this century vary, and these accounts themselves often bear traces of the literary bias that Harvie has identified in British theatre historiography. Throughout this history, legislation – in the form of copyright and censorship laws – has exerted significant influence on the practice of playwriting and on understandings of dramatic authorship, often provoking flashpoints in the disputed status of the theatre text. By the turn of the 20th century, a popular view of plays as authoritative literary documents had become established, prompting an opposing avant-garde movement. Although the reality is messier and more complex than this brief overview, a narrative linking radical experimentation with the overthrow of the authoritative dramatic play continues to shape understandings of the theatre text, especially among alternative and experimental artists. As Beth Hoffman has observed of live art-aligned performance practices since the 1960s, there remains a need 'continually to *re-perform that break* between tradition and experiment' (2009: 97, original emphasis), with the text often forming the fault-line between the two. This is what I suggest can be seen from the mid-20th century onwards in Britain.

Playwriting and performance in the post-war period

I turn now to the post-war period and the confluence of numerous factors – including public funding, a revived interest in new plays, and the end of theatre censorship – that served to drive a wedge between different theatre practices based on their perceived relationship to text. The late 1950s and early 1960s are often identified by scholars and commentators as a time of renewal in British playwriting, led by a 'new wave' of social realist plays at theatres like the Royal Court. This familiar account of the post-war period can be found in books like John Russell Taylor's *Anger and After* (1963), Arnold P. Hinchliffe's *British Theatre, 1950–70* (1974), and *Post-War British Theatre* by John Elsom (1979), while the version of events echoed across these texts has been challenged by Dan Rebellato in *1956 And All That* (1999), which offers an important critical re-evaluation of the British theatre landscape in the 1950s. The plays produced at this time and the critical discourse around them stressed a broadly literary understanding of the theatre text, which came to be seen as opposed to the vast array of experimental theatre practices that emerged on the fringe shortly afterwards. The alternative theatre scene that developed in the 1960s and 1970s on the one hand challenged the authority of the playtext in theatrical production, and on the other hand entrenched a view of plays as singular, stable objects set in opposition to the supposed fluidity of devising practices. This binary continued into the early 21st century, becoming characterised as a battle between so-called 'text-based' and 'non-text-based' theatre.

I want to suggest that the newly founded Arts Council of Great Britain played a central – if often unwitting – role in this process. Arts Council subsidy is widely accepted as crucial to the support of British theatre, and particularly to new work, although its role in this area has rarely been explored in great depth.[9] This part of the chapter draws on research in the Arts Council's extensive archive and builds on some valuable contributions to this relatively under-investigated field. Jane Woddis' PhD thesis (2005), for example, represents an early investigation into the role of arts practitioners in the cultural policy process. This work offers useful insights into the Arts Council's approaches to new writing and the extent of practitioner involvement in policy-making, though it is tightly focused on the case study of the playwrights' groups that formed from the mid-1970s onwards and its scope is restricted by the limited availability of Arts Council archival material at the time the research was produced. Woddis' work shares some ground with Jacqueline Bolton's doctoral project (2011), which I discussed in the Introduction. In particular, both in the thesis and in a subsequent journal article (2012), Bolton persuasively argues that the 'new writing boom' of the 1990s and 2000s should be understood as the result of a series of financial and structural developments rather than as a spontaneous flowering of talent. Finally, the *Giving Voice to the Nation* project (2009–2014) investigated the theatre archive of the Arts Council of Great Britain and began to explore the funding body's impact on theatre practice over time. The project resulted in a series of guides to the structure and content of the archive, three conferences, and a series of publications on specific aspects of the research team's findings in the archive.[10] This represents the most extensive investigation of the Arts Council's archive to date and has laid important foundations for other researchers. The survey of the archive undertaken by the research team has made it easier to access and navigate the labyrinthine folder structure, while the books, chapters and articles emerging from the project provide useful models for how the material in the archive might be applied and interpreted.

Archival evidence demonstrates that the Arts Council had a significant influence on the development of the so-called 'new wave' of plays in the late 1950s and early 1960s. Although the funding body was established in 1946 to *respond* to the work of artists and organisations, it also introduced policy that initiated or strongly encouraged specific theatrical developments, particularly in the area of new playwriting. In 1948, a proposal for the encouragement of new dramatists marked the beginning of a long focus on new plays, the shortage of which was initially bemoaned. In 1951, for instance, the Arts Council was disappointed by the response to its new play competition as part of the Festival of Britain (ACGB 1951). Two years later, it was still felt that '[t]here is a dearth of new plays of quality' (ACGB 1953: 42); the following year's results were 'unspectacular and a little disappointing' (ACGB 1954: 39). In 1952, the Drama Panel moved to address this perceived gap by establishing a subcommittee to oversee 'a more ambitious scheme to assist new drama' (ACGB 1952: 37).[11] There's evidence, moreover, that the Council was interested not just in supporting individual productions or playwrights, but in substantially changing the British theatre ecology. Reporting on its new play schemes in 1957, the Arts Council explained that 'they create a climate and establish the conditions which make the writing of plays attractive and rewarding' (ACGB 1957: 25). Surveying the improved outlook for new plays, it insisted that 'the Council's Scheme must take some credit for this' (37). Two years later, the Council reasserted that the apparent renaissance in new drama 'springs from seeds carefully disseminated from St. James's Square [the location of the Arts Council's headquarters], as a deliberate act of policy' (ACGB 1959: 11). The growth of new playwriting was therefore framed as a success for the Council, which emphasised its proactive approach, advancing this as a key example of policy-making and actively seeking publicity for its playwriting schemes. For example, at a Drama Panel meeting in 1958, '[t]he Chairman hoped it might be possible to persuade one of the leading daily or Sunday newspapers to publish a survey of the five years' work by the Council for the promotion of new drama' (Drama Panel 1958), while in 1960 the Drama Director proposed that a brochure should be published illustrating the achievements of the New Drama Scheme (TWC 1960). The Council was clearly keen to make its role in the renewal of playwriting known among the sector, which in turn may have stimulated further writing activity and cultivated the impression that new plays were a central part of post-war British theatre culture. In addition to its new writing schemes, the Arts Council highlighted the responsibility of subsidised theatres to develop and stage new plays, thereby positioning the support of playwriting as a key aim of drama subsidy. At the first meeting of the Theatre Writing Committee (TWC) in 1952, it was stressed that '[a]ll repertory companies in receipt of a normal Arts Council grant should be reminded that helping new authors was considered part of their work' (TWC 1952).[12] Existing plays, meanwhile, were regularly revived as a central part of the programmes of subsidised theatres.

It is important to remember that at this time theatrical censorship was still in operation. Until the Theatres Act of 1968 scripts for public performances had to be submitted to the Lord Chamberlain for approval, effectively prohibiting the creation of work that did not have a pre-existing script or that used improvisation in performance.[13] Companies such as Joan Littlewood's Theatre Workshop, for example, received fines for diverging from scripts that had been submitted to the censor (Freshwater 2002: 55). This had a significant impact on the funding of new work in the first two decades of the Arts Council's existence, helping to establish precedents that favoured plays and playwrights. The Council did in fact discuss the possibility of funding work that flouted or circumvented censorship, for example through performances in private theatre clubs, but it decided in 1967/68 not to support presentations of any unlicensed plays, despite receiving funding applications from theatre companies without pre-written scripts (Drama Panel 1967; Drama Panel 1968). Censorship also reinforced many of the misconceptions about the relationship between text and performance that I address elsewhere in this book. As Freshwater notes, '[t]he Lord Chamberlain's staff did their best to subdue theatre's unpredictable communicative potential by chaining it to a single text', thus denying the multiplicity of performance (2002: 53). This is another manifestation of the anti-theatrical text bias, as the Lord Chamberlain's examiners 'frequently drew comparisons in their reports and memoranda between the respectability of written text and the impropriety of live performance' (54). Yet Freshwater argues that the Lord Chamberlain's archive also reveals that 'the censors struggled with theatre's ephemerality and slippery elusiveness', illustrating 'performance's evasion of the authority of the text' (55). In several instances, performances of licensed scripts took on new and unpredictable meanings in performance even after careful vetting of the text. Indeed, despite the insistence of Lord Cobbold (Lord Chamberlain from 1963) that his role was 'to consider plays and *not* productions' (quoted in Johnston 1990: 200, original emphasis), at times the censor sought to intervene beyond the text. Playwright John Arden, for example, recalls the Lord Chamberlain's Office requesting further information about the performance of certain stage directions that were thought to be of concern in his play *Armstrong's Last Goodnight* (Johnston 1990: 191–192). This illustrates the ways in which – to the anxiety of the play examiners – performance exceeds textual regulation. These regulatory difficulties reveal something about the nature of the relationship between text and performance, which – as I am proposing in this book – is far more complex than popular understandings have allowed.

While it could be argued that the Arts Council's commitment in the post-war years was to new theatre in general, which because of censorship was effectively just new *writing*, the funder's emphasis on *playwrights* specifically suggests an interest in the creation of dramatic literature over and above a simple desire to generate more new theatre.[14] This emphasis was consistent with broader cultural discussions at the time about the need for more serious plays, thus reinforcing the notion that playwriting was at the vanguard of theatrical renewal. The narrative that critic Kenneth Tynan retrospectively constructs is one of the age of the actor being superseded in the mid-1950s by the age of the author – and, to a lesser extent, the director (1975: 11–14). Tynan had complained in 1954 that 'apart from revivals and imports, there is nothing in the London theatre that one dares discuss with an intelligent man for more than five minutes' (147) and famously decried what he called the 'Loamshire play' (148), painting a picture of British theatre in decline. His complaints were echoed in the pages of magazines such as *Plays and*

Players, which lamented the lack of homegrown 'serious' plays in early 1956 (Rebellato 1999: 143), and *Encore* (Marowitz, Milne, and Hale 1981 [1965]).[15] This view has been uncritically repeated by many later accounts, as Rebellato demonstrates in his summary of the literature (1999: 2–6). It's important, as Rebellato cautions, to be wary of the assumption that 'the history of writing is an undeviating regularity, that 1956 saw only a new chapter in the chronicles of inspiration, in which writers managed to throw off their shackles and emerge into the light' (74). In the historicising of this moment, the premiere of John Osborne's play *Look Back in Anger* at the Royal Court Theatre in May 1956 has been constructed as 'the point at which English drama of the modern period starts to become both serious and accessible, the moment at which drama starts saying something real again' (Shepherd and Womack 1996: 278). As Shepherd and Womack note, this idea has been influenced by the claim of naturalism 'to be truly human rather than merely arty' (ibid.), tacitly linking the 'truth' of this form to the 'authentic' voice of the writer, which is to be transmitted as directly as possible to an audience. Rebellato analyses this 'desired integration of thought and expression' (1999: 76), exploring its implications for the organisation of theatrical production. He argues that '[w]hat is at stake, then, in the "revolution" of 1956, is not simply the singular emergence of the repressed playwright, but a reconstruction of the writer's role' (82). At the Royal Court – the self-declared 'writer's theatre' – it's possible to see the emergence of the influential idea that director and production should 'serve' the text and that all other theatrical elements are subordinate to the written drama. This flagship theatre and its attitude towards the theatre text became a template for the development of new playwriting, held up by the Arts Council as 'the sort of playhouse which has long been recognised as the model structure for a creative theatre' (ACGB 1957: 26).[16]

This 'revolution' in playwriting was followed in the next decade by another fundamental shift in the British theatrical landscape: the emergence of alternative theatre.[17] Though this disparate collection of artists and companies was in many ways entangled with the development of new writing – and indeed there were several playwrights whose careers stretched across both alternative theatre and writer-focused institutions like the Royal Court[18] – it was often framed as existing in an antagonistic relationship with subsidised playwriting, as well as with the commercial West End. Sandy Craig stresses the heterogeneity of the alternative theatre that emerged in the 1960s and 1970s, which he characterises as a 'mixture of socialism, song, satire, community expression, twilight entropy and apocalyptic dada' (1980: 10), made up of an assortment of political, community, and experimental theatre companies. But ultimately he sets it in opposition to the 'espousal of literary values' (13) that he sees as constitutive of the subsidised mainstream in the 1960s. Craig notes that, with the exceptions of John Arden and Edward Bond, '[v]ery few of the older playwrights, no matter how angry and radical, have sought to work even sporadically in alternative theatre' (19), thus establishing a division between the text-led Royal Court tradition and alternative theatre-makers. Revisiting this divide from a 21st-century perspective, Hoffman makes the following astute observations about post-war British theatre historiography:

'Theatre', when bracketed to denote a particular kind of text-based, literary, proscenium-framed practice aligned with a particular formation of conservative British culture, has long stood in as the to-be-opposed or to-be-overcome in articulations of experimental, politically motivated performance work. (2009: 98)

The emphasis on text and the literary is particularly notable. Although companies producing new plays were a central part of the alternative theatre movement in these early years, there is nonetheless a widespread rhetoric that positions alternative theatre as revolting against a 'literary' model of theatre-making exemplified by theatres like the Royal Court.

In most accounts, 1968 is singled out as a key year for the emergence of alternative theatre.[19] In addition to the heady political atmosphere of the time, Craig (1980) identifies three other developments in this year that helped alternative theatre to develop: the founding of *Time Out* magazine (which provided listings and reviews of fringe theatre offerings), the establishment of the Arts Council's sub-committee to investigate experimental theatre, and the abolition of censorship. Although the alternative theatre movement was already underway earlier in the decade, as shown by the establishment of key companies such as the People Show and CAST (both formed in 1965), it grew exponentially after the Theatres Act.[20] While much of this alternative theatrical activity was concentrated in London, there also developed a wide touring network and thriving hubs in cities like Brighton and Leeds, as well as important alternative theatre companies outside England such as 7:84 Scotland and Cardiff Laboratory Theatre. Initially, the Arts Council sought to fulfil its responsive role and meet the increased demand, encouraging and offering support to new developments across the British theatre sector.[21] Because of its historical commitments, though, the Council found itself in the difficult position of trying to foster innovation while continuing to support existing clients; the Drama Panel could only fund new companies with the sum left over after its pre-established priorities – which soon included the playwriting schemes – had been fulfilled (Andrews 1977). Despite expressions of interest in alternative theatre from within the Arts Council, there was no coordinated way of responding to applications that challenged the funding body's usual categories and expectations, and there were regular disagreements between subcommittees about which part of the Drama Department should be responsible for funding new alternative theatre ventures. Lunchtime theatres, for instance, primarily came under the remit of the Experimental Drama Committee (EDC), even though one committee member described them as 'small versions of the English Stage Company' (EDC 1972b). Or consider a company like Portable Theatre, which was labelled alternative theatre yet was also regarded by the Arts Council as 'crucial to the burgeoning ecology of British new writing' (Megson 2012: 174). This confusing situation is reflected by the comments of the Assistant Drama Director in the early 1970s, who acknowledged the danger that 'an applicant spent more time deciding who to aim at than how to draw the bow' (EDC 1973).

Unlike the case of new playwriting, then, the approach to alternative theatre was responsive rather than interventionist. In its response, furthermore, the Arts Council reinforced the difference between this new work and the text-led mainstream. The New Activities Committee that was set up to investigate alternative theatre in 1969 found 'an indifference to existing forms and traditional methods of provision' among experimental practitioners and concluded that the 'normal methods of assessment [...] can hardly be applied' (ACGB 1969: 11). A two-track funding system accordingly emerged, though it seems that this was more due to inconsistency and flawed planning than to a concerted effort to prise apart different kinds of work. There was no long-term strategy for dealing with alternative theatre; as early as 1975, the Experimental Drama Committee (a successor of the New Activities Committee) observed that '[i]t was felt that the experimental area had been allowed to develop without the long-term financial implications being taken sufficiently seriously by the Council' (EDC 1975). Alternative theatre companies were funded on an ad hoc basis, often underpinned by the assumption that their activities were a temporary disruption to traditional theatre models. There was doubtless a commitment on the Arts Council's part to support alternative theatre, and by 1975 it was highlighted as 'an area of exceptional growth' (ACGB 1975: 20). Significantly, though, 'the Arts Council's support to experimental companies had always been on a different basis to that for repertory theatres' (Drama Panel 1970). Whereas other grants were generally offered on an ongoing basis, for alternative theatre groups 'each case was re-assessed annually' (EDC 1972), creating uncertain funding conditions. The shunting of alternative theatre from committee to committee, meanwhile, contrasts with the continued commitment to new playwriting, which was consistently represented (if not always adequately funded) by a dedicated subcommittee.[22] Therefore, while new playwriting was an early beneficiary of directed Arts Council policy, alternative theatre-makers suffered from the Council's erratic growth and disjointed network of panels and committees. This haphazard response, I suggest, is a key factor behind the later schism between different kinds of theatrical work.

'Text-based' versus 'non-text-based'

The longer-term effects of these funding decisions rippled outwards over the following decades. The move towards the more recent divide between 'text-based' and 'non-text-based' theatre began during the competitive, under-funded 1980s and was exacerbated by funding initiatives in the 1990s that – intentionally or unintentionally – seemed to pit playwriting against 'visual' and 'physical' theatre.[23] During the 1980s, there was much discussion about how the Arts Council was to both meet existing commitments and encourage experimentation with limited funds at its disposal. In 1987, for example, the Drama Panel noted that the Projects Committee had become a catch-all for new Arts Council initiatives, and that 'whilst the Committee welcomed these initiatives, without expanding resources, it felt it was not able to provide adequate assistance' (Drama Panel 1987). By the end of the decade, the Arts Council itself admitted that '[d]emand for funding under this scheme is so great that twice as many projects could be justifiably funded' (ACGB 1990: 13). This strained funding landscape intensified competition and deepened rifts between different ways of working. Writing in 1988, playwright David Edgar drew a distinction between

> the literary, cerebral, intellectually rigorous but visually dry work of the university-educated political playwrights of the 1960s and 1970s, and the visually stunning, but intellectually thin experiments of the performance artists in and from the art schools. (1988: 175)

John Bull argues that this divide was not, for Edgar, absolute, but that many interpreted it to be so and that this divide would 'become central to what is now a very contemporary debate about text-based and non-text-based performance' (2016: 97). Theatre-maker Neil Bartlett agrees that in the 1980s there were 'a pretty absolute set of divisions between plays and formally innovative work; between building-based "theatre" and project-funded touring/arts centre/small-scale "experimental theatre"' (2013: 112). There was further evidence of an emerging rift at a 1988 conference titled 'Theatre in Crisis', during which a debate opened up about the differences between 'visual and verbo-centric theatre' (Lavender 1989: 214). This was echoed at the 1992 Birmingham Theatre Conference, at which Edgar reported 'a contest between the advocates of the individually written theatre text [...] and the collaborative ethos of live art' (1999: 20).

This 'contest' can be partly ascribed to a feeling of threat on the part of playwrights. Over time, the evident commitment to subsidising new writing could not keep pace with the number of new playwrights emerging, much as Arts Council funding was overtaken by the proliferation of alternative theatre companies. One result of this over-abundance of writers and companies was a misplaced suspicion of devising methodologies. From the 1980s onwards, playwrights increasingly expressed concerns about the perceived threat from devised work, as will be seen throughout this section. The Theatre Writers' Union's (TWU) 1987 survey of companies in the West Midlands, for example, complained that of the 42 new plays presented over a three-year period 'no less than 36 [...] were either "devised" or written by company members, and only two of the companies commissioned writers in the normal way', a situation that the Union intended to 'ameliorate' (TWU 1987: 10–11). The Union was also concerned about 'the habit of small-scale companies evading their responsibilities to employ (and pay) writers by "devising" shows' (43), not considering that the use of devising methodologies might be an aesthetic rather than a financial choice.[24] The introduction of non-building-based franchise funding in 1989/90 allowed for a slight rearrangement of Arts Council priorities at a time of otherwise constrained funding, compounding this impression that playwriting was under threat from other ways of working. Under the new system, regularly-funded touring companies were put on fixed-term franchises for which they had to reapply every three years alongside project-funded companies, thus offering the opportunity for theatre-makers who had long relied on project-by-project subsidy to access more stable funding. By 1997/98, the effect of the franchise system was a net growth from 22 to 37 companies funded on this basis, with the largest gains in the areas of mime (an increase of six companies) and experimental, Black theatre and children's theatre (net gains of three companies each) (Brown, Brannen, and Brown 2000: 384). Discussing the demise of Gay Sweatshop, which benefitted from the franchise system in the 1980s but then fell apart in the 1990s when faced with a choice between new writing and experimental performance, Sara Freeman argues that in the 1990s '[c]ompanies were increasingly sorted by their focus on new writing, the identity groups they addressed or their formal preoccupation' (2015: 145) – an argument that seems to be supported by looking at the categories of theatre to benefit from these new funding arrangements.[25] Moreover, as writers like David Hare and Howard Brenton increasingly worked with the major subsidised theatres, 'new writing approaches initially central to alternative practice became mainstream [...] while non-text-based work became the cutting edge' (Freeman 2014: 137). There was a corresponding increase in aesthetic opposition, with the work of new companies in the growing area of physical theatre frequently distinguishing itself in contrast to the solo-authored play. As Freshwater notes, 'physical theatre's relationship to text has remained central to existing discussions of its definition' (2008: 172), while Simon Murray and John Keefe see the terminology of 'physical theatre' as a 'distancing strategy' from theatre that was perceived to be 'outmoded and laboriously word based' (2016: 13).

From the perspective of practitioners making work that did not involve solo-authored, pre-written plays, an emphasis on collaboration and innovation by the Arts Council in the 1990s offered new opportunities while reinforcing this divide. From 1994, the Arts Council of Great Britain devolved into separate funding bodies for each of the British nations, but these all shared an emphasis on artistic innovation and diversity in this decade (Tomlin 2015: 26–32). One example of this was Arts Council England's New Collaborations fund (later merged with its Live Art Development fund into the Combined Arts Projects Fund), which encouraged inter-disciplinary performance and provided a source of money for practitioners whose work could not necessarily be accommodated by play-led institutional structures. Theatre-maker Amanda Hadingue, however, has observed the dangers as well as the advantages of exploiting this new policy emphasis: 'we were marginalising ourselves again as weirdos doing something unclassifiable on the fringes that had nothing to do with the great traditions of British drama – playwrights, actors and plays' (2007). These schemes, while welcome, were primarily responding to novelty and innovation; as Hadingue adds, there was a 'relentless pressure on theatre makers in the '90s to innovate formally, above all else' (ibid.).[26] Ongoing support was by no means assured, and such grants still firmly placed the companies funded (the likes of Blast Theory, Forced Entertainment, and Gob Squad) outside of 'proper' drama.[27] While arts policy from the mid-1990s onwards undoubtedly offered new opportunities for some, it also contributed towards a deepening of divisions that had formed in the preceding years. Theatre-makers perceived to be 'doing something unclassifiable on the fringes' saw new funding avenues opened to them in these years, but they continued to be defined against the text-dominated mainstream. Despite numerous, noted areas of crossover, in 1995 it was still agreed by the Arts Council that 'it was the correct approach to deal with new work and new writing in separate sections' (Drama Panel 1995).

Going into the 21st century, arts funding boosts under the New Labour government primarily benefitted new play development, despite ongoing concerns from playwrights about an emphasis on devising. The continued centrality of text-led theatre and of new playwriting in particular was confirmed by three reports commissioned in the 2000s: the British Theatre Consortium's (BTC) *Writ Large, New Writing in Theatre 2003–2008* by Emma Dunton, Roger Nelson, and Hetty Shand, and Anne Millman and Jodi Myers' *Theatre Assessment 2009*. *Writ Large* found that 'new writing' was the largest single category of productions across the theatres surveyed by the BTC for the years 2003–2009, representing 47% of all shows, and that 'devised work and physical theatre remain a minority component' (2009: 8).[28] In smaller-scale theatre, meanwhile, new writing 'appear[ed] to have undergone a period of renaissance', and increased funding had 'enabled a wider variety of new writing/new work to take place in an extraordinary mix of venues across the country' (Dunton, Nelson, and Shand 2009: 3). This 'renaissance' can be understood as a result of targeted resources and subsidy, as Bolton (2011; 2012) has explored in greater depth. The authors of *Writ Large* found that 'there is a concentration of new plays in the national companies and the major regional repertory theatres' (BTC 2009: 55) – in other words, in those established theatre institutions that have been consistently funded over a long period and that benefitted from considerable uplifts in the 21st century.[29] In addition to the extra sums awarded to theatres producing new plays, new writing received support from Arts Council England's managed funds: £270,000 in 2003/04 and £100,000 in the subsequent four years (Millman and Myers 2009: 77). New writing also received the highest levels of investment through Grants for the Arts, Arts Council England's new funding programme for artists and organisations outside the regularly funded portfolio (ibid.). *Writ Large* concluded that '[t]he promotion of new writing in the repertoire is a major success story both for English theatres and the Arts Council' (BTC 2009: 8), recognising the significant role of subsidy. Although – following the devolution of arts funding – these reports were focused on new writing in England, they illustrate a wider trend across the United Kingdom in the early 21st century. For example, the *Review of the Theatre Sector in Scotland* published in 2012 stressed that '[n]ew work is the lifeblood of Scottish theatre – often, although not always, this starts with the playwright' (Christine Hamilton Consulting 2012: 4). The same report found a notable increase in new writing in Scottish theatres between 2001 and 2011 – though this was also accompanied by an expansion of experimental performance over the same period (25). Meanwhile, in his 2019 review of the previous decade of Welsh theatre, Nick Davies – formerly an employee of the Arts Council of

Wales – stressed the contributions of the Sherman Theatre, Theatr Clwyd and theatre company Dirty Protest to Welsh new writing, describing the 2010s as a 'golden era' for the nation's playwriting (2019).

Still, however, some of the playwrights interviewed for these reports felt threatened by the rise of other forms. *Writ Large*, for instance, observes a worry among writers that Arts Council policy was moving away from the written text, while Millman and Myers' report reveals a consensus that emphasis had shifted away from 'new writing' and towards 'new work' (2009: 76–77). Among the 'concerns' of playwrights listed in the introduction to *Writ Large*'s historical context, meanwhile, is 'an emerging trend towards collectively-written plays, excluding freelance writers from the process' (BTC 2009: 3). Contrary to perceptions of a swing towards devised work, though, *Writ Large* found that '[t]he overwhelming majority (77%) of theatre works produced are plays' (6). This also runs counter to playwrights' belief that Arts Council policies that 'advocated new, collaborative methods of playmaking' were 'privileging devised, performance-based work over individually-written new plays' (4). Nonetheless, the vocabulary of 'threat' and 'challenge' recurs again and again in the feedback from playwrights surveyed in these reports. The authors of *Writ Large* do point out that '[s]ome of the concerns expressed by playwrights […] appear not to be justified' (11), observing the disjuncture between playwrights' perceptions and the BTC's findings. They are still keen, though, to stress the success of new writing and the comparatively niche status of devising, thereby reinforcing a sense that that the two are in competition. Edgar's feeling that 'fashionable opinion has turned its back on text-based theatre' (2009) perhaps gets to the heart of this persistent discontent among playwrights.[30] The Royal Court's then literary manager Chris Campbell likewise reported in 2012 that the playwrights he worked with 'feel undervalued, they feel that they are being represented as old-fashioned, out of touch, a bit square and a bit dull' (Goode 2012). Such complaints echo Mark Ravenhill's analysis of the theatre landscape in the early 1990s, when he claims 'it wasn't cool to be a writer' and '[t]he figure of the playwright had taken a battering' (2004: 310) – mainly, he argues, from physical theatre and devised work. While there was a shift throughout the 1990s and 2000s towards greater acceptance and encouragement of various kinds of experimental and collaborative theatre-making within the theatre and arts funding establishment, this generated defensiveness among playwrights who felt that the innovation of other theatre-makers was being celebrated at the expense of playwriting – at the same time as, contrary to perceptions, new writing continued to receive a greater share of funding and support. As an indirect outcome of the Arts Council's public emphasis on innovation on the one hand and its funding of an expanded new writing infrastructure on the other, British theatre had become divided on the basis of its perceived relationship with text.

In the first two decades of the 21st century, the British theatre sector was frequently framed as an artistic and ideological battlefield. On one side – depending on the preferred terminology – was 'new writing' or 'text-based theatre';

pitted against it was 'new work', 'devised theatre', or 'non-text-based theatre'. According to some, this was possibly the 'defining theatrical schism' of the early 21st century (Haydon 2013: 61). As Bolton has observed, there was

> a tangible friction – sometimes creative, though typically obstructive – between practitioners who primarily engage with the production of individually-authored play-texts – 'text-based theatre' – and practitioners who primarily engage with the collaborative devising of non-script-led works – 'non-text-based performance'. (2011: 98)

Typically, 'text-based' theatre is seen to follow a national theatrical tradition of play- and playwright-led drama, in which the integrity, authority and vision of the script is enshrined at the centre of the theatre-making process, whereas 'non-text-based' theatre usually describes work that is perceived to be opposed to this tradition – whether or not the work itself actually includes text. Practices that have been grouped under the broad umbrella of 'non-text-based' theatre include devising, physical theatre, immersive and interactive theatre, site-specific theatre, and practices aligned with the traditions of live art. Liz Tomlin has similarly outlined this institutional divide, observing that the separation of development opportunities into 'text-based' and 'non-text-based' streams 'requir[ed] young theatre-makers to categorize themselves, for strategic development purposes, as either playwrights or non-text-based artists' (2009: 58). As demonstrated by my non-exhaustive list of the many different practices labelled 'non-text-based', this binarised view of the contemporary British theatre landscape belies its formal diversity. Furthermore, the proliferation of new theatrical forms during the period considered in this book renders a two-pronged understanding of British theatre insufficient, while the sustained drive towards collaborations of various kinds continues to blur the already porous boundaries between practices of writing and devising. The categories of 'text-based' and 'non-text-based' are therefore fluid and rather vague, and the practices they describe often have more in common than the opposing labels would suggest. This seems to confirm Hoffman's suggestion that 'it is precisely the ambiguous and ambivalent nearness of the two sets of practice that exacerbates [...] the desire to maintain distinction, autonomy and uniqueness' (2009: 97).[31] While I do not deny that there are differences in how text is treated in different theatre-making processes, as I will explore in later chapters, the stark demarcation of work as either 'text-based' or 'non-text-based' misunderstands the nature of playtexts and reduces the huge range of contemporary theatre-making practices, thereby eliding or misrepresenting the work of many artists.

The potentially reductive nature of this terminology was part of the fierce debate about 'text-based' and 'non-text-based' theatre in the late 2000s and early 2010s. Theatre-maker Andy Field was one of the first to publicly rail against 'a spurious divide in theatre between "text-based" and "devised" work' (2009), which as he observes was regularly agitating both practitioners and commentators on online forums.[32] Though distinctions between 'text-based' and 'non-text-based' persisted, as Cathy Turner observed the following year, 'at least their relationship now seems to be on the agenda' (2010: 77). A couple of years later, meanwhile, director and dramaturg Alex Chisholm expressed her desire to bring 'an end to the [...] unnecessary opposition between New Writing and New Work' (2012), provoking a fresh wave of discussion about the contending terms. In the seven years between first embarking on this research during my doctoral studies and the moment of writing, meanwhile, there has been a distinct easing of hostilities between the 'text-based' and 'non-text-based' camps. Reflecting back on the antagonism at the start of the century, Field writes that 'the amount of time I spent worrying about all this seems like a memory from another world' (2021: 63). He suggests that '[w]ith hindsight, these arguments were nearly always defined by mutual defensiveness and I think a lot of insecurity about our future survival in what was then a brand-new era of austerity' (ibid.).[33] While there has been little easing of the economic pressures that created this atmosphere of fierce competition, there are numerous indications that institutional structures are beginning to shift to accommodate multiple ways of working with text in the theatre-making process. Since the arrival of Vicky Featherstone as artistic director in 2013, the Royal Court has actively expanded the scope of its remit as the 'writer's theatre', launching collaborative experiments like The Site, a temporary theatre space which was led by design rather than text, and working with theatre-makers who were often previously situated on the 'non-text-based' side of the binary, such as Chris Thorpe and Complicite's Simon McBurney. Other prominent new writing venues like the Bush Theatre have also widened the ways in which they make work with artists. Whereas previously the Bush was known for supporting new plays, it now has a more flexible submissions policy and works with a number of theatre-makers whose processes do not begin with pre-written scripts.[34] And in 2015 the National Theatre combined the NT Studio – which previously supported the workshopping of many projects that might have been considered 'non-text-based' – with its literary department, bringing together all development initiatives in the New Work Department. Although these examples are all London-based, the national prominence of these institutions suggests a shift at the heart of the British theatre establishment. In Scotland and Wales, meanwhile, the national theatres established this century have similarly challenged divisions on the basis of text.

In the following chapters I will be moving fluidly between examples of practice typically separated into the categories of 'text-based' and 'non-text-based', in an effort to further erode the barrier that has separated different forms of British theatre-making over recent decades. While at times I will have cause to acknowledge the 'text-based'/'non-text-based' binary, I am primarily interested in exploring practices that are experimenting in interesting ways with text and performance, regardless of how these practices have previously been defined. Often, moreover, the pieces of theatre that I analyse defy categories based on a simplistic understanding of the theatre text, as with the Made in China performance discussed in the Introduction. This example also nods towards the way in which many of the practices that I explore are themselves actively questioning the relationship between text and performance. Drama has, as Bennett has noted, a 'curious but typical tendency to theorize about itself' (1990: 256). This is a shared characteristic of many of the plays and performances discussed in this book, which are often prodding at the very nature of theatre itself, revealing crucial fault-lines in popular understandings of the relationship between text and performance. That said, by focusing on pieces that complicate assumptions about the role of text, I'm not seeking to set these in opposition to other forms of theatre. It's important to be clear that, while these specific examples are of value to my study because of the ways in which they reveal the complexity of the relationship between text and performance, this same complexity holds for *all* theatre.

Conclusion

As I have briefly recounted in this chapter, the theatre text has been the subject of centuries of debate, with scholars, critics, and theatre-makers arguing for its place as literature on the one hand and material for performance on the other. Many have asserted that playtexts are complete on the page, while others have contended that they are incomplete until performed. Paradoxically, though, such texts are both complete and incomplete. They are autonomous works of literature *and* they are indeterminate suggestions for performance. As Rebellato observes, a play is 'complete on its own and it is complete in performance' (2015: 170–171). While – as Rebellato's comment suggests – the pre-written, solo-authored playtext has a particularly tricky ontological status in this respect, many of the same characteristics apply to other texts for performance, as I have begun to demonstrate. The history of perceptions of the relationship between text and performance in Britain, meanwhile, is discontinuous and disputed, with many tellings of this history having an investment in the essential literariness of the playtext. One important flashpoint in this history is the attainment of 'literary' status for (some) plays at the turn of the 20th century, which was met with an opposing rejection of dramatic texts in favour of theatre as art among avant-garde theatre-makers. This set up a binary that has since been reproduced in various guises. In Britain, specifically, a convergence of different factors in the post-war period has led to a subsequent division of theatre-making practices on the basis of their perceived relationship to text, which by the turn of the 21st century had become an opposition between 'text-based' and 'non-text-based' theatre.

While the 'text-based'/'non-text-based' battle may be waning, and while several promising signs point to the ascendance of a more complex interplay of page and stage, there remains a need to unpick the understandings of text and performance that have sat beneath this binary. If these misconceptions about the theatre text are not addressed, similar divides may emerge again in the future. Whereas much existing scholarship has separated performance from playtext and divided theatre-making into devising and text-led practices, the rest of this book focuses on the sometimes troubled relationships and leakages between these categories. It looks back at some of the key tensions in the battle between 'text-based' and 'non-text-based' theatre in order to dig down to the deeper causes of this antagonism. On the one hand, as I examine further in the next chapter, playwrights, directors, and critics have frequently engaged in a rhetoric of 'serving' the playtext, which they imbue with creative authority. Practices of devising and collective creation, on the other hand, have often been framed as acts of resistance against the perceived power of solo-authored plays and their frequent association with the literary, which many theatre-makers have found creatively limiting. I argue that both approaches are underpinned by a misunderstanding of the complex interaction between page and stage – a complexity that the following chapters continue to explore.

Notes

1 This production is a prime example of the porous national boundaries discussed in the Introduction: the text was written by a British playwright, produced by a Dutch theatre company, and first performed in Brazil before coming to the Young Vic Theatre in London.
2 Both Ian Shuttleworth (2015) and Andrew Haydon (2015), for example, described van Hove's production as minimalist, while Christopher Hart argued that 'it's pretty much a failure as a piece of drama' (2015: 862). In my own review, I noted that 'as theatre it has an oddly detached quality' (Love 2015b).
3 The relationship between text and performance has been a matter of long debate within Shakespeare Studies. Some key texts from just the last couple of decades include Lukas Erne's *Shakespeare as Literary Dramatist* (2013 [2003]), which argues that Shakespeare wrote for the page as well as the stage; *Shakespeare and the Idea of the Book* by Charlotte Scott (2007), exploring the role of texts in Shakespeare's theatre; and Robert Wiemann's essay "Performance in Shakespeare's Theatre: Ministerial and/or Magisterial?" (2010), in which he stresses the dual identity of drama as both writing and performance, avoiding a binarised or hierarchical relationship between the two. Worthen offers a summary of some of the competing literary and theatrical understandings of Shakespeare in his article 'Intoxicating Rhythms: Or, Shakespeare, Literary Drama, and Performance (Studies)' (2011), while another overview of changing scholarly attitudes towards Shakespeare, text and performance can be found in Barbara Hodgdon's introduction to *A Companion to Shakespeare and Performance* (2005).
4 This view of the anti-text orthodoxy in academia has also been observed – albeit somewhat more polemically – by playwright David Edgar, who railed against the academy's 'profound ideological hostility to playwriting and playwrights' in his comments at the 'Turning the Page' conference (Merrifield 2013).
5 See Julie Stone Peters (2000), who similarly emphasises the importance of these factors but also complicates this narrative of the emerging literary playwright by drawing on evidence of a rich visual theatrical culture in the 19th-century. I discuss this further in Chapter 4.
6 This tendency is exemplified by Anthony Jenkins' influential argument about the emergence of 'serious drama' in *The Making of Victorian Drama* (1991).
7 As Stephens notes, the 1833 Copyright Act did not necessarily benefit playwrights, as the copyright of many scripts was held not by their writers but by publishers, while the situation for playwrights was further complicated by the uncertain legal status of minor theatres (1992: 91–95).
8 Other playwrights who are commonly recognised to have played a central role in elevating the profession in the late 19th century and into the 20th century include Dion Boucicault, Henry Arthur Jones, Oscar Wilde, and Harley Granville-Barker.

9   This link is observed but not examined, for example, in Cathy Turner and Synne K. Behrndt's *Dramaturgy and Performance* (2008), while the *Modern British Playwriting* (Megson 2012; Milling 2012; Nicholson 2012; Pattie 2012; Sierz 2012; Rebellato 2013) and *British Theatre Companies* (Saunders 2015; Tomlin 2015; Bull 2016) series comment on Arts Council funding in their introductions.
10 Among the publications resulting from the project was the *British Theatre Companies* series of books (Saunders 2015; Tomlin 2015; Bull 2016).
11 The subcommittee had several different names over the years: the New Drama Sub-Committee, the New Writing Committee, the Theatre Writing Committee, the Theatre Writing and Bursaries Sub-Committee. For ease of reference, I subsequently refer to it as the Theatre Writing Committee (TWC).
12 It was also subsequently emphasised that the Council 'directly subsidises theatres on the grounds that they follow a deliberate policy of supporting new work' (ACGB 1959: 12) and that '[a] company's policy towards new plays is part of its annual application and is taken into account when assessing the subsidy to be offered' (ACGB 1977: 18–19).
13 For more detailed accounts of theatre censorship in Britain, see Steve Nicholson (2003, 2005, 2011, 2015), John Johnston (1990), David Thomas, David Carlton, and Anne Etienne (2007), Dominic Shellard, Steve Nicholson and Miriam Handley (2004), and Nicholas De Jongh (2000).
14 The emphasis on playwrights also continued after the end of censorship. In the 1974 annual review, for instance, the Arts Council boasts of 'this country's remarkable record in finding new playwrights in the past fifteen years' (ACGB 1974: 16). Discussing the support of experimental new work and its crossover into the mainstream, meanwhile, the Council asserts that '[a]t the centre of this process stands the playwright' (ACGB 1979: 15).
15 Similar views are expressed in the essay collection *Modern British Dramatists* (Brown 1968).
16 Taryn Storey (2012) has looked in greater detail at the alignment of the Royal Court's and the Arts Council's aims and the influence this had on state subsidy to theatre.
17 While this new breed of theatre was variously described as experimental, fringe, underground, and avant-garde, I'm choosing to refer to these practices as 'alternative theatre', which Sara Freeman (2006) notes is the term preferred by most practitioners.
18 Playwrights who moved from the fringe to the subsidised mainstream, or who moved back and forth between the two, include David Hare, David Edgar, Howard Brenton, and Caryl Churchill.
19 Craig (1980) identifies this as the turning point, in agreement with Peter Ansorge (1975). This year is also the starting point for Catherine Itzin's study of alternative political theatre (1980) and is accorded particular historical significance in *British Theatre Companies 1965–1979* (Bull 2017).
20 In 1966, the Arts Council was funding 61 theatres, companies and organisations (ACGB 1966); a decade later, this number had risen to 174, 96 of which were project-based clients – a group formed primarily of companies that might be categorised as alternative theatre (ACGB 1976). This growth was also partly enabled by increases in funding from government to the Arts Council. Between 1966 and 1976, the Arts Council's total grant-in-aid grew from £3,910,000 (ACGB 1966) to £28,850,000 (ACGB 1977).
21 In his history of alternative theatre, Steve Gooch acknowledges that the funding body 'was not slow – by its own standards – to respond to the new developments of the Fringe' (1984: 45). 'Fringe and experimental companies' were first mentioned in an Arts Council annual review in 1967, with a recommendation for continued support 'to be given in as flexible a way as possible' (ACGB 1967: 25).
22 Over the years, alternative theatre was variously dealt with by the New Activities Committee, the Experimental Projects Committee, the Experimental Drama Committee, the Projects Committee, and the Standards and Reassessments Committee. In the case of

alternative theatre companies who worked with writers, meanwhile, there was some overlap with the TWC.
23 While funding levels from 1979 are disputed because of disagreements about the level of inflation and therefore the real terms increase or decrease in subsidy (Peacock 1999: 44), Drama Panel and committee meeting minutes bear out a sense of embattlement in the 1980s.
24 That said, there may have been a financial element to some of these decisions to devise, as by this time the TWU had been successful in negotiating writers' fees that would have been beyond the means of some small-scale companies. For more details of the rights negotiated by the TWU, see Edgar and Wittington (2012a).
25 Freeman suggests that it was Gay Sweatshop's move away from new writing, which had formerly consolidated its status, that lost the company its Arts Council funding (2015: 150).
26 In the late 1990s, for example, Arts Council England was listing '[n]ew forms and collaborative ways of working' as one of its five key priorities (ACE 1999).
27 This is illustrated, for instance, by the Drama Department's advice in 1994 to Forced Entertainment, among other performance companies, to find funding from elsewhere in the Arts Council (Etchells 1996).
28 The 47% of the repertoire of reporting theatres and companies that consisted of new writing included not just new plays, but also new adaptations and translations, as well as 'some devised work' (BTC 2009: 6). This broad definition of new writing was responding to the remit of capturing the full range of work writers were doing in the theatre in the early 21st century.
29 Arts Council England received a £25 million funding boost under New Labour, with the theatre budget receiving a 72% increase. 83% of the additional money for theatre in England in these years went to producing organisations and companies (Millman and Myers 2009: 21).
30 It's worth noting that Edgar was one of the authors of *Writ Large*.
31 While Hoffman's article is primarily concerned with practices that define themselves as live art, her observations about 'a break between something like the dramatic or literary and something like the live or the visual' (2009: 97) also invoke the 'text-based'/'non-text-based' dichotomy.
32 This debate about 'text-based' and 'non-text-based' theatre took place in articles, posts, and comments on platforms including the *Guardian* theatre blog, the anonymously authored website *Encore Theatre Magazine*, sites run by theatre bloggers such as Andrew Haydon and Matt Trueman, and blogs written by theatre-makers like Andy Field, Chris Goode and David Eldridge. Several of these sites are now defunct. Haydon offers an overview of these and other outlets for online theatre criticism during this period (2016).
33 Debates about 'text-based' and 'non-text-based' theatre were largely happening in the context of the 2008 financial crash and its aftermath, including the economic austerity policies introduced by the Conservative-Liberal Democrat coalition government formed in 2010.
34 The theatre's associate artists, for instance, have included companies such as ANTLER, Sh!t Theatre and Gameshow.

2
DRAMATURGICAL INNOVATIONS AND EVASIONS OF AUTHORITY: AUTHORSHIP AND INTENTION

In the studio of the Royal Exchange Theatre, Gemma Paintin looks out at the audience. 'We can just sit and chat can't we?' she says invitingly, gesturing towards us as we sit quietly in the dark (2016: 48). 'They won't answer you,' says her co-performer James Stenhouse, explaining, 'it's not in the script' (ibid.). A moment later, Paintin responds by producing the playtext and handing it to a member of the audience. What follows is an entirely scripted interaction between performer and spectator, with the script itself visible throughout to the rest of the audience. After a few lines of chit-chat, Paintin asks: 'Does this feel like real dialogue to you?' (50). The audience member, as instructed by the script, responds: 'Neither of us sounds particularly convincing' (ibid.).

In this moment from Action Hero's 2015 show *Wrecking Ball*, Paintin and Stenhouse extend their authorial power beyond the confines of the stage by putting words in an audience member's mouth. The company describes *Wrecking Ball* as being 'about theatre' (2016: 6), adding that the show is about 'the power an artist holds and the ways in which well-meaning people might abuse that position of power unintentionally' (7). The story of a photographer exploiting a female celebrity is used as an analogue for the potentially manipulative power of the script, thus implicitly challenging the attribution of authority to playtexts, which are often understood as the set of instructions that other theatre-makers must 'serve'. *Wrecking Ball*'s narrative and its form both demonstrate abuses of power – the twisting of someone else's actions, or the scripting of their behaviour – that might be imputed to the 'authoritative' playtext. Like the Made in China show I discussed in the Introduction, the whole piece is something of an argument with scripted drama. In *Wrecking Ball*, Action Hero perhaps underestimate the extent to which all playtexts are open to interpretation and alteration, but the show nonetheless highlights the power that has accrued to text and playwright in mainstream British production structures.

DOI: 10.4324/9781003126812-3

In contemporary British theatre and performance, authors and texts keep appearing on stage like this. A whole sub-genre of plays has put creators in the spotlight – as unreliable narrators, as naïve interviewers, as frustrated artists, and as manipulative author figures whose authority is playfully toppled. As Dan Rebellato notes, 'not just writing but authorship itself has become a key area of theatrical experimentation' (2013: 11). Evoking Roland Barthes' famous essay (1977 [1967]), several playwrights have staged their own deaths (and, occasionally, resurrections), while others – like Paintin and Stenhouse – self-consciously wield their own power within their plays. At the same time, other writers appear to be withdrawing from their plays by refusing to specify details such as the speakers, setting, or order of scenes. But these apparent retreats similarly serve to underline and question the authoring role of the playwright. In this chapter, I propose that this recent trend is rooted in a long-standing anxiety about the location and operation of authorship in theatre practices. This, I suggest, is a key component in the problematic status of the theatre text. Within the British theatre sector, there have been many debates about who can claim authorship within the theatre-making process and what this authorship might look like, based on implicit and often opposing understandings of the relationship between text and performance. These debates are, in turn, founded on under-explored ideas around intention and authority, which this chapter interrogates through looking at several contemporary plays and productions in which authorship itself is under scrutiny.

The death – and rebirth – of the author

Authorship has proved to be a fertile area for theatrical experimentation over the last three decades, as Rebellato has discussed in his essay 'Exit the Author'. Drawing on various examples, from playwrights including Martin Crimp, Tim Crouch, Sarah Kane, and Dennis Kelly, Rebellato argues that 'authorship has become a ground for aesthetic and ethical questioning that stages the death of the author as a way of profoundly investigating theatrical meaning and our capacity for fundamental political change' (2013: 12). Rebellato resists seeing these instances of 'playwriterly withdrawal' (15) as evidence of a dissolution of authorship, as well as challenging the 'absolutist anti-authorial' position commonly attributed to post-structuralist thinkers such as Roland Barthes, Michel Foucault, and Jacques Derrida. He concludes from a re-reading of these theories that 'intention is not something that we can straightforwardly separate from a text and neither Barthes, Foucault nor Derrida believe that we can' (23). While Rebellato suggests that, by questioning and foregrounding authorship, the plays that he cites contain radical political potential, I am more interested in what they might reveal about the relationships between authors, texts, and performances, and the unease they expose around the fraught question of authorial intention. Beneath the experimentation that can be witnessed in these texts, there seems to be a persistent anxiety about the nature and role of authorship in a theatrical context, as also demonstrated in some of the discourse around text, performance, and the position of the playwright explored in the previous chapter. To more fully unpack what might be going on here, I want to briefly revisit some of the influential authorship theories discussed by Rebellato and further explore their implications for models of creation and ownership in British theatre, before going on to focus more closely on the idea of authorial intention.

An important place to begin is Barthes' essay 'The Death of the Author', which initiated an effort to shift analytic emphasis away from the biography and intentions of the author and onto the multiple interpretations of the reader. At the close of the essay, Barthes famously asserts that 'to give writing its future, it is necessary to overthrow the myth: the birth of the reader must be at the cost of the death of the author' (1977 [1967]: 148). Often, this has been read rather literally to imply the complete irrelevance and eradication of the author.[1] At the extreme end of this reading, it's suggested that Barthes denies all forms of authorial intention and sees language as operating entirely out of the control of those who write it. However, as Rebellato points out, 'in trying to show this move from author-centred work to the multiplicity of text, Barthes refers to a series of authors', as well as using 'characteristically intentional vocabulary to describe how writing happens' (2013: 21). Indeed, it is *writers* (such as Stéphane Mallarmé and Marcel Proust) who, according to Barthes, have 'attempted to loosen' (1977: 143) the power of the author – much like the playwrights discussed in this chapter are questioning their own authority in their writing. The evidence of the essay itself therefore suggests that Barthes' theory is not quite as radical as many of its critics – and its champions – have claimed. What Barthes is really asking for in his call for the death of the author is not an end to the idea of intending authors as such, but to the author's intention as the text's governing authority; he is rejecting the notion of 'the "message" of the Author-God' in favour of 'a multi-dimensional space in which a variety of writings, none of them original, blend and clash' (146). If authorial intention is toppled from its position of dominance, then 'the claim to decipher a text becomes quite futile' (ibid.). In a theatrical context, this implies not a doing away of writers, but a movement away from any attempt to faithfully decode writers' intentions in the transition from page to stage.

In the wake of Barthes' essay, the figure of the author has if anything become the subject of increasingly intense scrutiny, debate, and experimentation. Silvija Jestrovic argues that, after Barthes, the author can be seen as a performative figure, suggesting that 'the godlike authorial figure is deconstructed, but also almost immediately reassembled, sometimes as an intertextual reference, sometimes as a ludic, performative figure' (2020: 5). This certainly speaks to the various playful incarnations of the author that I explore in this chapter. The idea of the 'death of the author' has also captured the imaginations of many theatre-makers, who have sought to collectively create work in ways that resist or deconstruct the perceived authority of the 'Author-God'. In their overview of some of the typical definitions of devising, Deirdre Heddon and Jane Milling include – in somewhat tongue-in-cheek fashion – 'the embodiment of the death of the author' (2006: 5). Here, they are highlighting the way in which some practitioners have understood devising as a form of theatre-making that challenges and evades authorship by rejecting the perceived tyranny of the playtext. The rhetoric of many devising companies explicitly positions their work in opposition to play-led producing models and instead aligns it with a Barthesian turn away from the figure of the author. Even in companies that have a writer and/or an artistic director, this individual often seeks to distance themselves from any notion of authorship. Forced Entertainment's Tim Etchells, for example, stresses the role of quotation and borrowing in his writing, insisting that he is simply 'collecting, sifting and using bits of other people's stuff' (1999: 101). He has a markedly Barthesian conception of his role as writer, rejecting traditional tropes of authorship and instead seeing himself as 'a space this other stuff is flowing through and lodged inside' (99). Outlining the process of creating text with the company, Etchells describes it as 'a growing, generative process of improvisation, negotiation, discussion, more writing and eventual fixing' (105), contrasting this with the perceived rigidity and authorial control of playtexts and the 'frighteningly singular' (101) voice of the playwright. There is, as Mark Smith (2013) has identified, a tension at work here, between Etchells' regularly reiterated aversion to the written word and the role of author, and the prominent place of Etchells' own writing both within and around Forced Entertainment's work. Simon McBurney has likewise played down his creative authority within Complicite, generating a similar tension (Freshwater 2007: 183–191).

While the extent to which devising rejects authorship is somewhat overstated and often based on a misreading of Barthes' theory, collective forms of theatre-making do pose a certain challenge to conventional understandings of authorship within British theatre. There is the fraught question, for example, of the extent to which authorship can be shared and who ultimately holds responsibility and authority within a collaborative process. Although claims of completely collective and non-hierarchical creative processes are often not entirely reflective of the ways in which devised performances are actually made, as Heddon and Milling acknowledge (2006: 5–6), even the attempt to work in this way highlights the fact that identifying the author of a performance is inherently tricky (is it the writer? the director? the designer? the performers? all of the above?) and that there is no single, seamless model of page-to-stage enactment that can account for the complex relationship between text and performance. These debates are complicated further by copyright law. For legal and financial purposes, it's necessary to identify who is primarily responsible for creating a show, and this responsibility is typically assigned to a single, 'authoring' writer. While there are some examples of collective approaches to copyright – such as the royalty arrangements negotiated between Frantic Assembly and playwright Bryony Lavery, who share creative and financial credit for the shows on which they have collaborated (Smith 2013: 242) – these remain unusual. As Martin Puchner notes, 'it is almost impossible for directors and choreographers to copyright theatrical productions, while dramatic texts have long been integrated into the legal regime governing copyright' (2011: 293). There are practical difficulties and complexities associated with joint or split authorship in UK copyright law, which has led to a preference for simplifying ownership where possible – usually by assigning this to the playwright as default (McDonagh 2021: 113). The Copyright, Designs and Patents

Act does allow for joint authorship, which is defined as 'a work produced by the collaboration of two or more authors in which the contribution of each author is not distinct from that of the other author or authors' (McDonagh 2021: 83), but in practice this rarely extends to directors and other theatre-makers involved in the creation and development process.[2] There is, as Luke McDonagh observes in his study of theatrical copyright and authorship, relatively little case law to consult concerning the question of joint authorship. But those cases that do exist have tended to uphold the authorial rights of the playwright against the claims of collaborating directors, concluding that workshop and rehearsal development does not constitute joint authorship (McDonagh 2021: 83–84). Moreover, the one successful joint authorship claim that McDonagh cites was supported by written notes documenting specific suggestions about a scenario and characters; notably, 'the court emphasised writing over other forms of creative input' (85), thus reinforcing the authoritative position of text.[3] The collaborative model of creation seen in devising processes, meanwhile, 'does not lend itself easily to the traditional way copyright recognises authorship or joint authorship' (McDonagh 2021: 105).[4]

Therefore, while the collaborative nature of theatre-making inherently challenges the idea of a sole author, there is little doubt that authors continue to occupy a prominent position in British theatrical culture, whether they are seen as legal entities, as symbols of authority, as performative figures, or as tyrants whose role must be challenged. This is where Foucault's notion of the 'author-function' offers a useful reframing of authorship debates. Responding to 'The Death of the Author', Foucault argues that a focus on the concept of writing has 'merely transposed the empirical characteristics of an author to a transcendental anonymity' (1991: 104). The most obvious signs of the author's individuality have been erased in favour of a focus on writing as something seemingly autonomous, yet the features of authorship are simply displaced; this 'runs the risk of maintaining the author's privileges under the protection of writing's *a priori* status' (105). Foucault argues that we need to look instead at the 'author-function', suggesting that the often-unquestioned processes of authorship as a concept can reveal a lot about how readers understand and interpret texts. Helpfully for a theatrical context, where there is often not just one clearly identifiable 'author' of a piece, Foucault makes a distinction between the author as a concept or function and the writer as an actual person putting pen to paper: 'the author' is an interpretative construct that regulates the relationships between and the discourses surrounding certain groups of texts, distinct from the actual individual(s) who wrote the texts in question. What Foucault seems to be suggesting is that, rather than simply proclaiming that the author is dead, it's necessary to understand more fully how the author as a concept functions within a specific society and culture, thus allowing a more rigorous interrogation of the structures controlling the circulation and reception of discourse. While Foucault is primarily discussing literature, this equally applies to theatre, where the author or author-function is frequently appealed to as a regulating authority, either limiting or legitimating the multiple repetitions of performance.

Although there has been much academic debate about authorship since Barthes made his critical intervention, the poststructuralist discourses that have influenced many theatre-makers in what might be loosely described as devising or collective practices have left mainstream production structures in Britain largely unaffected. Perhaps the most notable impact of such discourses on script-focused theatre-making practices was the perception of some that they posed a threat to the playwright.[5] In reality, though, the ideas of thinkers like Barthes and Foucault have had relatively little impact on how the playwright's role has typically been conceived in mainstream professional contexts during the period under investigation. In these settings, the playwright is still often understood as the primary 'author' of the theatrical event, whose script directs the rest of the creative team. Simon Stephens, for instance, has discussed how actors are 'used to using the playwright's text as a bible' (2012: vii), while views about the importance of 'serving' the playwright's intentions in performance are expressed by many of the playwrights and directors interviewed in Duncan Wu's volume on contemporary dramatists (2000). The director's responsibility to realise the intentions of the playwright is also emphasised in textbooks such as Sally Mackey and Simon Cooper's *Drama and Theatre Studies* (2000), and in several 21st-century directing handbooks (Unwin 2004; Mitchell 2009; Swain 2011). The staging of new writing, specifically, has tended to emphasise the centrality of the playwright and their text. As director and dramaturg Alex Chisholm has observed from her experiences in the industry, '[t]he rhetoric of New Writing is all about "serving the text" and "serving the writer"' (2012). Similarly, Harry Derbyshire discusses how in British new writing 'the collective process of theatrical production' is 'harnessed in the service of an individual voice' (2008: 131) – though, unlike the staged authors that I discuss in this chapter, the playwright who possesses this voice is typically expected to disappear into their work. As Rebellato (2013) and Jacqueline Bolton (2012) both note, Britain's mainstream playwriting tradition and its practices of new play development often encourage the creation of 'coherent and transparent fictional worlds' (Rebellato 2013: 25), in which the author remains an invisible presence whose distinctive 'voice' speaks through the fiction they have constructed.[6] This has remained the dominant view in the staging of new writing in Britain, despite occasional disputes about so-called 'director's theatre' – a term that is frequently used with pejorative associations in a British context, as I discuss in Chapter 3.

Often, then, the question of authorship has sat at the heart of debates about the relationship between text and performance and oppositions between so-called 'text-based' and 'non-text-based' theatre. The former has been characterised – both positively and negatively – as subject to the authority of the author-playwright, while some proponents of the latter have claimed that it evades or democratises such authorship. I wonder, though, if existing interrogations of theatrical authorship are somewhat misplaced and fail to get to the bottom of how texts and their intersection with performance are understood. By focusing too heavily on the question of who is identified as the author of the live event, there is a danger of eliding the underlying issues that might render authorship problematic in the first place. The concept of the author (or the author-function, to echo Foucault) typically stands in for ideas around intention and authority. When asserting the centrality of the playwright's 'voice' in the staging process, what is at stake is the idea of that writer's intentions, which are seen as an authoritative set of meanings to be discovered and conveyed via performance. In processes of collective creation, meanwhile, similar notions of authorial intention and authority are often being actively resisted. Therefore, it is these ideas that need scrutinising. Despite the volume of literature about artistic intentions, intention in theatre-making remains relatively untheorised. In existing studies of literary intention, discussion of intention as it pertains to dramatic literature is marginal or absent,[7] while theatre and performance scholars have generally assumed, ignored, or rejected the relevance of theatre-makers' intentions to interpretation.[8] This is another symptom of the playtext's peculiar ontology: dramatic texts are *intentionally* written to be produced more than once by different interpreters. Debates about how to (or whether it is possible to) determine the 'correct' interpretation of a text based on the writer's intentions, therefore, are not applicable in the same way to dramatic literature. Still, though, a significant proportion of theatre-making in Britain remains wedded to a rigidly intentionalist approach.

While this chapter challenges such strict intentionalism, I agree with Rebellato (2013: 19–21) that it is not possible to entirely reject the idea of artistic intention. Separating *necessity* and *relevance*, which bleed unhelpfully into one another in much of the literature on this debate, I propose that intention is a *necessary* condition for recognising a piece of theatre *as* theatre (or a playtext *as* a playtext), regardless of whether such intentions are understood as relevant to interpretation. When watching a show, our understanding of it is predicated on the assumption that its makers have intended it as a piece of theatre. If we encountered a safety announcement (an expression of a different intention) or a scurrying mouse (not – we assume – possessed of conscious theatrical intention) on a stage, we would not understand these incidents as theatre unless it seemed to us that they were *intended* aspects of the event. Similarly, we're able to recognise a playtext thanks to a combination of the conventions of language and genre and the implied intention of a writer (or writers), the latter usually indicated by the attachment of an author's name. If we did not believe that an intending playwright had conceived a text *as a play*, then the lines conventionally marked out as stage directions, for instance, would not make sense. When such conventions are broken, meanwhile, the role of intention becomes even more apparent. For example, a text like Sarah Kane's *4.48 Psychosis* (1999) might appear to be a poem or a collection of textual fragments were a reader not aware that Kane *intended* it to be a play. While it remains theoretically possible to imagine scenarios in which some sort of meaning is read from texts that have not been produced by an intending author but that nonetheless conform to linguistic conventions,[9] these would be unlikely to be understood as art. This same argument holds for plays that are anonymously authored, or where the identity of the writer is uncertain, because there remains a tacit understanding of intention involved in those acts of creation, whether or not the intending individual can be identified. The enduring centrality of intention to our collective thinking about theatre will also be seen later in this chapter in the ways in which I and other critics discuss theatre-makers' experiments with authorship. Even where aspects of intentionality are questioned, the language of intention stubbornly persists. Without completely denying the relevance of intention to our understanding of plays, then, I nonetheless believe it's necessary to rethink how artistic intentions impact on theatrical practice and to do away with a limiting and monolithic notion of authorial intention.

Within new play producing structures in Britain, as already identified, the director and creative team are typically perceived to be 'serving' the intentions of the playwright. There are objections that might be made to this characterisation: many playwrights complain that their plays have been misinterpreted in production, while directors who proclaim to be 'serving the text' may in fact be more interested in their own interpretations. Nonetheless, though it may be that serving the intentions of the writer is just what British theatre *says* it does, this broadly intentionalist position still privileges playtexts. To clarify what I mean here by intentionalist, I am borrowing Alfred R. Mele and Paisley Livingston's spectrum of attitudes towards intention, within which they identify four positions: absolute intentionalism, strong intentionalism, moderate intentionalism, and absolute anti-intentionalism. The absolute versions of intentionalism and anti-intentionalism involve, respectively, a belief that a text means only what its author intended it to mean, or contrastingly that the author's intentions are entirely irrelevant to interpretation. Strong intentionalism holds that interpretations should be limited to what the author *could* possibly have intended, constraining admissible readings to the artist's context; moderate intentionalism maintains the relevance of authorial intentions to readings of a text while also allowing for interpretations that go *beyond* what the author could have intended (1992: 941–944). Absolute intentionalism and absolute anti-intentionalism are virtually never realised in theatre practice. A production of a play can never mean solely what the playwright intended it to mean because plays are in- or under-determinate texts. In performance, the meanings of the text cannot be limited to those intended by the playwright in composing it, because staging must always supply some elements that are absent from the script. The very act of performing a writer's script, meanwhile, implies a relationship with that writer's intentions – what they *intended* to be conveyed on stage – even if most of those intentions are subverted. A script is an instrumental text, written with the end goal of performance(s) in mind, and so to create a performance from the starting point of a playtext is to refer to an intentional series of suggestions. It was the writer's *intention* that the script be staged, regardless of other intentions about the staging that might be ignored or contradicted. Productions of playtexts, then, might be loosely classed as adopting either strong or moderate intentionalist approaches. Strong intentionalism sets boundaries on interpretation, using the playwright's reconstructed (possible) intentions – or, if the playwright is present in the rehearsal room, their self-reported intentions – to limit the meanings of a play. A moderate intentionalist production, meanwhile, would treat some of the playwright's intentions as relevant and maintain a relationship with what the writer was (believed to be) attempting to achieve, but without allowing these intentions to rule out other interpretations that speak to, supplement or even conflict with what's offered in the text.[10] In Britain, the staging of most new plays could be classed as adopting a strong intentionalist approach, whereas moderate intentionalism is more characteristic of productions of classics seeking contemporary relevance (which I go on to explore in Chapter 3). This is partly the result of a theatre culture in which new plays rarely receive a second production until many years after their first – if ever. There is therefore a perceived ethical imperative to grant the playwright 'their' version of the play and to not misrepresent their intentions, as well as an understandable need to give developing playwrights the opportunity to see their work 'on its feet'. When staging plays from the dramatic canon, by contrast, it's often assumed that audiences will already possess some degree of familiarity with the text and therefore there's more room to diverge from the author's presumed intentions.

In the analysis that follows, my aim is to dispute the strong intentionalist tendency that can be witnessed in many play-led producing processes and to question the understanding of artistic intentions that underpins it. Throughout the rest of this chapter, I explore some of the ways in which contemporary theatre-makers have experimented with authorship and suggest what these experiments might reveal about understandings of intention and authority within British theatre-making. While these examples are arranged in a loose taxonomy, gathered under four headings that represent some of the forms of experimentation I have most frequently observed in contemporary British theatre, this is by no means an exhaustive categorisation of theatre-makers' playful investigations of authorship. Rather than offering a comprehensive survey, I engage with specific instances of creative practice as a means of animating some of the central ideas of the chapter. I begin with plays in which (a version of) the creator appears on stage. In these shows, the author is no longer a shadowy, unseen individual or an omniscient figure of authority; they are an onstage presence, either represented by the playwright themselves or by an actor. By underlining the role of the author in this way, these plays often paradoxically unsettle authorial intention. Similarly, some playwrights and theatre-makers have made the text itself part of the visible fabric of the theatrical experience, reminding spectators of the relationship between stage and page. I also explore how a number of playwrights are – to an extent – withdrawing their own authority from the text by leaving aspects of their plays open or undecided. Finally, I look at the ways in which theatre-makers have engaged with notions of the impossible or unstageable as a way of once again foregrounding the tension between author, text and performance.

Staging the writer

Placing the author onstage is not an entirely new phenomenon. The long-standing Western dramatic convention of the prologue is one way of bringing the playwright into the space of the theatre, making them visible (if not physically present) to the audience, and sometimes comically undermining their authority as creator.[11] From the historical avant gardes onwards, meanwhile, the role of the artist and their authority over the work they produce has been questioned by several successive generations of Western theatre-makers, some of whom have creatively centred and displaced the author from the stage. One might think of examples ranging from the playful absence of the author in Luigi Pirandello's *Six Characters in Search of an Author* (1921) to the Wooster Group's disruption of authorial power in their irreverent reimaginings of various classic plays.[12] In the United Kingdom, alternative theatre-makers have been challenging the model of individual authorship through various collective practices since the mid-20th century, as mentioned above. The last few decades, though, have seen this depiction and interrogation of authors in their own work increasingly move from the margins of British theatre into more mainstream spaces, emerging as a recurring preoccupation within the practice of many playwrights, as well as in the work of what might be loosely termed devising companies and performance artists.

As observed by Rebellato (2013), the 'death' of playwrights within their own scripts – cheekily invoking Barthes' essay – is a recurring feature of several contemporary British plays. Frequently, author figures are staged only to be killed or maimed. In *The Author* (2009), Tim Crouch kills off his fictional alter ego at the end of the play and knowingly cites Barthes in his stage direction: '*The death of the author*' (2011: 203). As part of the confrontational deconstruction of authorship in *Tonight I'm Gonna Be the New Me* (2015), Made in China's Tim Cowbury writes himself a heroic fictional death – only to be undercut by Jess Latowicki's mocking delivery. In David Greig's *San Diego* (2003), the character 'David Greig' is similarly dispatched, only to miraculously reappear later in the play. Meanwhile, a series of other characters named David pepper the play like echoes or ghosts of the murdered author. Michael Pinchbeck's *The End* (2011) is framed as one long prelude to the author's departure – only the creator (that is, Pinchbeck) is reluctant to leave. Throughout the show, Pinchbeck and his co-performer Ollie Smith (who, as co-deviser of the piece, can also be understood as its author) repeatedly mime shooting one another, dying, and being reborn. And at the end of Part One of Dead Centre's *Chekhov's First Play* (2015) – to which I return in Chapter 3 – the Director (played by actual director and co-creator Bush Moukarzel) seems to shoot himself in the head. While this character is not positioned as the author of the show, per se, he has up until this point been the chief mediator of the audience's experience, providing a constant running commentary through our headphones. From this moment onwards, his controlling voice recedes, giving way to a dreamlike succession of images that audiences are left to decipher by themselves. In all these examples, the 'death' or near-death of the author figure is a dual manoeuvre that simultaneously spotlights the role of the writer and gestures towards a (partial) freeing of the performance from their intentions.

In plays like Crouch's *The Author* and Ella Hickson's *The Writer* (2018), meanwhile, a concern with writing and authorship is explicitly signalled in the title. In the premiere production of Crouch's play at the Royal Court, the playwright himself depicted the eponymous author, the writer of a fictional play that bears all the gory hallmarks of 'in-yer-face' theatre.[13] Audience members – who are arranged in two banks facing one another – never see this play. Instead, they are told about it by the fictional Tim Crouch, the two actors who appeared in the play, and an audience member who saw it. The graphic violence and abuse depicted in this fictional script are not represented on stage but instead reside in the imaginations of the audience, provoking questions about the ethical responsibilities of both creator and spectator. While most audience members will presumably be (or become) aware that the play being discussed is not real, they will likely know that they are watching a play written by Tim Crouch, who is revealed to be sitting and speaking amongst them, thus blurring the line between fiction and reality. In this way, Crouch at once discloses and obfuscates his role as playwright. He takes on the self-reflexive persona of 'the author' while deliberately wrong-footing the audience as to what is and is not real, both flirting with and frustrating the intentionalist desire to read the author into the work. While the author's self-regard is gently mocked, his words – in the form of the fictional play being discussed – are shown to have terrifying power. The character Vic, who has had a violent breakdown after performing in this play, explains: 'It's not me, it's the writing. You know it's well written when it gets inside you. It really got inside me' (Crouch 2011a: 185). In a similar way, the writing of *The Author* 'got inside' audience members who were invited to imagine horrific, unseen acts of abuse, often provoking walkouts and even vocal outrage from spectators (Crouch 2011c).

As well as playing with ideas to do with the playwright's power, presence and persona, *The Author* illustrates the oscillation that exists in any theatrical text between authorial control and lack of control. It's stated in the stage directions, for example, that there is '*freedom in ADRIAN's speech to improvise if needed*' (Crouch 2011a: 165), but the implication is that such freedom is curtailed elsewhere. I have previously suggested that Crouch's work contains 'a simultaneous movement of relinquishing certain aspects of control and underlining others' (Love 2017: 31). The playwright character in *The Author* even reflects upon this paradoxical authority and powerlessness, prodding at the responsibilities (or lack thereof) that a writer has when their work is handed over to others. He notes that after the writing process, the playwright must 'hand over' their play: 'You leave it to the actors. They will make their own discoveries. You leave it to your audience' (Crouch 2011a: 190). He adds, as though to absolve himself of any guilt, '[t]hat's the job of the writer. Not to go in and solve things. But to reveal things, things for other people to solve' (ibid.). In *The Author*, the staging of the writer is used as a device to question the distribution of interpretive control and ethical responsibility among theatre-makers and audience members. At the same time, as I've argued elsewhere, Crouch's work purposefully 'underlines the slippages between text and performance' – and, it might be added, between text and author – 'that are present in any piece of theatre' (Love 2017: 2). By setting this play inside its audience and stripping away many of the usual signifiers of theatrical performance, Crouch focuses attention tightly on the words he has written, while also illustrating the many ways in which these words escape his control once they are released into the auditorium and the unpredictable imaginations of spectators.

Written almost a decade later, *The Writer* tackles some of the same concerns as *The Author*, but from the distinct perspective of a female playwright in a patriarchal society. While Hickson does not explicitly identify the writer character in the play as herself, nor did she appear in the play's first production, *The Writer* similarly foregrounds the process of writing and the role of the playwright. Much like Crouch's play, *The Writer* is constantly pulling the rug out from under the audience by shifting its meta-theatrical frame and moving between different levels of fiction and reality. It begins in the aftermath of another fictional play, as a Young Woman argues with an Older Man – who turns out to be the director – about the sexist and commercialised show she has just seen. Soon this too is revealed to be a play within the play, which is followed by a post-show discussion with the (female) Writer and (male) Director (on whom the characters of the scene that has just been performed appear to be based). In subsequent scenes, it's frequently unclear at which level of reality the action is operating. Are we seeing scenes from the play that the Writer is working on, or snapshots of the Writer's 'real' life? – which is, of course, a fiction invented by the *real* writer, Ella Hickson, who has experienced many of the theatre industry structures against which her protagonist chafes. The third scene of the play appears to offer an alternative to these structures, only to be immediately undermined, leaving the impression that the only way to succeed is to imitate the masculine power of those who have traditionally dominated the profession.

As Hannah Greenstreet has noted, '*The Writer* is structured upon deep ambivalence' (2019: 349). It is ambivalent about how to deconstruct capitalism and patriarchy (and, indeed, about whether such a thing is even possible), about the political power of art, about different forms of theatrical representation, and about the very activity of authoring. In the act of writing about a writer, who is working within a theatre establishment exemplified by the institution for which the play was written,[14] Hickson is posing a series of unanswered questions about artistic genius (and how genius has been gendered), the patriarchal structures of dramatic language and form, the embeddedness of art within capitalism, the (im)possibility of an authentically 'female' form of theatrical representation, and the relationship between text and performance. Throughout the play, the location of theatrical authorship is contested, as the Writer's desires and intentions are repeatedly manipulated by the Director, who moulds her ideas into a more commercially palatable shape. In performance, moreover, this is of course overlaid with the collaboration between Hickson and the actual director (Blanche McIntyre in the premiere production). And as much as the writer character in the play expresses anger about her intentions being squashed or reshaped, the script itself implies a deep understanding of the collaborative nature of theatre and a desire to experiment with this collaboration. As I discuss further below, Scene Three plays with seemingly unstageable images, while stage directions elsewhere in the text suggest a dialogue of challenge and creativity between page and stage. This is especially clear in Scene Two in the following stage direction: '*No pressure, but just in terms of defending the whole of art, this should be totally magic*' (2018: 47). Rather than giving any instructions, this note throws down the gauntlet to the director and actor, while being written in a conversational tone that suggests the back-and-forth of theatrical collaboration. Karen Quigley also draws attention to this particular stage direction, which she suggests exemplifies the idea of the playtext as 'a provocative document of challenge' (2020: 43). In *The Writer*, therefore, Hickson questions the process of authorship from multiple angles, at the same time as situating such questions politically.

Similarly to *The Writer*, Arinzé Kene's *Misty* (2018) puts its creator on stage as a means of highlighting and deconstructing inequities within both British theatre culture and the wider society. Where *The Writer* confronts patriarchy and capitalism, *Misty* engages with structural racism and gentrification. As with *The Writer*, *Misty* initially appears to be one thing, before its opening sequence is revealed to be a scene that Kene's authorial persona – played in the premiere production by Kene himself – is writing for a new commission. The rest of the show switches back and forth between the 'urban play' that Kene is writing and self-aware criticisms of the way in which this play panders to the racialised tropes expected by white middle-class audience members, with its '[g]eneric angry young black man' protagonist, as one of Kene's fictionalised friends puts it (2018: 13). Like the Writer in Hickson's play, the character of Arinzé has to constantly navigate the limiting and exclusionary structures of the British theatre industry, as well as the disapproval of friends and family who think he's writing a play that conforms to racist stereotypes of Black masculinity and fulfils the desire of white audiences to watch representations of Black trauma. Facing pressure from both sides, Arinzé asks: 'Can a play from a person like me just be a fucking play already?' (54). Like Crouch in *The Author*, Kene is questioning the responsibility of the playwright, but from his specific position as a Black British writer in an industry in which voices like his remain under-represented – and, as a result, are freighted with expectations to speak for an entire community.

In each of these three plays about playwriting, there is an implicit question about the extent to which any piece of theatre is ever a 'true' representation of its writer's intentions. While these interrogations of authorship are wielded to different aesthetic and political ends, they also underline the inadequacy of any pretence to 'serve' the intentions of the writer and their text in performance. As demonstrated by these examples, the strong intentionalist tendency that I have identified in British new writing is inherently problematic. Intention as typically imagined in this context has a rigid and singular character that is misrepresentative of artistic intentions. The notion of 'serving' the playwright's intention assumes that there is just one main intention or set of intentions that can be discovered and pursued – an idea that is belied by the complexity and ambiguity of the texts discussed in this section. Moreover, this oddly monolithic intention is often conceptualised as a pre-existing blueprint in the playwright's mind. Together, these assumptions construct intention as something prior to and divorced from the process of writing: a singular, external 'plan' that can be discovered and translated onto the stage. This view also undermines the creative contributions of directors and other artists and implicitly devalues theatre-making methodologies that do not possess a sole writer and are therefore perceived to lack a strong, guiding 'voice', in turn cleaving these methodologies from 'text-based' practices. This is a common criticism in reviews of devised theatre and is exemplified by the view of Michael Billington, who critiques the 'meaningless ghetto' of what he calls 'visual theatre' (2007: 396) and concludes that only the playwright is able to 'investigate, explore and even to influence the society we actually inhabit' (397).[15] The construction of intention as prior to, separable from and singularly authoritative over the playtext (and, by extension, performance) is therefore one that I am keen to dismantle.

Artistic intention as typically understood is too simple and singular, and intentionalist and anti-intentionalist arguments alike ascribe too much internal clarity and coherence to intentions. Consider, for instance, W. K. Wimsatt Jr. and M. C. Beardsley's definition of intention as 'a design or plan in the author's mind' (1946: 469). Kaye Mitchell also notes the prevalence of this blueprint model in the literature on intention (2008), while W. B. Worthen has observed the frequent use of the blueprint metaphor in discussions of the relationship between text and performance (2010: 12–13). It is my argument that, contrary to these models, intentions are nowhere near this determinate and detailed. Here it's useful to refer again to Barthes, whose critique of author-centred interpretations speaks to what I am suggesting about how artistic intentions function:

> The Author, when believed in, is always conceived of as the past of his [sic] own book: book and author stand automatically on a single line divided into a *before* and an *after*. The Author is thought to *nourish* the book, which is to say that he exists before it, thinks, suffers, lives for it, is in the same relation of antecedence to his work as a father to his child. In complete contrast, the modern scriptor is born simultaneously with the text (1977 [1967]: 145, original emphasis)

While I'm not adopting Barthes' terminology of scriptor (which has not been taken up by critics, despite the influence of this essay), I do find his idea of the writer – and their intentions – being 'born simultaneously with the text' a useful way of reframing the relationship between playwright, text and performance. The playwright's artistic intentions are not a complete, pre-existing blueprint that give birth to the text, and likewise the text is not a complete, pre-existing blueprint that gives birth to the performance.

Intentions, and thoughts in general, are by their nature (and to greater and lesser degrees) indeterminate. As a number of thinkers in the field of philosophy of mind have discussed, mental images can be distinguished from visual perceptions by their indeterminate nature: a mental image 'leaves open certain facts about its object' (McGinn 2004: 25).[16] I can picture a table, for instance, without knowing what colour it is, or I can imagine a dog without specifying its breed. The imagined object is no less table-like or dog-like because of the lack of these details. An intention to express something in artistic form can be understood in a similar way to my incomplete mental images of tables and dogs: the outline of an intention can exist without being fully fleshed out. The finer details of that intention are subject to change over time and as required, just as I must add detail to my mental image of a table if someone asks me what colour it is. To imagine intentions as clear and comprehensive, then, is to impose order and completeness on indeterminate thought processes. It's thus necessary to reject the blueprint model of a separate, pre-existing and complete intention that can be discovered through examining works of art. Instead, it's more accurate to imagine an interconnected multiplicity of intentions, none fully determinate and each with different implications for interpretation. Consider the intentions a playwright might have in writing a play. The overarching intention is the intentional act of setting out to create something, beneath which is the more specific intention to write a play. It is these two sorts of intention that permit interpretation, allowing us to consider the play an intentional object that was conceived and written *as* a play. Related to these, though, are many other intentions. These include intentions about the writing: the characters' objectives, or the desired emotional impact of a scene. But they may also include intentions that anticipate the play's performance, over which the playwright has limited control. The playwright is, furthermore, likely to have some more abstract, aspirational intentions for the play. Not all these intentions are equally relevant for those staging the play. The intentions that interpreters are generally more interested in are those concerned with aspects of the writing and their desired effects; these are the intentions that directors often claim to be 'serving'. These complex aims are what Michael Hancher would call 'active intentions': 'the author's intention to be (understood as) acting in some way or other' (1972: 829). None of the playwright's active intentions, I suggest, are necessarily irrelevant, and equally none of them can fully determine the meaning of the play. That is, these various intentions *may be* relevant to any given interpretation, but they *cannot* govern the proliferation of meaning, as I will discuss further in later sections of the chapter.

Before moving on, I want to consider one further instance of the staging of the author. Within the field of verbatim theatre, there's a growing tendency to reveal the writer(s) behind the dictaphone, staging the process of the investigation as well as its findings. In Alecky Blythe's work, for example, Blythe herself is often present, either as a recorded voice, a character portrayed by an actor, or – as in *Little Revolution* (2014) – playing herself. Though nominally an investigation of the 2011 London riots, *Little Revolution* is also a knotty meditation on the impossibility of Blythe – as a privileged, white, middle-class theatre-maker – understanding or representing the voices of those involved in the unrest. Blythe's guiding hand as the author of this piece is most strikingly evident in the play's epilogue, in which she returns to Hackney after several months to speak to barber Colin, who has been portrayed as something of a local sage. Here there's an implicit acknowledgement of the way in which Blythe has shaped the testimony she has gathered, elevating voices like Colin's and transforming him into a character. The epilogue also contains a gentle rebuke of the way in which Blythe has dropped into this community, used its voices, and left it behind; as Colin says to her: 'You sort of disappeared' (2014: 95). We learn that Blythe has returned because the trial of the police officer involved in the death of Mark Duggan – which sparked the riots – is about to conclude, and she's keen to capture Colin's reaction. Colin, however, is unaware of the impending verdict, leading Blythe to laboriously engineer the scenario. Rather than editing out this manipulation of events, Blythe closes the play with a conspicuous indictment of her own failures as an author, highlighting her paradoxical authority and powerlessness. Similarly to Blythe's authorial self-deconstruction, in other verbatim or semi-verbatim plays like Gregory Burke's *Black Watch* (2006) and David Hare's *The Power of Yes* (2009) the playwrights are characters in the text, depicted by actors in performance and often mocked within their own creations. This self-aware style of verbatim has also been used by theatre companies such as Breach, whose work is as interested in the form of documentary theatre as it is in the subjects being investigated. Typically, the company explores events with only fragmentary documentary evidence, underlining the gaps in historical documentation and raising complex questions about storytelling, authorship and truth. In *Tank* (2016), for example, Breach offers multiple possible reconstructions of the events surrounding John C. Lilly and Margaret Howe's experiments teaching English to dolphins in the 1960s, using the many gaps in the records of this study as an opportunity to highlight and critique the multiple ways of interpreting this historical narrative. In doing so, they reveal the implications of different renderings of the truth and the power structures – including patriarchy, scientific mastery, and colonialism – that shape how stories are told, once again deconstructing the process of authorship and questioning its ethical responsibilities.[17]

In these examples from verbatim and documentary theatre, the staging of the author serves to critique the documentary form, pose questions about the nature of truth, and simultaneously unsettle and reinforce the controlling position of the author, who ultimately shapes the evidence they have gathered. In these ways, such onstage authorial presences might be understood as doing something distinct and removed from the experimentation of Crouch, Hickson, and Kene. But while being differently motivated and exploring different theatrical traditions, these various stagings of the author(s) all draw attention to the writer(s)' intentions and control (or lack thereof), the creative dialogue between text and performance, and the responsibility associated with authorship. They also speak interestingly to an element of Foucault's analysis of the author function. At the outset of his essay, Foucault states that he wants to examine 'the manner in which the text points to this "figure" that, at least in appearance, is outside and antecedes it' (1991: 101), but his later argument that the individual qualities and intentions that are attributed to an author 'are only a projection [...] of the operations that we *force* texts to undergo' (110, my emphasis) appears to contradict this. Here he's suggesting that it is the interpretive operations of the *reader* that construct the author and impose this on the text, rather than the text itself pointing to an author figure. However, Foucault then returns to his earlier position and asserts that 'the author function is not a pure and simple reconstruction made secondhand from a text given as passive material. The text always contains a certain number of signs referring to the author' (111–112). When considering these seeming contradictions, one might think about how the modes of discourse in operation at the time a text is written, as well as the time and culture in which it is read, affect how the presence of an author is marked (or not marked) in the text. Indeed, as Foucault goes on to explain, the signs that point to the author 'do not play the same role in discourses provided with the author function as in those lacking it' (112). This resolves the apparent paradox in Foucault's thinking: the author function *is* a construct, produced by our interpretative practices, but this changing discursive norm in turn impacts upon how authorship is or is not manifested in particular texts. Extending this proposition to theatrical texts, it might account for the recent experiments in authorship discussed here. The appearance of characters such as 'Tim Crouch', 'The Writer', and 'Alecky Blythe' indexes a set of contemporary discourses and attitudes towards authorship; these features of the texts mark their authors in ways that are constructed by current interpretive procedures. The very possibility of this playfulness with language and the figure of the author is historically specific – and could even be seen as arising from the 20th-century questioning of authorship of which Foucault's essay is a prominent part. These various stagings of the author, then, perhaps point to an ongoing shift in how authors, texts, and performances are culturally understood.

Making the text visible

The text as a physical object shown in performance is another recurring feature that can be seen across a range of contemporary British theatre. This displaying of texts on stage might be traced back to a late-20th-century tradition of what Elinor Fuchs calls the 'literalization or textualization of the theater event' (1996: 74), which she observes in experimental US theatre and performance in the 1970s, 1980s, and 1990s. But while Fuchs is primarily concerned with how this emergence of text and writing on stage 'complicate[s] the spectator's experience of theatrical presence' (ibid.), I am suggesting that one of its principal effects in the following examples of contemporary British theatre practice is to deconstruct the perceived text/performance hierarchy. I agree with Karen Jürs-Munby that what she has called 'exposed textuality' has the ability to 'highlight, rather than obscure, the gap, tension and conflict between text and performance' (2010: 102). I've already discussed one example of this in Action Hero's *Wrecking Ball*, which the company describes as 'a script in inverted commas' (2016: 9). Having started as a live art company, *Wrecking Ball* was Action Hero's self-aware attempt at writing a 'proper' play, but in a way that staged all their apprehensions about the authority of author and text. Including the play itself as a material object within the performance is one of the ways in which Paintin and Stenhouse make visible both the scripting power of the text and the inevitable gaps and slippages that always exist between text and performance, no matter how tightly the former appears to control the latter. In a number of other contemporary performances, the playtext – usually an unseen presence – has been conspicuously shown on stage, emphasising its existence as an object separate from its live enactment and again foregrounding and unsettling the role of its author(s) and their intentions.

Action Hero had already played with putting the script on stage in its durational performance *Slap Talk* (2013): a six-hour scripted slanging match between Paintin and Stenhouse, during which they read from scrolling autocues while filmed close-ups of their faces were shown on two large TV screens. The performance was often mounted in galleries, with audience members free to come and go and walk around the space. It was possible, then, for spectators to catch a glimpse of the words on the autocue, confirming that the insults exchanged between the performers were indeed being read from the script. There are also several moments throughout this piece when Action Hero deliberately highlights the relationship between text and performance, with the performers appearing to offer unscripted digressions before it becomes clear that – like the sequence of audience interaction in *Wrecking Ball* – these lines are also directly taken from the text. For example, one performer interjects with 'that's too far' after the line 'I'm gonna pour bleach down your throat', only to be told 'I'm just saying what it tells me to say' (2015: 137–138). Action Hero thus explores multiple layers of meaning-making, pointing to Paintin and Stenhouse's roles as both writers and performers and playing with the ways in which text does and does not dictate performance. By making the text a visible presence in the form of the autocue and by exerting pressure on the text-performance relationship by elongating the duration of the piece, they repeatedly draw attention to the role that language plays in live performance. In doing so, the company also places pressure on the everyday violence it enacts, with the scripting of theatre becoming an implicit analogy for the ways in which various power structures aggressively script our speech. Meanwhile, as time wears on and exhaustion affects Paintin and Stenhouse's performances, mistakes are made and (in my experience of watching the show across a few different iterations) unexpected moments actually do disrupt the text. As spectators, we can be less and less sure if these apparent slippages are scripted or ad libbed. Because the text is present in the space, moreover, we are reminded of its role in performance, perhaps prompting us to reflect on how text functions in other performances.

Other uses of the script on stage similarly explore ideas around text, performance, power, and authorship. In Deborah Pearson's solo piece *The Future Show* (2013) – which culminates in yet another authorial death – the text is laid out as a series of pages in a binder on the desk in front of Pearson, from which she reads throughout. As the title suggests, the show predicts the future, from the moments immediately following the performance right through to the end of Pearson's life.

The play opens by informing the audience of its final line: 'I will say "the length of a breath," breathe in, breathe out, and then stop speaking. I will look at you and you will clap' (2015: 20). We later discover that this final line represents the moment of Pearson's future demise – the death of the author. It is the most definitive of endings, yet it also takes us right back to the beginning of Pearson's narrative; it's both a death and a resurrection. One of the final thoughts that Pearson narrates as her future self 'dies' is 'this is exactly as I'd said it would be' (33) – a knowing moment, but a line that also refers simultaneously to the power of the script in front of Pearson and the impossibility of this text actually representing what it claims to represent. As well as underlining the impossibility of the task Pearson is undertaking and playing with the fuzzy line that exists in all autobiographical performance between truth and fiction, the constant physical presence of the script and the references made within the play to the veracity of its predictions can also be read as a self-reflexive deconstruction of authorial control. An act of authoring that extends decades into the future is, on the one hand, a hubristic over-reach of creative control. On the other hand, though, it's an authorial gesture that contains its own failure, highlighting the author's *lack* of control. Moreover, *The Future Show* implicitly challenges common understandings of the script as a complete authorial blueprint that is realised in performance, as the instability and changeability of the text is integral to the structure and concept of the piece. Though it now exists in published form, while Pearson was performing it *The Future Show* was written afresh before each new performance – because, of course, the future kept changing as her previous futures became the past and the present.[18] In performance, Pearson kept all earlier versions of the script in the binder and visible to the audience – another reminder that what we are seeing is just one ephemeral iteration, not the authoritative master work of the author.

The use of text on stage can also be an index of manipulation and exploitation. In Kieran Hurley's play *Mouthpiece* (2018), projected text represents the stories that Libby, a middle-class, middle-aged playwright, appropriates from Declan, a working-class teenager whose life she condescendingly decides to improve. The whole play is framed by Libby, who uses the vocabulary of playwriting handbooks to set up the key story beats: the opening image, the break into two, the midpoint. She repeatedly cites the 'rules' of good storytelling, forcing Declan's life into the mould of 'successful' drama. As she increasingly takes control of Declan's narrative, her spoken words become projected stage directions, which become the actions that Declan performs on stage:

Libby I write: *He takes out a small pocket knife and stabs the pillow.*

Projected text: He takes out a small pocket knife and stabs the pillow.

He takes out a small pocket knife and stabs the pillow. (2018: 55)

Here the audience sees scripting in action, as Libby's text becomes performance in real time, taking on the authoritative role that pre-written plays are often imagined to have. But at the end of the play, the character of Declan rejects the story that is written for him. As the projected text states that he 'violently thrusts the knife across his neck', the stage direction instructs that he '*does not thrust the knife across his neck*' (65), refusing the tragic ending that has been scripted by Libby. But an audience is also aware that this act of defiance is itself scripted by Hurley, who knowingly throws himself open to the same questions he asks of Libby and the way in which she attempts to give voice to the supposedly voiceless, without anticipating that they might speak back. The presence of text on stage adds another layer to this interrogation, inviting us to question the power and responsibility of the playwright, as well as the ways in which performance exceeds their writing.

The example of *Mouthpiece* illustrates the potential for script on stage to be wielded as a critical tool. Jürs-Munby suggests that the 'resistance of performers against text and vice versa can function to disturb ideological normalization and "business as usual"' (2010: 112) – thus noting a political dimension to the use of visible texts in performance, which resonates with some of the examples discussed in this section. She concludes that

> Texts on stage as resistant players remind us not only of the ways in which we are continually being 'scripted' and 'conscripted' by dominant ideologies but, equally, of the ways in which writers are engaged in creating spaces to expose these dominant scripts. (113)

The writers and theatre-makers whose work I have explored here are frequently exposing the dominant scripts of the political status quo, as well as revealing and challenging the dominant scripts of (British) theatrical convention. I want to mention just one further example, which connects the use of scripts on stage to this chapter's central questions about authorship and authority. Elsewhere, I've explored how the text manifests in various ways on stage – from printed scripts to scattered cue cards – in the different pieces comprising Michael Pinchbeck's *The Trilogy* (2014). In all three performances, Pinchbeck is playing with authorial absence and presence and using the assorted material incarnations of the text as one way of doing so. As I wrote about these shows, the device of making the text visible on stage 'reveal[s] the complete-yet-incomplete status of *all* playtexts and performances', as well as serving to 'disrupt the presumed authority of play and playwright, acting as a reminder that both plays and performances endlessly refer to one another' (Love 2020: 30, original emphasis). Although such experiments with putting the script on stage as a material object remain relative outliers in British theatre practice, rather than the norm, they expose the gaps between writer, text, and performance that are constitutive of theatre as an art form.[19]

To account for the contradictions revealed by these experiments and to move away from the flawed blueprint model that I discussed in the previous section, I want to suggest that artistic intentions can be thought of in terms of *doing*. Although I'm not convinced by her separation of textual intentions from an intending consciousness, Kaye Mitchell's objection that '[t]he mentalistic conception of intention ignores the practical aspect of intention involved in doing or acting'

(2008: 17) prompts a useful rethink of intention in relation to process. Intentions are not necessarily prior to acts, such as the act of writing; they may be considered inextricable from the *doing* of those acts themselves. To explore this suggestion, I find it helpful to draw on Ludwig Wittgenstein's discussions of language and thought.[20] It's important to recognise that Wittgenstein is dealing with thought as a concept and a grammatical construct rather than as a set of processes located in the brain; his interest lies in our use of words, not in psychological phenomena. It does not reveal anything about our use of the word 'think', Wittgenstein argues, to say that it represents an inner mental process. He thus questions the assumption that thought and speech are detachable from one another and that a thought precedes a spoken statement, much as intention is assumed to precede artistic expression. To see how intention might be located in doing, we can reflect on how we typically describe speech and thought. Rarely would we claim to have formulated a sentence as a specific string of words prior to speaking. We might say we have a basic intention immediately before speaking, which if interrupted we would later be able to recall ('I intended to say … '), but the precise *form* of that intention emerges during the utterance, which constitutes it. Wittgenstein suggests that the 'lightning-like thought' that we understand as preceding a statement 'may stand to a spoken thought as an algebraic formula to a sequence of numbers which I develop from it' (2009: 112e). That is, the thought, like the formula, provides certainty that one will be able to go on to solve the problem, but it does not itself express the solution. It might be thought of as the key to the intention rather than the full intention itself. The statement (or, for my purposes, the line in the play), not the 'lightning-like thought', is the expression of the intention, though the multiplicity of meanings immediately opened up by language means that even here intention cannot be seen as complete and transparent.

Similar reasoning may be applied both to artistic intentions and to the ways in which we interpret them. Wittgenstein argues that the image of an unseen mental process which animates and gives meaning to speech does not accord with the circumstances in which we say that someone thought or intended something; we attribute thought and intention in line with observable patterns of behaviour, whether embodied or written. In this sense, to talk of a separate set of intentions that are located somewhere in the hidden depths of the brain contradicts the procedures through which we identify intention in the first place. The notion of an inner process, Wittgenstein concludes, has nothing to do with the role of the words 'think' and 'intend' in what he calls our 'language-games'. Artistic intentions can therefore be thought of as embedded in creative processes and outputs in the same way that an intention to say something is embedded in the spoken statement. Seeing intention as rooted in the act of creation in this way resonates with the inherent unfinished-ness of playtexts, which are not complete documents of prior authorial intentions that may be straightforwardly enacted, but are constantly evolving through the processes of writing and staging, embodying many complex intentions along the way. This is made explicit in a piece like *The Future Show*, which demonstrates the enmeshment of intention and doing through its ever-changing script. Moreover, the displaying of the text as an object on stage can serve to undercut some of the mystical, authoritative properties it is often invested with, frustrating the futile desire to mine it for some kind of authorial essence. A more process-oriented understanding of intention has the additional advantage of dissolving the stubborn mind-body dualism entrenched in many theories of intention, as well as applying equally to the making-through-doing model of devising as to the isolated writing of the solo playwright – which is often far from isolated and is as much a making-through-doing as devising is. Here, then, is a possible way forward that might account for the variety and complexity of different modes of creation that can be found within contemporary British theatre.

Playwrights abdicating authority

As discussed above, there remains a relatively widespread assumption within British theatre culture that the playtext is something of a blueprint for performance which may be followed by directors and actors, and that the text itself can be traced back to a similar blueprint of intentions in the mind of its author. Like an architectural blueprint, there's an expectation that the playtext will lay out the relationship between the various elements of the theatrical event – or, at least, those elements that have conventionally been within the purview of the writer, such as character, dialogue, plot, setting, and dramatic structure. However, several British plays written since the 1990s have subverted, challenged, or entirely rejected some or all of these elements. At the risk of over-extending the metaphor, these plays are like blueprints with missing walls or interchangeable rooms. Their primary disruption of playwriting conventions lies in their refusal to determine certain components of the drama, be that the order of the scenes, the number of speakers, or the scenario in which the words on the page are to be spoken. In so doing, these plays offer a provocation to other theatre-makers. One of the most striking aspects of this mode of playwriting, as I discuss in this section, is the way in which it resists the conventional modes of reading, interpretation and production that have dominated the British theatrical mainstream, while simultaneously revealing something that is true of all texts for theatre.

Martin Crimp and Sarah Kane were at the vanguard of this form of playwriting in the late 1990s. Crimp's *Attempts on Her Life* (1997), for example, consists of 17 'scenarios' which lack specified settings or speakers. The play has no unifying plot or narrative; the only connective thread between the various scenarios is the central yet absent female figure, who is variously referred to as Anne, Anya, Annie, Anny, or Annushka. In *Crave* (1998) and *4.48 Psychosis* (2000), Kane also eschews dramatic plot and named speakers. In both plays, the language is fragmented and there is often no readily apparent connection between page and possible performance, leaving it up to theatrical interpreters to decipher some kind of meaning. Similar invitations to directors and performers can be found in a series of other contemporary British plays. At the start of *Pornography* (2007), for example, Simon Stephens writes: 'This play can be performed by any number of actors. It can be performed in any order' (2008a: 2). While Caryl Churchill's *Love and Information* (2012) has a more circumscribed structure, with sections that are to be performed in a specified sequence, she notes that 'the scenes can be played in any order within each section' (2012: 2), and she also includes a series of 'random' scenes which can be inserted at any point. Stef Smith's play *Swallow* (2015) is preceded by an explanation that the script contains no stage directions, inviting readers and theatre-makers to 'imagine it as you wish' (2015: 4). Similarly, the note at the start of Lulu Raczka's play *Nothing* (2013), which was developed with and originally performed by Barrel Organ Theatre, invites future interpreters to '[h]ave fun' with the text (2014: 9). Raczka explains that 'the pieces can be performed in any order, by any number of people, in any space, at any time. They can be cut and pasted in any way you would like' (ibid.). The play as written consists of a series of monologues, which were intercut in an improvisatory way by Barrel Organ's actors at each performance. The cut, the order, and even which performer was to deliver each monologue were all determined live. Having seen the show multiple times, my experience as an audience member was markedly different on each occasion. Another note in the published text stresses that '[t]he show is not finished' (2014: 10), suggesting the incompleteness both of the play as printed on the page and of any individual performance. *[BLANK]* (2018) by Alice Birch, meanwhile, consists of 100 scenes from which a director may pick and choose to construct their version of the play. Birch frames the text as 'a challenge and an invitation' to theatre-makers to 'make your own play' (2018), explaining that anyone who chooses to stage the text may select as many scenes as they like, in whichever order they like, with whatever casting they like. It feels particularly significant that in her note to the play Birch explicitly hands over ownership of the piece to its future directors and performers, at least partly relinquishing her role as author.

Such disavowals of authorial control have led to these sorts of plays being described as 'open' texts (Jürs-Munby 2006; Barnett 2008) – a label that usefully identifies the dramaturgical innovations employed by these writers, but that ignores the incompleteness of *any* playtext as a record of its author's intentions. In her analysis of what she calls 'indeterminate' playwriting, Emilie Morin persuasively argues that plays like the ones cited above can be understood as 'attempts to expose the processes and conventions which sustain the event of performance', arising out of a 'weariness with the conventional modes of dramatic representation' (2011: 80). This is where, for me, the real interest of these texts lies. By subverting or rendering indeterminate the usual markers of character, plot, setting, and so on, these plays draw critical attention to the relationship between text and performance and the conventional ways in which that relationship has been calibrated. At a surface level, they appear to be acts of refusal, excising certain ostensible statements of authorial intention from the text. But by removing these conventional markers, they in fact reveal the ways in which theatrical interpreters typically approach playtexts, exposing the assumptions that are often made about where and how the writer's intention is expressed and how this is expected to translate into performance.

The complicated nature of artistic intention in relation to both text and performance can be further elaborated by looking in more detail at a specific example. With *Pornography*, Stephens made what appeared to be a shift away from the relatively realistic dramatic worlds of his previous plays. Importantly, this text was written specifically for German director Sebastian Nübling and responds to a German-language theatre culture that has a very different attitude towards texts than the British mainstream. As Bolton explains, in this culture

> [a] play-text may be rewritten, edited, spliced, fused and/or collided with other texts; ideas that have been conceptualised in words may be transposed onto other layers of theatrical presentation such as space, design, music, costume, rhythm and the actors' bodies. (2014: lxiv)

Pornography was written following Stephens' encounter with this culture during the German-language premiere of his play *Herons* in 2003 (directed by Nübling), and the play is – according to Stephens' account – a direct response to the exhilaration that he felt about this way of working.[21] It consists of a series of scenes revolving around the week of the 7/7 terrorist bombings in London in 2005, but there is no linear progression or other obvious connection between the separate sections of the play. As already noted, these scenes can be performed in any order, explicitly empowering theatre-makers to construct their own version of the text in performance. It is *intentionally* written to be de- and re-constructed by directors, while the absence of any other instruction challenges the assumed transparency of the playwright's intentions in their script. In Nübling's production, some of the dialogue within scenes was reordered and the implied gender of certain characters was subverted, while the British premiere directed by Sean Holmes intercut the various scenes, demonstrating just some of the many possibilities of the text. In his framing of *Pornography*, Stephens echoes scholars' claims of openness, explaining: 'I wrote [Nübling] a text that was as open as possible. It not only invites directorial interpretation, it is unstageable without it' (2009: xix). As in *Attempts on Her Life* and *4.48 Psychosis*, there's no assigning of lines to speakers, although a sense of dialogue between distinct characters often emerges from what Stephens has written. In 'Five', for example, contextual cues suggest that the lines of speech are between two siblings. Moreover, when faced with the bewilderment of British directors Stephens wrote a revised version that included character names but did not make any other changes to the dialogue, thereby making the script more comprehensible to those who might stage it in the United Kingdom (Bolton 2014: lxvi). This demonstrates the inflexible attitude of the British theatrical mainstream towards theatre texts and the somewhat arbitrary conventions through which a playwright's intentions are interpreted, as well as revealing the extent to which the structure of *Pornography* remains shaped by dramatic conventions of speech and narrative. As I've previously argued, despite the apparent departure represented by this play, it's more accurate to view *Pornography* as 'a disruption to British new writing conventions [...] than as a rupture in the fabric of [Stephens'] creative output' (2016: 325). By stripping away key elements that are conventionally included in the playtext, Stephens 'simply draws attention to possibilities that are always available in the movement from text to performance' (326).

As this example suggests, the defining features of so-called 'open' texts can in fact be identified as characteristic of *all* texts written for theatre. No text can ever be entirely 'closed', because there will always be elements of performance that cannot be accounted for on the page. Yet there is still an understandable desire to differentiate between – for want of a better word – 'conventional' plays and the dramaturgically experimental texts explored here. The solution to this seemingly intractable problem is to understand all plays as comprising a varying mixture of open and closed elements. In any play, there will be details that are determinate on the page and those that are indeterminate. Typically, determinate details include things like the number and names of characters and the settings for each scene – the conventions from which those texts that are often described as 'open' depart. But even in a play with long and detailed stage directions, there are elements of indeterminacy. The play cannot specify *everything* about its enactment. On the other hand, even the most apparently open plays have certain fixed parameters. While the text of *Attempts on Her Life* may seem unfixed, it is still organised into those 17 scenarios, of which Crimp specifies only the first may be cut entirely; a director staging *[BLANK]* has a huge number of scenes to choose from, but there is still a limit to what Birch has written. Indeterminacy is only possible within certain determinate limits. This shifting balance of determinate and indeterminate elements on the page once again demonstrates the multiplicity and complexity of artistic intentions, which cannot be straightforwardly interpreted and followed. Key to the kinds of experimental playwriting discussed here is the idea that, as Matthew Roberts argues of Kane's work, 'language can undermine its own traditional function as what brings consistency to, and what determines the meaning of, theatrical performance' (2015: 98). In many cases, these playwrights are *intentionally* using language to deconstruct itself and, paradoxically, to challenge its assumed status as a vehicle for authorial intention. By questioning the authority of the written word, by crafting images on the page that resist any notion of frictionless staging, and by using conspicuous gaps in the text to underline the necessary interventions of performance, these plays draw attention to and perhaps even reconfigure typical perceptions of the relationship between writer, text, and performance.

Playing with unstageability

One further way in which contemporary British playwrights have experimented with authorship is through flirting with impossibility and unstageability in their scripts. As Karen Quigley (2020) argues in her study of unstageability as a persistent but ever-changing phenomenon, notions of the unstageable are inherently tangled up with the relationship between text and performance. Texts which test the staging capacities of theatre invoke a dialogue with performance, alluding to the gap between the imaginative provocations of the page and the practical possibilities of the stage. As Quigley's book demonstrates, there's a long history of what might be called unstageability, which is itself a contingent concept. What is considered unstageable in one moment in time may be seen as stageable in another, and vice versa, dependent on changing stage technologies, audience tastes and social values. Throughout theatre history there have also been texts that, while dramatic in conception, have deliberately been written *not* to be staged, or to exceed the possibilities of staging. Typically referred to as closet dramas, these texts – which have been explored at length by Martin Puchner (2002) – were produced with the intention of being read rather than performed theatrically (although many have subsequently been staged in one way or another). My interest in this section, though, is not in plays that attempt to sidestep the theatre altogether in this way, but instead in texts that – either as a whole or in specific moments – create a productive friction with performance through challenges to the conventions and/or technical abilities of the stage. These are plays that are written to be performed, and that often demonstrate an acute theatrical awareness, but that present images or concepts that may seem (for a variety of reasons) unstageable.

One of the most formally provocative British plays of recent years, Jasmine Lee-Jones' *seven methods of killing kylie jenner* (2019), is a compelling example of this productive friction between page and stage. The play follows the fallout from protagonist Cleo's online tirade against Kylie Jenner and the ways in which the celebrity has made money by appropriating Black culture. It alternates between relatively naturalistic scenes of dialogue between Cleo and her friend Kara and what Lee-Jones dubs 'Twitterludes': streams of tweets, peppered with emojis, gifs, and memes. As the play goes on, its two realities – referred to in the script as the 'Twittersphere' and 'IRL' – bleed into one another, with Twitter language invading Cleo and Kara's speech. In the published text, these various elements are formatted as they would be on Twitter (with the exception of the gifs, which are shown as collections of still images), with little to no indication of how they might be theatricalised. In her notes to the play, Lee-Jones simply recommends that the tweets are performed by the actors playing Cleo and Kara, who are challenged to find ways of embodying emojis and gifs. Elsewhere in the text, Lee-Jones provides more oblique and poetic stage directions, such as: '*the most present sense of the present tense*' (2019: 1); '*The bird expands and suddenly we are on Twitter*' (2); '*A tumbleweave may cross the stage*' (45). Lee-Jones' abstract instruction before the play's climactic speech is especially challenging:

> Over the course of the following, Cleo @INCOGNEGRO goes into heartspeak. Her two heretofore separate identities as the IRL Cleo and TL @INCOGNE-GRO conspire to cross over and become one as she allows the truth to pour from her. As she does so, she expands and swells in the space. In doing all of the above, she breaks the form of Twitter and eventually the internet itself ... (74)

How do Cleo's online and offline selves collide? How can she be shown to expand and swell? What does it look like to break the internet on stage? Lee-Jones' script prompts a host of such questions to be negotiated by director, actors and designers. Her stage directions hint at this collaborative relationship between playwright and other theatre-makers, with notes that are phrased as suggestions rather than instructions: '*The whole room might go dark*' (81); '*Then all of a sudden Saartjie's spirit is summoned and appears in all its might. Or maybe they're just high as fuck*' (ibid.). In these moments, Lee-Jones invites a playful partnership with theatrical collaborators, demonstrating a perceptive and imaginative awareness of performance while not seeking to shape the details of future stagings. The inclusion of images or ideas that might seem impossible to stage can also be read as an implicit comment on what – and who – has traditionally been considered stageable in British theatres. Lee-Jones' play is deeply concerned with representation and appropriation; her young, Black, female protagonists inhabit the sort of story that is rarely told on mainstream British stages.

There are some similarities between *seven methods of killing kylie jenner* and Eve Leigh's *Midnight Movie* (2019), another play that attempts to stage the experience of existing online. But where *seven methods* is about being Black and female online, *Midnight Movie* explores the relationship between pain, disability, and the internet. The play theatricalises the experience of being awake in the middle of the night and browsing the web, punctuated by pain. The text is largely composed of long descriptions of online wanderings, meandering in the non-linear fashion that is characteristic of internet browsing, with very few indications of how this speech might be rendered theatrically. The frequent note '*new tab*' signals changes of direction, while also posing the unanswered question of how this might be shown on stage. Like Lee-Jones, Leigh often frames her stage directions as open, uncertain offerings – '*Maybe we're in the video*' (2019: 18); '*There is probably quite a long silence*' (37) – while other instructions are striking in their seeming unstageability, such as: '*There is an ocean onstage. / There is a real danger of drowning*' (39). Her opening note on the play is similarly ambiguous, stating only that it is 'being performed by too many people' (5) and asking interpreters to consider factors such as 'whether and to what extent [the performers] are visibly disabled' (ibid.). Another play that dramatises the experience of the internet while posing challenges for staging is *Teh Internet Is Serious Business* (2014) by Tim Price, which contains no stage directions and does not clearly distinguish (either through instructions, page layout, or typography) between text typed in web forums and text spoken in offline dialogue. Another recent play that likewise resists staging in ways that challenge theatrical conventions and assumptions about who or what can be represented is Ellie Kendrick's *Hole* (2018), a dramatic expression of female rage. Kendrick's text presents a series of audacious images to be staged, from chasms opening beneath performers to fists punching up through the floor, alongside poetic, choral sequences of speech. In her notes on the play, Kendrick states that her text is 'neither a series of instructions nor a poem' (2018: 6), displaying a knowing awareness of what is conventionally considered stageable and an openness to the varying interpretations of theatrical collaborators. In all these examples, playwrights are articulating – or seeking to articulate – under-represented or hard-to-represent experiences and developing a new language in which to do so.

Their often ambiguous or provocative prompts to other theatre-makers push playwriting into new territory, while also reminding audiences and readers of the gap that always exists between the suggestions of the text and the material enactment of live performance.

Other plays contain specific moments – often stage directions – that appear impossible to realise in performance. Quigley sees these unstageable stage directions as 'a form of creative resistance' (2020: 42), which reveal that the relationship between text and performance is not a rigid hierarchy but a 'fluid spectrum' (43). Stage directions also occupy an interesting position within the playtext because their status is uncertain and disputed; they are often not seen as an untouchable statement of authorial intent in the same way as words spoken by characters.[22] As Quigley puts it, the stage direction is 'fragmentary and hybrid', 'occupy[ing] liminal space' (42). Stage directions that push at the limits of theatrical realisation or actively resist performance, therefore, can be understood as another form of self-reflexive experimentation with authorship. Quigley discusses a series of illustrative examples, such as the stage directions in Sarah Kane's *Cleansed* (1998) – including demands for graphic violence, rats that carry away severed feet, and flowers that suddenly spring up from the floor – and the call for a bird several times larger than a human performer in Alistair McDowall's *X* (2016). To these might be added Caryl Churchill's famously ambiguous instruction for the parade scene in *Far Away* (2000): '*five is too few and twenty better than ten. A hundred?*' (2008: 132). Or one could consider the sole, recurring stage direction in *Pornography*: '*Images of hell. / They are silent*' (Stephens 2008a). In Ella Hickson's play *Oil* (2016), meanwhile, the 'Interscenes' that transport her protagonist May between different continents and historical eras contain a series of strange, provocative and/or seemingly impossible-to-stage directions: '*She walks through lands, through empires, through time*' (2016: 26); '*A small army of Iranian men walk obediently, in line, like ants*' (54); '*She flies above time*' (85); '*A child flies backwards into the future*' (101). There are echoes of this approach to stage directions in Scene Three of *The Writer*, which Hickson explains as '*an attempt at staging female experience*' (2018: 57) and which contains instructions such as '*The tribe dissolves*' (63) and '*A chalk circle. A structure. A system. A scheme. For a new world: the whole earth changes its face. Buildings rearrange*' (64). In both these plays, Hickson seems to be reaching for a novel form of theatrical expression – one that has the potential to enlarge the imaginative scope of performance and that can tell stories in politically significant new ways, whether it be responding to the representational challenge of the Anthropocene (in *Oil*) or resisting the structures imposed by patriarchal capitalism (*The Writer*). These stage directions all present either an imaginative leap, an image that initially appears impossible to create using the available technologies of the stage, or an ambiguous instruction that allows countless interpretations by other theatre-makers.

Rory Mullarkey is another playwright who has repeatedly experimented with unstageability in his stage directions. In *The Wolf from the Door* (2014), for example, he calls for moments of seemingly impossible stage violence, such as the instruction: '**Leo** *pulls a sword out of his bag and chops* **Derek**'s *head off*' (2014: 11).

Scene Fourteen, meanwhile, consists of a long list of outrageous 'sights' that must somehow be realised on stage, including the following:

A women's fencing association pulls down Nelson's Column.

Buckingham Palace is raided by an over-seventies golf team.

A life-drawing class sets fire to all the trees in Green Park.

Westminster Abbey gets napalmed by a ceilidh group. (42)

In this play about an unlikely armed insurrection fomented in Middle England, the comic impossibility of such sequences can perhaps be read as a sardonic comment on the apparent impossibility of overthrowing the government. One of the joys of the play is its slipperiness; it's hard for an audience to know how seriously we should take such suggestions of violent revolution by polite hobbyists. Even more strikingly, the entire first act of Mullarkey's play *Each Slow Dusk* (2014) consists solely of stage directions – an example that Quigley uses to cement her argument about the potential for unstageable stage directions to 'push theatre beyond its conventions and limits' (2020: 81). However, the first staging of *Each Slow Dusk* also demonstrates the inadequacy of considering the writer's intentions as one homogenous set of aims that can be collectively fulfilled or discarded. Much like the dramaturgically experimental texts discussed in the previous section, the play was composed with the self-reported intention of provoking innovative staging solutions from other theatre-makers. However, in Pentabus Theatre's production this challenge was – in Mullarkey's view – not fully taken up.[23] Director Elizabeth Freestone chose to have three actors simply speak aloud the stage directions that are assigned to the three characters in the text; in Mullarkey's words, 'essentially this thing that I had hoped would be open and explosive became a kind of monologue play' (Love 2015a). But it was equally Mullarkey's *intention* to hand the script over to collaborators and leave it to them to resolve the problem posed by his writing in whichever way they chose. Texts may present provocations and challenges to other theatre-makers, but they cannot guarantee inventive stagings. Moreover, there are countless other implied intentions in Mullarkey's script – from the setting to the character arcs – that Freestone's production did preserve. This example reinforces my earlier point about the complexity and multiplicity of artistic intentions. In individual instances, certain intentions may be judged more relevant than others by interpreters. Assumed intentions that relate to the plot, for instance, might be perceived as more important than those suggested in the stage directions, or vice versa (or, in other instances, the two may not be separable). None of these intentions can be definitively discovered by interpreters, who must always make guesses and approximations. Furthermore, an understanding of intentions as multiple, indeterminate, and at times even contradictory undermines any simplistic idea of 'serving' them.

In these moments of apparent unstageability within their plays, playwrights are implicitly engaging in a form of collaboration with other theatre-makers.

This then underlines the tension between text and performance, rather than attempting to elide it. Notably, many of the theatre-makers considered in this chapter are also harnessing such experiments for ideological critique. As discussed in the Introduction, scholars such as Rebellato and Julia Jarcho have even suggested that the gap that is opened up between text and performance in such plays *allows* for this political and philosophical questioning in a way that is not possible in plays that maintain the illusion of a complete, internally coherent fictional world, with the author kept out of sight. By disrupting the perceived unity of performance, it is suggested, these plays might also disrupt the uniformity of capitalism in the way proposed by Theodor Adorno in his insistence upon 'non-identity' in art. The problem with performance, from Adorno's perspective, is its here-and-nowness, given the manifold horrors and suffering of the present. But through asserting its status *as writing* within the live event of theatre, a play might claim to 'hijack the performance here-and-now in the name of that which is neither' (Jarcho 2017: 115); this, for Jarcho, is where its resistance lies. According to this view, then, the sorts of plays that I have discussed are doing something politically valuable by introducing a friction between text and performance.

Yet, while it's clear from the examples in this chapter that such experimentation has created productive opportunities for ideological questioning, I'm also wary of generating another binary – between politically radical plays that underline their own instability and politically regressive plays that seek to maintain a closed fiction. As Sheila Stowell has persuasively argued in her defence of realism, 'dramatic forms are not in themselves narrowly partisan' (1992: 87) and need to be understood in relation to specific historical, political, and social contexts. Likewise, Liz Tomlin makes the crucial point that 'the conclusive alignment of ideological characteristics on the basis of form alone is ultimately self-defeating' (2013: 12), threatening to calcify once 'radical' forms into new orthodoxies. Moreover, it is my argument that these experiments with authorship illuminate truths about how *all* theatrical texts function. The friction that Rebellato and Jarcho identify between text and performance always exists to some extent. Text and performance have each always already infiltrated the other, yet neither can be fully assimilated by the other. The difference that can be observed is between those artists who welcome and underline this incommensurability between text and performance, and those who seek to minimise it. In that sense, the examples examined in this chapter do perform a radical role in this specific context by unsettling assumptions about the assimilability of text and performance, or the authority of script over staging, but not in a way that necessarily marks them out as inherently more politically questioning than other theatrical forms. Their particular value lies instead in how they foreground the trickiness of dramatic writing. As opposed to the dramatist whom Peter Szondi sees as absent from drama – 'He [sic] does not speak; he institutes discussion' (quoted in Jarcho 2017: 8) – the artists whose work I have explored here make themselves present in their plays, disrupting the fictions of their own creation in ways that place authorship at the centre of critical discussion.

Conclusion

While interrogations of authorship are not unique to this period, this has become a notable preoccupation among a range of British theatre-makers in the late 20th and early 21st century. By foregrounding the act of scripting, the plays and productions discussed in this chapter reveal assumptions of authorial control that might otherwise recede into the background and remain unquestioned. Their especial interest, for the purposes of this study, lies in how they prod at the perceived hierarchy of text over performance and direct attention towards areas of friction or tension between text and performance. This invites a re-evaluation of how authorship is understood in relation to both texts and performances. Focusing on the notions of intention and authority that sit beneath the concept of authorship, I have argued that rather than comprising a singular, comprehensive blueprint that exists prior to the writing of a play and may therefore be discovered by reading it, artistic intentions can be more accurately described as indeterminate, multiple, and contained in creative processes. My conception of intentions – which applies not just to the sorts of playful, self-reflexive texts discussed in this chapter, but to *all* theatrical scripts – thus invites interpreters to adopt a flexible approach to what the playwright(s) may have intended. What I previously described as a strong intentionalist production of a play is not ruled out – a director may choose to treat all presumed intentions (or as many as they can identify) as relevant – but it is unseated as the interpretive norm and revealed to be ultimately futile. Indeed, given the array of different, indeterminate intentions involved in a play, the likelihood of ever truly 'serving' the playwright's intentions is vanishingly small, even when – as in many British productions of new plays – the writer is present during rehearsals. Furthermore, when understood as multiple, indeterminate, and embedded in process, artistic intentions might cease to be considered the primary possession of a playwright who is interpreted and 'served' by others, and instead become the shared preserve of theatre-makers working in countless different ways.

Notes

1 This is reflected in the title of Adrian Page's essay collection *The Death of the Playwright* (1992), while Steve Waters exaggerates the implications of Barthes' argument when he asserts that 'the isolated author has been deemed anachronistic' (2011: 264).
2 The difficulty of accommodating collaboration within existing copyright, royalty, and working arrangements is also illustrated by the Writers' Guild's guidelines on collaborative development (Edgar and Whittington 2012b: 25–27).
3 However, McDonagh does remind readers that 'courts inevitably require evidence in order to make their determinations, and clear written evidence tends to persuade judges more readily than vague oral remembrances' (2021: 85).
4 McDonagh does suggest, though, that recent UK case law suggests possibilities for a more flexible legal recognition of collaboration and joint authorship in the future.
5 In a 1989 lecture, David Hare noted that this 'depressing philosophy was not one to cheer the heart of a playwright' (2005: 164). Steve Waters likewise expresses concerns about what he sees as a backlash against playwrights, claiming that 'individual authorship

in some theatrical circles has been imagined as inherently fascistic, patriarchal, phallocentric, phallogocentric – only collective creation is able to overcome such thought crimes' (2011: 264).

6   Maggie Inchley (2015) has also discussed the preoccupation with finding new 'voices' in British playwriting, with a particular focus on the drive to stage previously marginalised voices during the New Labour era.

7   For a selection of this literature from throughout the 20th and 21st centuries, see W. K. Wimsatt Jr. and M. C. Beardsley (1946), E. D. Hirsch (2001), Alfred R. Mele and Paisley Livingston (1992), Colin Lyas (1995), and Kaye Mitchell (2008). Even in Livingston's (2005) study of artistic intention across multiple media there is not a single mention of theatre.

8   For one of the few discussions of intention in theatre, see Rebellato (2013).

9   See, for example, Mele and Livingston (1992: 933–934). It's interesting that thought experiments imagining intentionless meaning are often rather fanciful, perhaps suggesting how integral intention is to our way of thinking and the lengths to which one must go to attempt to get away from it. Another example is the 'wave poem' (Knapp and Michaels 1982).

10 Here it's also worth noting the distinction between a *reader*'s interpretation and a *theatremaker*'s interpretation. A director will read and interpret the text themselves and then add a further layer of interpretation in the act of presenting that text to an audience. It's therefore possible for a moderate intentionalist directorial concept to convey what is essentially a strong intentionalist reading of the play's meanings.

11 Examples include the comic prologues of Roman playwright Plautus, which often comment on the construction of the play and its plot, and Francis Beaumont's 1607 play *The Knight of the Burning Pestle,* in which the deliverer of the prologue is interrupted by a grocer and his wife from the audience who demand changes to the play. Though it's worth noting Tiffany Stern's warning that in the early modern period prologues were not always composed by the same writer as the rest of the text (2009: 2).

12 The Wooster Group have created deconstructive re-workings of classic plays including *Our Town* in *Route 1 & 9* (1981), *The Crucible* in *L.S.D. (… Just the High Points …)* (1984), *Three Sisters* in *Brace Up!* (1991), as well as putting their own spin on *Hamlet* (2007).

13 Aleks Sierz (2001) offers an overview of the tropes of what he calls 'in-yer-face' theatre in his book of the same name .

14 *The Writer* was commissioned and produced by the Almeida Theatre, a prestigious, state-subsidised venue in a wealthy area of London which has a history of receiving criticism for its under-representation of female playwrights.

15 In my PhD thesis, I discussed several reviews which made similar criticisms of devised theatre (Love 2018: 266–276).

16 See Rebellato (2009: 21), Colin McGinn (2004: 12–39), Daniel Clement Dennett (1993: 92–93), and Edward S. Casey (1976: 104). This is also something that Ludwig Wittgenstein explores, as acknowledged by McGinn.

17 Breach's other shows include *The Beanfield* (2015), a self-aware historical 're-enactment' of the Battle of the Beanfield, and *It's True, It's True, It's True* (2018), which engages with the difficulty of reconstructing a 17th-century rape trial from incomplete, translated court transcripts.

18 The published version of *The Future Show* contains three different iterations of the show as performed by Pearson, together with a score designed to help other performers make their own version of the show.

19 Other examples of putting the text on stage include Christopher Brett-Bailey's *This Is How We Die* (2014), in which he read from pages on a desk, and the practice of theatremaker Andy Smith, whose performances often involve reading from scripts on music stands.

20 My approach here is partly inspired by Lyas (1995), who likewise applies Wittgenstein's ideas to a consideration of artistic intentions.
21 I have written at greater length about Stephens' relationship with German-language theatre in the article 'New Perspectives on Home: Simon Stephens and Authorship in British Theatre' (2016).
22 Quigley offers a helpful overview of the history and uses of stage directions and how scholars have written about them (2020: 39–58). I return to the marginal status of stage directions in Chapter 4.
23 Mullarkey discussed his attempt to write something 'completely unrecognisable' which would challenge collaborators during a conversation as part of the 'Are We on the Same Page?' symposium (Love 2015a).

3
CONTEMPORARY APPROACHES TO CLASSIC TEXTS: SUPPLEMENTATION AND ITERABILITY

Chekhov's First Play (2015) opens with a theatrical in-joke. Bush Moukarzel, one of the two directors and adaptors of the play, enters as The Director with a gun in his hand. It's a knowing visual reference to 'Chekhov's gun': the idea that – as The Director later explains – 'if in the first act you put a gun on stage, then in the last act it must be fired' (2016: 37). Already, before a word has been uttered, spectators are primed to engage as much with the myth of Chekhov-as-author as with his unwieldy first play. Throughout the first part of the performance, a pointedly traditional Chekhovian aesthetic of period costume and samovars knocks up against a 'director's commentary' delivered to the audience through headphones. Dead Centre offers a strikingly self-aware approach to the conventions of reviving classics in Anglophone theatre cultures, combining a mock-reverent rendering of the script with a commentary that parodies literary criticism. There's even a tongue-in-cheek invitation to audience members 'who are comfortable with the classics' to remove their headphones and experience the play 'as Chekhov intended' (12). The implication is that to really recreate the play 'as Chekhov intended' is an impossible task. This dialogue with impossibility continues throughout the show, as Dead Centre playfully deconstructs cultural expectations of Chekhov, of productions of the classics more broadly, and of the assumed authority of the canonical author. Bit by bit, the performance starts falling apart – a page skipped here, a forgotten line there. Eventually, the whole world of the play self-destructs, as a wrecking ball smashes through the middle of the set. The Director's futile effort to distil some essence of Chekhov in performance is abandoned and revealed as the sham it is. 'Actually', he admits when he returns at the end, 'we changed quite a lot' (54).

There is, to borrow Karen Quigley's words, a 'dialogic engagement' (2020: 93) between the adapted text and the adaptation throughout *Chekhov's First Play*. She suggests that the use of the director's commentary 'calls to mind Linda Hutcheon's

DOI: 10.4324/9781003126812-4

sense that the spectator of adaptation is [...] oscillating between the adapted text and the adaptation' (96). In this sense, adaptations or versions of classic plays – especially where the source text is well-known or, as in the case of *Chekhov's First Play*, audiences are likely to be familiar with the aesthetic typically associated with the playwright – offer an instance of (potentially) heightened awareness of the relationship between text and performance. This is one of the reasons why, in this chapter, I turn to revivals and adaptations. Having re-examined theatrical authorship, here I explore the implications this has for the Western dramatic canon, treatments of which are often plagued by an even more intense anxiety about the authority of the author – especially where that author is widely regarded as a genius. Later in the chapter, I investigate and challenge the idea of the dramatic 'work', which has often functioned as another stand-in for authorial authority. The chapter also considers the ways in which texts and performances transform over time as plays are revived in new cultural contexts. First, though, I explore the contemporary trend for interventionist treatments of the canon, which are often described as 'radical' revivals. These playful appropriations of texts that have traditionally been revered as authoritative templates for performance have begun in some ways to dismantle the perceived power of play and playwright, while at the same time their interventions are frequently justified through an appeal to presumed authorial intentions. I also look at the critical backlash with which these productions have sometimes been greeted, analysing some of the common tropes found in reviews. This response from reviewers, as well as the anxieties expressed by theatre-makers themselves, reveals the tensions around authority, ownership, and fidelity that sit at the heart of this chapter.

Staging classic texts

In July 2013, Michael Billington asked in a comment piece: 'is it OK to rewrite classic plays?' (2013). The premise of his article is representative of much of the popular critical discourse surrounding productions variously labelled as 'versions', 'adaptations', or 'radical' revivals, which are celebrated by some for reimagining classic plays and bringing them to new audiences, while others fret that they are defying the intentions of their long-dead authors. In this case, Billington concluded: 'If we are to revive old plays, which inevitably contain obscure words and allusions, surely it is the job of the actor' – not the adaptor or director – 'to make us understand them' (ibid.). He adds that the 'only alternative is to shrug our shoulders, admit defeat and say that the past is a foreign country – and now utterly dead' (ibid.). Billington's comments allude to the paradox that sits beneath common understandings of the classics in British theatre culture: these plays are assumed to still resonate with audiences today, yet any production that goes 'too far' in its temporal or imaginative relocation of the drama is condemned, at least by some reviewers. As critics like Billington see it, a 'radical' effort by theatre-makers to make a centuries-old play speak to contemporary spectators by significantly cutting, altering, or theatrically intervening in the text is an admission that the past is 'dead', rather than an acknowledgement that plays constantly change in relation to changing historical contexts. This attitude once again lodges authority with the text and with the assumed intentions of the playwright at the time of writing, in ways that I have already shown to be reductive.

Along similar lines, playwright David Hare has pejoratively characterised the approach of many of the practitioners discussed in this chapter as 'director's theatre where you camp up classic plays and you cut them and you prune them around' (quoted in Alberge 2017). His use of the phrase 'director's theatre' alludes to a tradition of theatre-making that has strong associations with continental Europe and that has often been resisted and maligned within British theatre culture. Peter M. Boenisch defines 'director's theatre' as 'the production of plays, in particular from the canonical dramatic repertoire, staged by an ensemble of resident theatre artists, usually at the public state and city theatres of Continental Europe' (2015: 1), with the implication that such productions will 'rethink the play afresh' (3) rather than attempting fidelity to the intentions of the author. This tradition of directing has been explored by Boenisch in his study of Regietheater and in Maria Delgado and Dan Rebellato's edited volume *Contemporary European Theatre Directors* (2020). In contextualising his attempt to rethink so-called 'director's theatre', Boenisch perceives an 'irreconcilable cultural divide' between 'the insular English theatre culture and its geographically not too distant Continental equivalents' (2015: 2). This is reinforced by the objections of Hare, who refers to 'all that directorial stuff that we've managed to keep over on the continent' and expresses his fear that it is 'beginning to infect our theatre' (quoted in Alberge 2017). Similarly, British director Joe Hill-Gibbins has commented on 'a fear and suspicion of European theatre and the idea of what is dismissed as "director's theatre" in some quarters of British theatre' (quoted in Gardner 2020). As he identifies, there's an oddly isolationist attitude embedded in these complaints about 'director's theatre' , which is seen as a somehow non-British approach represented by figures such as Thomas Ostermeier (a German) and Ivo van Hove (a Belgian), whose productions have frequently appeared on British stages in recent years. Criticisms of these productions are thus bolstered by a view of text-led, playwright-centred theatre as distinctly British, set in opposition to the director-led traditions of other European theatre cultures.

Nonetheless, an approach to the dramatic canon that broadly aligns with what has been called 'director's theatre' has become more widespread in Britain over the last couple of decades, as exemplified by the practitioners discussed later in this chapter. As I go on to explore, these contemporary directors have made various interventions in classic plays, prompting some – like Billington and Hare – to question the relationship that such productions have to their canonical texts. Less pejoratively, various scholars have sought to analyse what it is that such productions are doing and how these approaches differ from (for want of a better phrase) more conventional treatments of the classics. The terminology of adaptation has sometimes been used as a way of distinguishing such 'radical' versions of the classics from 'traditional' revivals. In such instances, adaptation is applied not to the transfer of a narrative from another art form (such as a novel) to the stage, but to the contemporary transformation of a pre-existing playtext. For example, John Bull applies the label 'Add-Aptation' to Simon Stephens' new English-language versions of plays by Ibsen and Chekhov for directors Carrie Cracknell and Katie Mitchell. Bull characterises this approach as one that 'does not concern itself overmuch with a fidelity to the original language' or with 'the traditional claim that the spirit of the original text is still being respected' (2018: 282–283), but he still distinguishes this from what he refers to as 'appropriation', in which new versions of classic plays are identified as 'after' or 'based on' their source text. Bull's reference to 'appropriations' draws on the work of Julie Sanders, who states that 'appropriation carries out the same sustained engagement as adaptation but frequently adopts a posture of critique, even assault' (2006: 4). Similarly attempting to differentiate between 'appropriation' and 'adaptation' in the introduction to her volume on theatre adaptation, Margherita Laera notes that 'appropriation emphasizes the idea of "taking for one's own use" [...], and is thus often preferable in contexts in which there is little or no concern, and productively so, with "staying true" to the source' (2014: 11). However, these definitions all prompt a question that is never fully resolved: at what point of remove does a production become an adaptation or appropriation of its text, rather than simply a new version of it? Working along similar lines, Nora Williams has argued that Hill-Gibbins' production of *The Changeling* (2012) is better considered an adaptation than a revival. Williams stresses the extent to which Hill-Gibbins and dramaturg Zoë Svendsen made changes to the text of the play, noting that 'scenes were cut, swapped, and/or combined, jokes were updated and rewritten, whole characters were excised' (2018: 319). She asserts, based on this, that Hill-Gibbins and Svendsen created 'an undeniably adaptive *Changeling*' (ibid.), but without offering any framework for determining how one might differentiate between revival and adaptation.

While still drawing on ideas from adaptation studies, Jozefina Komporaly instead uses the term 'radical revival' to 'denote the audacious and game-changing intervention that has taken place in the adaptive process' (2017: 2). The central argument of her book is that such radical revivals are themselves a distinctive and innovative type of adaptation. She further defines such radical revivals as 'practices that treat the source work as raw material towards an independent artwork' (ibid.); these practices encompass 'revivals of existing plays, dramatizations of other genres as well as the staging of other "found" material' (ibid.), with examples ranging from Punchdrunk's immersive theatrical events, which are loosely based on classic narratives, to directorial interventions in canonical plays such as *Hamlet* and *Faust*. For Komporaly, furthermore, a 'radical revival' is 'an intervention that is not only rooted in the critical re-evaluation and fragmentation of a precursor, but also offers a risk-taking and innovative remake within the framework of a significantly different reconstruction' (4). This is a potentially helpful way of differentiating between 'radical' and 'conventional' approaches to revival and/or adaptation that speaks to several of the examples discussed in this chapter. However, the challenge once again lies in the decision about where one draws the line between these approaches in practice. The idea of a 'radical' revival, meanwhile, often relies on a flawed rhetoric of textual fidelity and transgression – a rhetoric that has long haunted both adaptations and revivals.

There have been some productive challenges to the notion that any adapted or revived performance can or should be judged by how 'faithful' it is to its source text. Linda Hutcheon, for example, asserts that an 'adaptation's double nature does not mean [...] that proximity or fidelity to the adapted text should be the criterion of judgment or the focus of analysis' (2013: 6). However, many assessments of both adaptations and revivals continue to use fidelity as a yardstick. This can be seen in some of the critical responses cited elsewhere in this chapter, in which reviewers object to the ways in which theatre-makers have seemingly transgressed or betrayed the play they are reviving. There is still an assumption by many within the British theatre establishment that a new version of a play should maintain an ill-defined degree of fidelity to its text, or if not to the letter of the text then to some 'spirit' thought to inhere in the play. But the many different ways in which the idea of fidelity is deployed as a measure of both success and failure reveal the instability of this idea. As will be seen throughout this chapter, 'fidelity' has been variously applied to a production's use of language, integrity of plot and character, acting style, stage aesthetic, 'spirit', tone, or atmosphere. Rejecting this imprecise discourse of fidelity and infidelity, W. B. Worthen argues that 'texts are always a field of transgression' (1997: 36), which is useful as a starting point for critically approaching the revivals discussed in this chapter and the rhetoric of radicalism that often surrounds them. According to this view, all new versions inevitably remake the drama they are claiming to represent. From this perspective, distinctions between conventional treatments, 'radical' revivals, and adaptations begin to blur. However, I still find it helpful to hold onto a distinction – however shaky and contingent – between revivals and adaptations. No matter how imprecise or contested the terminology of adaptation may be, it still usefully describes a transposition of material from one medium, genre, culture, language, and/or historical or ideological context to another (including various possible combinations of these transpositions)[1] in a way that remains distinct from new productions of plays that explicitly frame themselves as revivals, even where they make significant textual or directorial interventions. On this basis, I consider *Chekhov's First Play* an adaptation rather than a revival, as it transposes a relatively small proportion of the (translated) content of Chekhov's untitled first play into a new dramaturgical framework.[2]

In this chapter, I extend Worthen's idea that playtexts, rather than offering source material which can be faithfully or unfaithfully performed, are always inevitably 'fields of transgression'. To do so, I refer to Jacques Derrida's work on supplementation and iterability, which I argue can be usefully applied to the relationship between text and performance. My thinking here owes a debt to Marvin Carlson, who has argued for a similar application of Derrida's theory of the supplement to playtexts and performances.[3] As an alternative to the theoretical models of illustration, translation, and fulfilment, Carlson proposes the supplement as a concept that resolves the tensions inherent in earlier frameworks. While illustration theorists see performance as 'a supplement joined to the already existing plenitude of the written text' and fulfilment theorists have 'stressed the other signification, of performance as supplement in the sense of filling a void' (1985: 9–10), Derrida's dual interpretation of the term allows for both senses at once. Carlson writes that

> a play on stage will inevitably display material lacking in the written text, quite likely not apparent as lacking until the performance takes place, but then revealed as significant and necessary. At the same time, the performance, by revealing this lack, reveals also a potentially infinite series of future performances providing further supplementation. (10)

The supplement, in Carlson's view, 'den[ies] plenitude for either written text or performance' (ibid.) and 'avoids the problems attendant upon privileging either performance or written text' (11). I similarly find the doubleness of the supplement as theorised by Derrida a useful corrective to hierarchical models of text and performance, while also building further upon Carlson's analysis.

Before going on to look at specific examples of how contemporary British theatremakers have approached the dramatic canon, I want to briefly address the commonly held belief that texts, as opposed to fleeting, ephemeral performances, offer a stable repository for the meanings of the play. This logic might seem to support the claim that it's in the text, rather than in any of the countless possible performances, that the definitive version of any play can be located. Here, though, I find it helpful to draw on Worthen's argument that typical constructions of the relationship between text and performance are based upon 'reductive assumptions of the formal consistency of published texts, of texts as material objects that house the work of the author' (1997: 7). He illustrates the flawed nature of these assumptions by looking at the process of creating new editions of Shakespeare's plays, which exist in various textual versions. As Worthen notes, 'the multiplication of texts complicates the unity of the work and its relation to authorial intention' (10). While this is perhaps especially so in the case of Shakespeare, whose plays exist in many different forms and have been reproduced and disputed in countless editions over the centuries, it's an insight that might be applied to *all* plays. Even a new play that is immediately published when first produced is subject to this textual instability, existing as an unpublished manuscript prior to rehearsals, a series of working documents during the rehearsal process, and a version typically published before the end of rehearsals (and therefore potentially differing from the version used in performance, as stated in the disclaimer at the front of many published playtexts). And in many cases – as I explore in Chapter 4 – the same play will go on to have future lives in print, either in revised new editions or in collected volumes of plays by the same writer. In this sense, then, texts share the same quality of instability that is characteristic of performances, demanding a rethink of the relationships between texts, performances, and what is typically thought of as the authorial 'work'.

Reinventing the canon

The critical discourse discussed above is responding to contemporary British productions that are – in a variety of ways – reimagining, challenging, or updating the dramatic canon. Like the experiments with authorship discussed in the previous chapter, this critical conversation with the classics is not an entirely novel development in the last 30 years. Across much of continental Europe, director-led theatre has for several decades been engaged in a project of interrogating, politicising, and re-energising the canon, while experimental North American theatre companies like The Wooster Group have been intervening in classic texts since the 1980s. These treatments of the classics occasionally toured to the United Kingdom , while some British alternative theatre-makers staged their own confrontations with the canon.[4] But since roughly the turn of the 21st century there has been a notable increase in British productions taking what might be perceived as a radical approach to the canon, accompanied by an often fraught public discourse around the staging of classic plays. This has been spurred in part by greater theatrical exchange between Britain and continental Europe, with a new generation of directors and other theatre-makers being inspired by practices from across the Channel. In a range of ways, contemporary British theatre practitioners are now playfully unsettling the authority of canonical texts, going beyond the well-established practice of staging classics in modern dress to more fundamentally question how these plays relate to 21st-century society and culture. While I have questioned the sharp differentiation of 'radical' and 'conventional' treatments of classic plays, Komporaly's list of the assorted processes used in radical revivals and adaptations usefully captures the diversity of these approaches: theatre-makers are variously making use of 'restructuring, remixing, remerging, remediation, re-enactment, re-scaling, re-culturing, replotting, re-dating, reconfiguring, resetting, reimagining and relocating' (2017: 5). This ranges from the deconstructive commentary of *Chekhov's First Play,* to the strikingly contemporary theatrical idiom of the Robert Icke production of *The Oresteia* cited in the Introduction, to revisionist versions that approach classic plays from a perspective of feminist, Marxist, or anti-colonial critique – to suggest just a few examples.

As already noted, the terminology of 'radical' revivals has often been used in relation to the approaches of specific directors who are seen as intervening in some way in the classic texts they stage. Practitioners making theatre in the UK whose work has been referred to in these terms include Rupert Goold, Katie Mitchell, Maria Aberg, Joe Hill-Gibbins, Ellen McDougall, Robert Icke, Emma Rice, Sean Holmes, Carrie Cracknell, Natalie Abrahami, and Ben Kidd (who is part of Dead Centre, as well as working as a freelance director). While these directors' productions are aesthetically diverse, they often make significant cuts and/or changes to canonical scripts and they share a tendency towards striking, irreverent, and often gleefully anachronistic visual images, from Goold's insertion of an Elvis impersonator in his production of *The Merchant of Venice* (2011) to the abundance of blow-up sex dolls in Hill-Gibbins' *Measure for Measure* (2015). Occasionally, as in *Chekhov's First Play*, these productions offer meta-theatrical commentary on the texts they are staging, taking a deconstructive approach to the canon. Other recurring characteristics of this broad category of theatrical work include the use of multi-media elements, modern music, movement sequences, stripped-back and/ or abstract set designs, and the insertion of contemporary colloquial language. Such features have often been dismissed as 'gimmicks', with some reviewers suggesting that these staging flourishes get in the way of the plays.[5] For example, Paul Taylor's assertion that Aberg's controversial production of *King John* (2012) – which switched the gender of the Bastard, transferred key lines from one character to another, and brought a retro party aesthetic of balloons, neon lights, and sequinned hats to Shakespeare's history play – demonstrated 'a lack of trust in the play' (2012: 410) is particularly revealing of the expectations attached to classic texts. For Taylor and many other critics, the play's the thing, which must be trusted and 'served' by the director. Here and in other negative reviews of 'radical' revivals, there's a commonly expressed indignation that directors are imposing their own ideas and images on the text, rather than allowing it to 'speak for itself'. For many of these directors, on the other hand, text is 'there to be engaged with and reformulated' (Delgado and Rebellato 2020: 19).

Alongside the trend for controversial directorial treatments of the Western dramatic canon, ensemble and devising companies have been similarly reimagining and deconstructing the classics. Filter Theatre, for example, has created riotous 'remixes' of plays including *Twelfth Night* (2006), *A Midsummer Night's Dream* (2012), and *Macbeth* (2015), irreverently cutting and restructuring the texts and adding raucous live music. Meanwhile, immersive adaptations of classic plays such as Punchdrunk's *Sleep No More* (2003), ZU-UK's durational *Hotel Medea* (2009), and dreamthinkspeak's *The Rest Is Silence* (2012) provide multiple perspectives on the familiar narratives of *Macbeth, Medea,* and *Hamlet* respectively, dismantling the single frame supplied by the playwright. On a much smaller scale, Forced Entertainment has offered its take on the Bard in *Complete Works: Table Top Shakespeare* (2015), a series of performances in which individual members of the company told condensed versions of Shakespeare's plays using everyday objects as the characters. One prominent British theatre company that had a sustained engagement with the canon, and which received both praise and criticism for its playful versions of classic texts, is Kneehigh (particularly under the artistic directorship of Emma Rice between 2002 and 2016). The company adapted a wide range of dramatic and non-dramatic texts, including plays, novels, and fairy tales, as well as films and television shows. Kneehigh's approach was characterised by 'a theatricalization of everyday objects, an adventurous use of the performance space and an enthusiasm for the full use of the performers' bodies on stage' (Radosavljević 2013a: 73), as well as an urge to democratise and popularise classics that are often perceived as elitist. In the company's production of *The Bacchae* (2004), for example, newspaper was used to craft everything from the severed head of Pentheus to headwear for the worshippers of Dionysus, while a tutu-clad chorus explained ancient Greek mythology with the help of a blackboard. Rice has explained that the company's process would always begin with story rather than script, working from the ensemble's 'instinctive feelings' (quoted in Radosavljević 2013b: 102). In these mischievous reimaginings of the canon, text was displaced from its usual position of authority; as Rice puts it, 'I work on the iceberg and the words are the sprinkle on top of the point' (103). In these and other ensemble productions, moreover, authorship is dispersed among company members, moving away from any monolithic notion of authorial intentions.

Finally, a range of intercultural dramaturgical interventions in the Western canon have simultaneously disrupted the perceived authority of text and author and decentred the assumed cultural norms associated with these classics. Interculturalism, as both a term and a practice, has a problematic and contested history, as helpfully summarised by Ric Knowles (2010). Here, I'm not addressing forms of interculturalism which have involved white, Western theatre-makers borrowing from (and arguably appropriating) other cultures and traditions. In response to this tainted history, some have rejected the vocabulary of 'interculturalism' altogether; Victor Ukaegbu (2013), for example, favours the term 'cross-cultural', while Tara Arts' co-founder Jatinder Verma has variously employed the terms 'intercultural', 'multicultural', 'transcultural', and 'cross-cultural'. But the sorts of dramaturgical interventions that I'm interested in here are best captured by Royona Mitra's term 'new interculturalism' (2015). Drawing on Ted Cantle's definition of interculturalism, and looking specifically at the creative practice of British-Bangladeshi dancer and choreographer Akram Khan, Mitra defines new interculturalism as constituting not a one-way borrowing of non-Western performance traditions, but instead a hybrid, insider-outsider perspective that brings different cultures into dialogue through the 'fundamentally intercultural' bodies and experiences of the artists involved (2015: 23). She also stresses the contrast between intercultural theatre projects that have 'relied on intercultural exchanges and translations in textual terms' and the 'open-ended corporeal aesthetic' of Khan's work (ibid.), suggesting a self-reflexive, processual meeting of cultural elements that moves beyond textual meaning. This definition speaks to versions of the Western canon by Black British and British Asian theatre-makers in which these texts are negotiated through the hybrid identities of practitioners, in the process questioning and/or displacing the plays' perceived whiteness and, in some cases, their historical use as tools of colonialism.[6] Companies working in this vein include Talawa, Tribe Arts, New Earth (previously known as Yellow Earth), and Tara Arts.[7] The latter's hybrid methodology of 'Binglishing' Western classics disrupts the idea of a 'norm' or 'centre' and resists the marginalisation of artists of colour and/or artists of immigrant heritage within British theatre culture. 'Binglish' refers to 'a theatrical language and philosophy that integrates Western European conventions and much older classical Asian theatre writings' (Ukaegbu 2013: 125).[8] Emphasising the non-textual elements of this practice, Ukaegbu identifies the following features of 'Binglishing':

the use of detailed, stylised bodily movements/physicality, actors' voices, visual and imagistic spectacles, stylised costumes, elaborate non-naturalistic make-up, and emotions integrated with music and song [...] minimal props, open stage, continual on stage presence of all performers, absence of section breaks, direct address, invocatory preludes, a narrator, and a dramatic convention in which actors and audiences make no pretence about the event as theatrical encounter. (126)

Verma, furthermore, explains that Tara Arts has increasingly moved towards a practice in which 'movement and music [...] are not ancillary to the spoken word but form an integral part of the "text" of performance' (quoted in Hingorani 2010: 45–46). The integration of Asian performance traditions and the prominent use of music and movement can be seen, for example, in the company's production of *Macbeth* (2015). The drama is accompanied throughout by a visible onstage drummer, whose underscoring pulse is integral to the production, and the fights in the play are transformed into extended, stylised movement sequences. The witches, meanwhile, are reimagined as singing and dancing hijras: members of a recognised third gender in India and Pakistan who live on the margins of society and are known for their ritualised performances. In Verma's version, the two worlds of the play – the spiritual realm of the witches and the world of the other characters – come to represent the different cultures that migrant communities exist in and between. Significantly, in the context of this investigation, Verma has also described Tara Arts' approach as a 'rejection of the dominant convention of the modern English stage – the spoken word' (1998: 129). As Colin Chambers puts it, 'Binglish ideologically and physically decentres English and all the power that flows from this' (2011: 161). While this is primarily – and importantly – a decolonising move, it also disrupts any perceived hierarchy of text over performance and language over other forms of theatricality.

The examples introduced here involve a mix of different approaches to the text, from productions that would – despite their critical interventions – be commonly recognised as revivals of existing plays, to extensive reworkings that are typically thought of as new plays in their own right. But all these approaches involve a complex dialogue between the playtext, its position in the canon, and the new production, which exists within a distinct set of social, cultural, and political contexts. In her consideration of the intercultural revivals of the Western canon produced by companies like Tara Arts, Varsha Panjwani makes the crucial point that these directors and companies 'do not just employ Shakespeare' – or, one might add, any other canonical playwright – 'for political purposes, but they also transform Shakespeare performance' (2017: 54). There's a two-way exchange between play and context, in which the fraught concept of fidelity recedes into impossibility. This is an important point to pick up on when challenging the notion of any definitive performance of a text. As already noted, one of the peculiar characteristics of playtexts is that they are written to be performed multiple times in multiple different contexts. This iterability – to borrow a term from

Derrida – is inscribed in their essential structure: the possibility of numerous future performances is a constitutive characteristic of dramatic writing. As Rebellato observes, 'a play is an object designed precisely to be placed in a variety of new contexts generating new meanings and associations each time' (2013: 23). In a brief discussion of this phenomenon, he adds that '[g]ood plays, one might say, display maximal iterability' (ibid.) – an idea that I want to explore further here. Iterability, according to Derrida, is a necessary part of the structure of *all* language: linguistic signs are characterised by the inherent possibility of repetition. Derrida argues that for written communication to function as such, it must remain readable after the disappearance of both writer and receiver – indeed, writing that was not readable in these circumstances would not be writing. If I write a note that is intended for a particular recipient and it gets lost, for example, it may just as easily be read by someone else who later finds it. Derrida thus conceives of writing as 'an iterative structure, cut off from all absolute responsibility, from consciousness as the ultimate authority' (1988: 8). Writing cannot be controlled by its author because, for it to work *as* writing, it must function in that author's absence, opening it up to countless different meanings and uses. Writing is, therefore, 'a sort of machine which is productive in turn' (ibid.). A play might thus be understood as a particular type of meaning-making machine. Once written, it generates meanings independently of the playwright and their intentions, both in reading and in performance. This necessary and inherent feature of all playtexts unsettles the notion of any one context (say, the playwright's context or the context of the original production) commanding authority over the countless iterations and interpretations that the playtext makes possible.

Importantly, Derrida's theory of iterability holds even for apparently unique instances of writing: 'iter*ability*, which is not iteration, can be recognized even in a mark which *in fact* seems to have occurred only once' (48, original emphasis). A script written for a specific one-off event, or a script that is considered (at present) to be unstageable, can still therefore be understood as iterable; its medium relies upon the theoretical *possibility* of its repetition. Iterability is a useful concept because it further elucidates the way in which plays are separable from and beyond the control of their writers, and because it captures the combination of continuity and deviation involved in a play's multiple performances. Derrida states that 'the structure of iteration […] implies both identity and difference': in each repetition, there is a 'minimal remainder' that allows us to identify the sign, but it will also be different every time it's repeated (53). Likewise, a play must have a certain self-identity that allows for it to be recognised and repeated, even as each iteration alters it. While the idea of an unchanging essence that the director can dig down and access is problematic, as I go on to discuss, there is something familiar that remains alongside the inherent difference in any new version of a play; this is what allows us to identify it as, for instance, *Hamlet*. Throughout the play's various iterations, meanwhile, the text itself also alters, changing in response to new contexts and performance conditions. To characterise a playtext as the enduring document that produces various fleeting performances is, in Derrida's way of thinking, to mistakenly attribute permanence to the written word. He argues that 'the structure of the remainder, implying alteration, renders all absolute permanence impossible' (54). The notion of iterability also brings back the question of intention, which Derrida displaces as the 'organizing center' (15) of meaning. He is clear that 'the category of intention will not disappear; it will have its place, but from that place it will no longer be able to govern the entire scene and system of utterance' (18). He notes also that the structure of iterability reveals that intention can never be fully present to itself; iterability 'leaves us no choice but to mean (to say) something that is (already, always, also) other than what we mean (to say)' (62). In other words, meaning is immediately divided in the moment of writing because of the possibility of its repetition and alteration, and therefore it's impossible to describe a writer as simply saying what they mean to say. This aligns with my argument in the previous chapter that artistic intention *allows* for meaning but cannot exclusively *govern* it.

One consequence of the iterability of playtexts is that they can be 'cited' and 'grafted' (to use Derrida's terminology) onto countless different contexts. It's crucial to understand here that Derrida is not denying the importance and indeed the absolute necessity of context. When he writes that every sign, in being cited, 'can break with every given context, engendering an infinity of new contexts in a manner which is absolutely illimitable' (12), he is not asserting that signs can function *independently* of contexts, only that they can function *within* a variety of contexts that are – theoretically at least – limitless. The ability of writing to be detached from one context and inserted into others is a *necessary possibility* that is inscribed in the very structure of signs. What this necessary possibility does mean, however, is that no one context can be distinguished as the absolute – and therefore regulating – context of a given text; 'no context can entirely enclose it' (9). This includes the context of a text's creator(s), which has often been used by intentionalists to police interpretations. For the playwright's context in the moment of writing the play to be 'exhaustively determinable', in Derrida's terms, 'conscious intention would at the very least have to be totally present and immediately transparent to itself and to others' (18). But the very nature of iterability and its concomitant division of meaning forbids this presence and transparency. Different contexts, then, have different impacts on playtexts, with no one context ever able to supply the text's completion. Worthen's metaphor of tools and technologies is useful here as a way of conceptualising this relationship between plays and their performance contexts. He suggests that the relationship between the written play and the stage performance may be 'modeled by the relationship between tools and technologies' (2010: 21). Playtexts, like tools, have an immediate purpose but can be put to many other uses; these uses are, in turn, altered by the changing technologies of the theatre. A tool's 'instrumental properties may change as the perceived technologies of its use change', and therefore 'tools afford different acts in different technologies, which redefine the *affordance* of the tool' (ibid., original emphasis). New stage conventions alter what possibilities a given playtext affords and therefore what meanings might be interpreted from it. While the same alteration might be claimed of all language, it is true of dramatic texts in a particular way as a result of their interaction with different stages. This is not to suggest that a play's original conditions of production are entirely irrelevant as soon as it is performed in a different context, which furnishes it with different meanings, but it demonstrates the futility of attempting to police a play's interpretations according to the circumstances of its composition and initial performance. It may be useful, for instance, for a director to research specific words in a Shakespeare play to determine what they suggested at the time of writing and therefore understand what they might have meant in their original context. However, this does not restrict the director to *only* what *could* have been meant at that time. The specific features of any individual text yield certain affordances, but these affordances will vary in relation to different performance contexts. My understanding of theatre texts is not based on the idea that performance should just ignore the text and what it does – as I hope is clear from my own attention to what texts do. Any performance depends to an extent on what the text itself affords, but this does not entail confining the performance to a narrow range of options. Performance is never wholly independent of the text, but neither is it wholly confined by its limits.

Discussing the 'transcendent genius' (1997: 54) commonly attributed to Shakespeare, Worthen makes a further important observation about how the relationship between classic plays and changing temporal and cultural contexts is typically configured by both theatre-makers and commentators:

> That plays can be produced to have new meanings for new audiences is not at issue here. What *is* claimed for plays of genius is a special property, the ability to *contain* such new meanings. Historical change is anticipated by such plays, and theatrical practice succeeds in 'making it new' largely by claiming to find a new language to preserve this mysterious essence. (55, original emphasis)

In other words, it's claimed that only 'classics' or 'masterpieces' can function in this way over time and that this is the reason why such plays have entered the dramatic canon in the first place. According to this view, which I expand upon in the next section, classic plays possess some mystical quality that enables them to transcend time and space, carrying an essence or spirit that may be faithfully communicated in countless different contexts. What I am arguing is that, by contrast, *all* plays are both endlessly iterable and historically contingent. As can be seen in the examples discussed above, from Kneehigh's playful take on *The Bacchae* to Tara Arts' geographic and cultural relocation of *Macbeth*, these texts mean differently in different contexts, without any of these contexts ever fully realising or containing their meaning.

The author's return and the absent 'work'

Just as the previous chapter illustrated that the author is far from dead in contemporary British theatre, playwrights of 'transcendent genius' still hold a grip on the collective imagination. Despite the framing of many contemporary revivals as 'radical', deference to the authority of the canonical author continues to haunt British theatrical practice, even where theatre-makers are not seeking to preserve a 'faithful' or 'authentic' version of the plays in performance. This is a phenomenon that was observed by Worthen in his analysis of the rhetoric of directors of Shakespeare working across Anglophone theatre cultures in the 1990s, leading him to conclude that 'a theatrical practice that necessarily works to displace, disrupt, or disintegrate the Shakespearean text is sustained by a constant assertion of fidelity to the globby essence of "Shakespeare"' (1997: 63). The same appears to be true of many British practitioners working with the classics in the 21st century, who – for all their apparent disruption of the canon – often appeal to the 'globby essence' or 'spirit' of classic texts and their authors. Meanwhile, as has already been seen, many reviewers have criticised revisionary and/or playful theatrical interventions on the basis of a similar appeal to the author and the integrity of their enduring, canonical text. Here, I want to explore a few instances of this rhetoric that serves both to censure and to defend 'radical' treatments of the classics, before deconstructing the idea of the authoritative, authorial 'work' that sits beneath such discourse.

Among the directors mentioned in this chapter, Mitchell has received perhaps the greatest critical backlash against her approach to the classics. The title of an article in the *Guardian* concisely captures the negative response to her work: 'Katie Mitchell – director or destroyer?' (Tripney 2008). In another profile piece, Charlotte Higgins states that Mitchell 'stamps such a strong authorial mark on her work' (2016), suggesting that this is at the root of reviewers' consternation. Indeed, Mitchell is frequently described as an '*auteur*', a word with primarily negative associations in British theatre culture.[9] Yet Mitchell herself often reinforces a rhetoric of 'serving' the text – albeit in a way that departs from British theatrical traditions. Her 2006 production of *The Seagull* provides a particularly interesting example in the context of this discussion, with its striking disjuncture between claims of vandalism from the critics and Mitchell's own framing of her work as uncovering the 'spirit' of Chekhov's play. Her production used a new version of the script by Martin Crimp, which cut all asides and soliloquies; it relocated the action of key scenes and inserted deliberate visual anachronisms; and it added symbolic touches, such as sudden, exaggerated gusts of wind blowing through the house. The critical response to Mitchell's production is notable for the repeated assertions that this version rejects, ignores, or rewrites Chekhov's authorial intentions. Nicholas de Jongh describes Mitchell's production as 'a pallid version of the real thing' and condemns her 'itching urge to interfere with Chekhov' (2006: 764); Claire Allfree laments that 'the play's inner music is lost' (2006: 767); and Jane Edwardes writes that 'director Katie Mitchell and adapter Martin Crimp are guilty of slashing rather than scraping' Chekhov's play (2006: 767). In the most indignant reviews, the main charge against Mitchell's version is that this is no longer Chekhov's play. Billington, for example, concludes that Mitchell's production is 'director's theatre at its most indulgent in which the play, as Chekhov wrote it, is definitely not the thing' (2006: 763), while Alastair Macaulay simply claims that 'it isn't the play Chekhov wrote' (2006: 765).

Even positive reviews are often still couched in the authority of playwright and text. Dominic Cavendish, for example, concludes that 'ostentatious though Mitchell's signature is as a director, it always serves to underwrite the genius of Chekhov' (2006: 763). Susannah Clapp similarly praises the way in which Mitchell's direction 'gets into the dark corners of one of Chekhov's trickiest plays' (2006: 765), implying that its success lies in the way in which it excavates usually hidden elements of the playwright's genius. What all these comments – both positive and negative – have in common is an investment in the essence of the Chekhovian 'work', which Mitchell's production is perceived as either transgressing or recovering.

Despite the accusations of directorial interference and imposition, Mitchell saw herself as engaged in a project of discovering and re-animating the intentions of the playwright. Speaking about the critical reaction to *The Seagull* in an interview a decade later, Mitchell explained that a 'lot of very careful thought went into understanding the material Chekhov had written', adding that it is 'very difficult when there is a feeling that a travesty has been created when you have handled it so carefully' (quoted in Higgins 2016). She understood her interventions to be aimed not so much at the play itself, but at production conventions that she found deadening. Discussing her approach to Chekhov, Mitchell suggests that

> the production history and traditions that came into being around the 1970s got mixed up with the plays. That's why you can offend a lot of people if you do Chekhov as radically as the material actually is, because everyone mixes up the productions that were done in the 1970s and 1980s with the material. (Mitchell and Icke 2016)

Mitchell insists here that it is Chekhov's drama that is really radical and that her approach is simply serving the spirit of this material. In the same conversation, she joked that Chekhov is 'sort of undoable. You can't do it. It's better to read' (ibid.). Though the laughter accompanying this statement suggests that Mitchell is not entirely serious, she echoes the belief of some – as discussed in Chapter 1 – that Shakespeare's plays have their fullest lives on the page and cannot be adequately staged. This highlights some of the limiting ways in which (classic) plays are understood in British theatre culture and demonstrates the authoritative place that ideas of author and 'work' still have, even in the practice of a director who has been repeatedly criticised for smashing up the classics.

Icke has expressed a similar desire to return to the radical original intentions of canonical authors, which can be seen most clearly in his approach to Shakespeare. On the one hand, Icke directs Shakespeare with an understanding that there is no single, authentic text that might be faithfully presented in performance, acknowledging that directors 'always cut and change Shakespeare, and yet we pretend that there's such a thing as authentic, "full text" Shakespeare' (Lewis 2020: xxii). His production of *Hamlet* (2017), for example, is alive to the multiplicity of possible versions of this play, leaving many of its central questions deliberately unanswered. There's no attempt in this production to solve the problem of whether Hamlet is mad, and at times doubt is cast on the guilt of Claudius. The constant use of live filming and screens during the performance, meanwhile, serves both to subject the royal family to a very modern form of surveillance and to further fragment the drama and its possible interpretations. Yet Icke has repeatedly defended his directorial style on the basis that he is excavating the 'original' radical qualities of classic plays. In conversation about *Hamlet*, Icke and lead actor Andrew Scott appealed repeatedly to Shakespeare's 'intentions', suggesting that they were trying to 'reclaim' those intentions from a dusty academic tradition that has stifled the theatricality of Shakespearean drama (Icke and Scott 2017). In departing from some of the orthodoxies of verse speaking and opting for a more accessible and colloquial acting style, Icke insists that he is staying true to Shakespeare's aims as a playwright who 'wrote sheet music for actors, and was a practical person of the theatre' (ibid.).

Elsewhere, Icke has explained that he likes the word 'radical' because it means going back to the roots; it implies a digging down to the 'original' spirit of the play (Mitchell and Icke 2016). He argues that 'it is OK to create a live, now, contemporary version of this old text, because that's what the writers would have wanted' (ibid.), holding fast to the intentionalism discussed in the previous chapter. In her introduction to Icke's collected volume of adapted plays, Helen Lewis summarises his approach to the classics: 'To successfully adapt a play, you have to forget that it is a classic, and think instead about why it became a classic. Forget the reverence: every performance is an adaptation' (Lewis 2020: x). While this appears to be a more radical approach than many mainstream British productions of the dramatic canon, there is still a sort of reverence embedded in this seeming irreverence: a reverence for 'why it became a classic' and, associated with this, an attempted (or at least claimed) fidelity to the playwright's 'original' intentions and the integrity of their 'work' – in spirit if not in letter. Other theatre-makers likewise share a belief that there is some spirit in the original that can best be brought to life by reviving it in a way that speaks directly to contemporary audiences. Writing about her work as dramaturg alongside Hill-Gibbins, for example, Svendsen is clear that they aim to challenge British conventions of staging the classics and to subvert the assumed primacy of the text, but she also suggests that their approach of taking the play apart ultimately allows them to 'serve' it (Svendsen 2013a). Holmes, meanwhile, explained that in his production of *Three Sisters* (2010) with Filter Theatre they were attempting to 'release the spirit of the play' (quoted in Gardner 2009).

Kneehigh's production of *Cymbeline* (2006) likewise illustrates the tendency towards framing both approval and disapproval in relation to the classic dramatic text or its 'essence', as well as starting to suggest a more productive way of thinking about canonical plays. The show, which was directed by Rice and adapted by Carl Grose in collaboration with the company, added modern, colloquial language, made deep cuts to Shakespeare's text – one academic reviewer counted 'about 200 lines' that remained intact (Wayne 2007: 230) – and added the new character of Joan, who comically shepherded audiences through the narrative twists and turns of the play.

It received mixed reviews, many of which commented on the extent to which it altered Shakespeare's play.[10] In her overview of the critical response, Duška Radosavljević draws attention to the way in which some reviewers understood the production as getting to the 'heart' of Shakespeare's play, even as it played fast and loose with the text (2013a: 57). Examining Kneehigh's process of adaptation, which involves working from the theatre-makers' emotional memory of the source, Radosavljević concludes that 'the respect towards the text on which the performance is based is bestowed on it by a respect and a deep understanding of its inner meanings which […] can only ever find a different form in another idiom' (80). This is a welcome alternative to the rhetoric of textual fidelity, based on an understanding of the fundamentally different idioms of text and performance, yet there remains a lingering attachment to the nebulous idea of the authorised 'work' in Radosavljević's emphasis on the 'heart' or 'spirit' of a play and its 'inner meanings'. In a similar vein, but more promisingly for my purposes here, Heather Lilley considers Kneehigh's style of storytelling in the context of oral culture, explaining that this allows 'a much broader conceptualization of source texts as cultural memories owned by no-one and everyone' (2018: 6). This is one potential way of sidestepping notions of fidelity. Kneehigh's idea of texts and stories as multiple, shared entities, not belonging to any one originator and available for endless possible re-presentations, gestures towards the sort of dispersal of authority and authorship that may be possible if limiting notions of the complete dramatic 'work' are abandoned as a standard against which to judge individual performances.

It is to this idea of the 'work' that I now turn, in an effort to further interrogate common critical attitudes towards contemporary re-workings of classic plays and the claims to authority that undergird them. Another of Icke's revivals offers an intriguing introduction to the ideas I want to address here. While he might hold onto the idea that he's recovering the original radical intentions of the playwrights whose work he stages, Icke's production of *The Wild Duck* is explicit in its challenge to the notion of a 'real version' of this play. Acknowledging audiences' desire for 'faithful' productions of the classics, the character of Gregory (Gregers) in Icke's reworked script says: 'People say they want to see the real version, true to Ibsen' (2020: 343). But as he goes on to point out, the promise of a 'real version' is a fiction. The play that Ibsen wrote in 1884 was written in a now outdated form of another language, in a different cultural and historical context, for a different set of stage technologies, in a theatre culture with a different series of conventions and expectations. Icke's take on *The Wild Duck* also simultaneously flirts with and disavows the common rhetorical tactic of seeking legitimacy through an appeal to the author's intentions and biography. In the commentary that the performers offer on the play, there are references to the details of Ibsen's life, yet these facts are undermined by the assertion that 'probably none of them are relevant' (344). At a climactic moment, the commentary reveals that Ibsen himself fathered and neglected an illegitimate child and that therefore '*The Wild Duck* is a lie' (440). But this statement has to be understood in relation to the context of *all* revivals as, in some sense, lies that inevitably betray the absent 'truth' of the text. Icke's version both reframes *The Wild Duck* for a new social context and deconstructs popular understandings of what theatrical productions of the classics are for. While the critical response was broadly positive, some reviews expressed irritation with this framing device, preferring the later sequences in which Icke more fully embraced the naturalism traditionally associated with Ibsen.[11] Billington, meanwhile, described Icke's production as 'an example of the arrogance of director's theatre', damning it as a 'parasitic rewrite' and arguing – in precisely the terms Icke's version seeks to debunk – that 'audiences deserve the real thing' (2018: 960).

It is this idea of the 'real thing' that I am disputing. Plays, as solo-authored scripts written (usually, but not always) prior to performance, can appear to be the definitive dramatic 'work', which different performances merely interpret.[12] Just as the playwright's intentions are commonly seen as a blueprint for the script, the script is then seen as a blueprint for performance, against which any subsequent productions can be judged. This is another misunderstanding of the ontology of playtexts: the idea of a complete and authoritative 'work' has become conflated with the individual playtext, the intentions of which many performances strive to fulfil. Some performance scholars, on the other hand, have attempted to invert this relationship, arguing that 'organic unity is achieved *only* in performance, and that the text as written is incomplete' (Carlson 1985: 8, original emphasis).[13] For them, the performance represents 'the work', the completion of something that is only partial in the playtext. I am arguing, instead, that 'the work' is a forever absent ideal that cannot be located in either playtexts or performances. My reference to 'the work' responds to Benjamin Bennett's identification of 'our sense, when we read a dramatic text in a book, that we are not receiving the *whole* work' (1990: 61, original emphasis). Bennett argues that what distinguishes drama from other literary genres is the fact that its on-the-page identity is dependent on the external idea of the stage: to understand written drama, we must have some notion of theatrical performance. He continues:

> If we agree that there is such a thing as the 'work' (the opus, the whole culturally effective entity), and that the dramatic text by itself is markedly defective [...], then it follows that performance in a theater contributes to *constituting* the very object (the work) of which it is an interpretation. (67, original emphasis)

What I want to take from Bennett here is his diagnosis of that nagging feeling that – at least in one sense – neither playtext nor performance quite provides the full picture. When I discuss 'the work', then, I'm referring to that elusive completeness that we often sense is absent in both our reading of plays and our viewing of performances, however well they may stand alone. Bennett expands on this sense of absence, noting that when we are reading it the playtext 'markedly fails to represent the whole "work" for us', yet in the theatre, 'when we are confronted with an actual performance that we recognize as a *mere* interpretation, the text [...] now paradoxically does represent the object of interpretation (the work) after all'

(73, original emphasis). Similarly, Worthen writes that '[p]erformance signifies an absence, the precise fashioning of the material text's absence, at the same time that it appears to summon the work into being, to produce it as performance' (1997: 17). Texts and performances thus point perpetually towards one another, while there remains (or appears to remain) a central absence around which they both circle – a gap that, in an echo of Bennett, I'm calling 'the work'. This is not a perfect terminology, but it suggests a sense of completeness and canonicity that is pertinent for the use to which I am putting it.[14] 'The work' is, in my usage, a reference both to impossible wholeness and to what Derrida calls 'pure presence'.[15]

Derrida's concept of the supplement offers a theoretical solution to the problem identified by Bennett of performances seeming somehow to constitute what they interpret. The etymology of the word 'supplement' points to its dual meanings: historically it has referred both to 'something added to that which is already complete' and 'something added to supply a deficiency or make up a whole' (OED 2017). This duality is seized upon by Derrida in his use of the term. For him, the supplement is 'both a surplus, a plenitude enriching another plenitude' (1976: 144) and at the same time 'adds only to replace' (145), filling a gap in that which it supplements. Crucially, Derrida insists that 'this second signification of the supplement cannot be separated from the first' (145); the supplement's necessity, therefore, is ambiguous, and its status is inherently paradoxical. I suggest that both playtexts and performances can be productively thought of as supplements – in the Derridean sense – which forever defer the absent 'work'. The supplement is 'maddening because it is neither presence nor absence' (154); rather it has 'the power of procuring an absent presence through its image' (155). According to Derrida, the endless 'sequence of supplements' reveals a necessity, 'that of an infinite chain, ineluctably multiplying the supplementary mediations that produce the sense of the very thing they defer: the mirage of the thing itself, of immediate presence, of originary perception' (157). Texts and performances can both be seen as supplements in this 'infinite chain', acting as 'supplementary mediations' of one another and of 'the work', 'produc[ing] the sense' of completion while always gesturing towards an absence.

As already noted, a similar argument has been made by Carlson, who likewise suggests that we see the performance of texts in terms of supplementation. What Carlson does not discuss, however, is 'the work' in the sense that I am employing it here. His model sees texts and performances – each denied plenitude – as supplements of one another, with neither privileged in any kind of hierarchy. I am suggesting, though, that 'the work' is seen as the equivalent of the desired but always absent 'pure presence' that Derrida argues does not exist. The supplement, Derrida proposes, compensates for the lack of a kind of full and immediate presence that can never be achieved – that, indeed, relies for its identity upon those very supplements that seem to conjure it. The playtext or performance thus produces the sense of 'the work' while acting as a supplement in its perpetual absence. Using Derrida's model of the supplement as a theoretical lens through which to view texts and performances illustrates that 'the work' cannot be located in either. For example, I would suggest that most of us have a fuzzy idea of an entity that we typically refer to as 'Shakespeare's *Hamlet*'; this is what we think of as 'the work'. While this 'work' might be thought to inhere in the text, the multiplicity of different available editions and the many theatrical questions that remained unanswered in any given version of the script reveal that 'the work' cannot, in fact, be found here. Likewise, when we watch an individual production, such as Icke's, we as audience members are made aware of both the text (which itself is just one of many possible textual versions of the play) as an absent-yet-present referent, and of the countless other ways in which this text might be interpreted in performance. Here, too, we find not 'the work' but one of many supplements. While this is more readily apparent when studying classic plays that consist of many different textual and performative supplementations, the same theory applies equally whether looking at a new production of an existing text or at a new playtext that can theoretically be supplemented by countless other productions in the future.

Before moving on, it's worth briefly considering whether this theory of supplementation and 'the work' can be applied to devised performances. The text for Kneehigh's shows, for example, was collaboratively generated by writer(s), director, and actors in the rehearsal room and then delivered more-or-less unaltered at performance after performance. While it's a truism that no two performances are the same, the small differences between one performance of Kneehigh's *Cymbeline* and another clearly cannot be equated with the differences between two separate productions of a playtext. In this instance, it could be argued that the live performance of *Cymbeline* was virtually self-identical with the collaboratively adapted text. Is it the case, then, that (some) devised performances possess the rigidity and stability of which their text-led counterparts are often accused? Might it be that 'the work', in these instances, is not absent at all but is embodied, in all its completeness, in performance? While there's a distinction that can be drawn here between different theatre-making practices, there will always remain a gap between the playtext or performance score and any individual performance. Performance, by its fleeting yet repeated nature, cannot be complete and definitive. Furthermore, devised productions, while often inextricably associated with the companies who created and performed them, do not rule out the possibility of future reinterpretations by other artists. Though they might not be intentionally written for countless future productions in the same way playtexts are, pieces created without a pre-written playtext still leave traces that can be reconstructed.[16] Moreover, as I discuss in the next chapter, more and more theatre-makers are choosing to publish documents of their work in various forms, further opening up the possibility that these works could be re-performed by others in the future. Although devised performance and the role of text within it offer an intriguing challenge to this theory of supplementation, 'the work' still represents an absent, unreachable, and desired-for ideal. In an art form characterised by ephemerality and repetition, the wholeness that the concept of 'the work' indicates is always impossible.[17] Completeness and self-presence of intention can no more be sought in the rehearsal room or in live performances of a devised show than in the pages of a playtext. It may be possible, though, to discuss the *degree* to which there exists a gap between the playtext – or, in the case of shows that do not have a pre-existing playtext, whatever constitutes the performance score – and performance(s). In this sense, the peculiarity of the playtext as an object once again becomes apparent. It is, as Rebellato puts it, a 'multiple thing' (2015: 172) which opens up the space for countless versions, all of which are held at a distance from the text they interpret. There's also a distinction to be drawn here between different productions (as distinct interpretations of a playtext) and individual performances of those productions, each of which is slightly different and more or less imperfectly represents the production (which might be understood as the ideal version that the creative team has in mind). Each performance thus supplements the production, while the production is one of countless possible supplements for the text(s) – none of which can embody 'the work'.

What I have primarily been disrupting here is the authority that accrues to 'the work' when it is mistakenly located either in the text (as the source of performance) or in the performance (as the completion of the text). In essence, I maintain that there are only ever playtexts and performances, all of which are at once complete and incomplete and which endlessly supplement one another. Conceptualising and giving a name to something that is always absent – 'the work' – might therefore seem superfluous. However, theorising this absence makes it possible to see the ways in which this false idea of completeness has operated as a shorthand for authority, whether located in the text or in performance, and to unpick the premises of that authority. Understanding 'the work' as an absent, ideal edifice deconstructs the perceived hierarchy of text and performance, as opposed to performance-oriented critiques that have merely upended it, and begins to dissipate the authority that has restricted texts and performances alike.

After Chekhov

I end this chapter by returning to Chekhov, who was first encountered haunting the stage in Dead Centre's performance. Despite being composed in Russian, Chekhov's plays have become a central part of the dramatic canon performed in the United Kingdom, alongside other frequently revived scripts including Shakespearean drama, Greek tragedy, and the plays of fellow naturalist playwrights such as Ibsen and Strindberg. The two productions of *Three Sisters* that I discuss in this final section actively disrupt the canonical authority of Chekhov's plays and question the power dynamics of canon formation itself. In each of these re-imaginings, the notion of a transcendent Chekhovian essence is both alluded to and unsettled, illustrating some of the arguments made throughout this chapter about the iterability and supplementarity of theatre texts.

In a British context, the idea of the stable Chekhovian 'work' is filtered through the process of translation from Russian to English, further complicating any claims to authentically staging the text. Translation is complex and contested, with no simple or transparent movement from source to target language.[18] For example, as Svetlana Klimenko (2001) has observed, attempts to 'faithfully' translate Chekhov's syntax from Russian to English can result in a very different affect for the reader or audience member due to key differences in the grammatical structures of the two languages. As a Russian, Klimenko struggles to recognise aspects of what English-speaking critics describe as 'Chekhovian', arguing that British Chekhov tends to over-emphasise nostalgia and melancholy. Discussing the reception history of Chekhov in Britain, meanwhile, Philip Ross Bullock notes that the plays have typically been 'heavily anglicized and romanticized' (2017: 76), coming 'to stand for a kind of idyllic and elegiac response to social change in late Imperial Russia that could readily be carried over into the context of post-war England' (ibid.). Cynthia Marsh succinctly captures the dominant British impression of Chekhov: 'an insistently self-reinforcing image of landed estates, 1890s to turn-of-the-century fashion, trees, gloom, isolation, tea drinking and samovars and endless talk often going nowhere' (2020: 130). Susan Bassnett concurs that in Britain audiences are now accustomed to 'a specifically English Chekhov, a playwright whose work has acquired a new set of signifiers in a changed cultural, political and theatrical context' (2014: 157).

Yet in much of the British rhetoric around Chekhov – as already seen in the discussion of Mitchell's production of *The Seagull* – one can still witness appeals to the authority of the canonical author, claims of fidelity, and suggestions that these plays contain an essence that transcends history and geography. In his analysis of critics' descriptions of these texts, Bull notes three key features of the discourse surrounding acclaimed translations of Chekhov and Ibsen:

> One: that there is no stated separation between the translation process and the production of the play text as it will be staged, one person being responsible for both in each case. Two: that the supposed veracity, the fidelity of their texts is vouched for in great part because they have 'literally' translated them from one language to another. Three: that it is claimed that the texts offer a strikingly contemporary dialogic form, whilst at the same time being true to the originals – both modern and universal at the same time. (2018: 289)

Here it's possible to see how the additional anxieties of fidelity and authenticity associated with translation are negotiated through an appeal to the authority of Chekhov's 'original' text and its supposed timelessness. These plays are imagined to have some unique quality that enables them to rise above time and space, carrying an essence that may be faithfully communicated in countless different contexts. But two recent productions of *Three Sisters* dismantle this illusion and some of its tacit assumptions about the universality of the Western canon.

In RashDash's riotous deconstruction of *Three Sisters* (2018), Chekhov is centred and then displaced. Before we see any of the all-female cast of performers and musicians, a bust of Chekhov is placed in the middle of the stage, suggesting both the assumed centrality of the playwright-as-author and his distance from contemporary audiences. Here, Chekhov is rendered in stone: revered, unchanging, museum-like. This is everything that RashDash's production then goes on to challenge. Some of the features of the play's basic architecture remain, such as the sisters and their stranded stasis, but the majority of the show is best characterised as a mutinous meditation on Chekhov, the dramatic canon more broadly, and the expectations associated with the classics. Above all, RashDash's version questions what is needed to create, interrogating the privilege of being able to author. These questions are viewed through a specifically feminist lens, in a reimagining that focuses on the eponymous women and critiques what female characters are and are not allowed to talk about in classic plays like this. As Masha comments on their conversations: 'All of this is so small' (2018: 15). Throughout the show, meanwhile, movement and music both serve to interrupt and disrupt the text, layering on different, non-verbal modes of theatrical communication that implicitly challenge the centrality of the spoken word in British theatre culture. The performance is also engaged in a constant dialogue with other versions of *Three Sisters*, which are visually referenced in the movement sequences and explicitly cited in the 'reviews song', which splices together extracts from reviews of recent productions of the play written by male critics. The audience is made aware of the fact that this is just one of many iterations, which exists in relation to – and in resistance against – countless other productions. RashDash has a quarrel not just with Chekhov and the conventions associated with staging his plays, but with the theatre industry structures which uphold the centrality and authority of the dramatic canon. This is made explicit within the play with a speech from an unnamed artistic director who tells RashDash: 'If you want to be taken seriously and to work on bigger stages and with more resource then at some point it would be sensible to engage with the classics' (9). The company both follows and skewers this suggestion, engaging with the classics as a way of asking why these plays – most of them written by straight, white, male playwrights – remain revered at the heart of British theatre culture.

Though taking a very different approach, Inua Ellams' adaptation of *Three Sisters* (2019), directed in a production at the National Theatre by Nadia Fall, also uses this canonical text as a means of questioning larger power structures. His version, which is framed as 'a new play by Inua Ellams after Chekhov', resituates the plot and characters within a postcolonial context. While retaining the dramaturgical structure of Chekhov's play, Ellams' adaptation is set very specifically during the Biafran War in Nigeria, with the action playing out between 1967 and 1970. Unlike productions that shift a classic play to a new period or location purely through visual signifiers such as set and costume design, Ellams changes the names of the characters, transforms their speech into a Nigerian idiom, and inserts numerous references to the events of the Biafran War. This transforms the stakes of the play, as Lagos (the equivalent of Moscow) is not only an ideal that the sisters long for in vain, but a location that is materially shut off to them as a consequence of conflict. The military backdrop acquires a different significance, while the political urgency of the play is enhanced. Philosophising talk of work, suffering and future happiness, which will be familiar to viewers of other Chekhov productions, is given a sharper edge by the context of conflict and postcolonial nation-forming. Although Ellams' play is in some ways more recognisable as *Three Sisters* than RashDash's version is – there's a greater ratio of sameness to difference in this iteration – it still makes an implicit political statement on the Western dramatic canon and its associations with whiteness and colonialism. Ellams and Fall use this well-known symbol of Western culture, which has accumulated such emotional and aesthetic baggage in its long British production history, to interrogate Western – and specifically British – values. This is most evident in oldest sister Lolo's speeches about neo-colonialism, which bluntly delineate Britain's role in the war and its wielding of economic power over its former colony. As she puts it, 'this is their plan. After colonisation, neo-colonisation. To always control' (2019: 59). Ellams' version also wittily undercuts the custom of duelling in the fourth act, in a critical gesture that speaks more broadly to tacit assumptions about the supposed superiority of Western traditions. In this production, the fatal duel at the end of Chekhov's play becomes a traditional Nigerian wrestling match – 'our way of doing things', which the characters contrast with the 'madness' of duels between white men (89). Although Chekhov himself is not the main target here, with the production instead critiquing the violent legacy of British colonialism and subsequent neo-colonial interference, this reworking of the play nonetheless deconstructs the image of privileged ennui that is understood by British audiences as quintessentially Chekhovian. And through (often humorously) undercutting the expectations of British Chekhov performances, this version also prompts an audience to consider the role of culture in upholding certain values and power structures.

Both RashDash's and Ellams' versions of *Three Sisters* announce themselves as 'after Chekhov', a phrase that I've pointedly echoed in the title of this section. Sanders offers a fascinating meditation on all the different ways in which the word 'after' might function in that phrase, capturing many of the questions and anxieties with which this chapter is concerned. 'After' can be a chronological signifier, an indication of reference – and perhaps deference – to a source that has come 'before', or an implicit endorsement of 'postmodernism's beloved idea of belatedness' (2006: 157). But Sanders also seizes on another meaning of the word: to 'go after' something, 'to pursue or to chase it', which might be seen as characteristic of certain appropriations that question and critique their canonical source texts (ibid.). And coming after, as Sanders adds, 'can mean finding new angles and new routes into something, new perspectives on the familiar' (158). Both the idea of new angles and routes and the notion of the revival or adaptation as 'going after' its source text seem apt for RashDash's and Ellams' deconstructive rewritings of

Chekhov, which reveal the instability of the imagined 'work' and some of the ways in which this concept has shaped and regulated the dramatic canon. This is not *Three Sisters* 'as Chekhov intended' – or as British notions of the Chekhovian 'work' assume he intended. These versions are, in every sense, *after* Chekhov.

However, there are also potential drawbacks to engaging with the classics in this way. As Sanders observes, adaptation (and, one might add, revival) 'both appears to require and to perpetuate the existence of a canon, although it may in turn contribute to its ongoing reformulation and expansion' (2006: 8). The colonial histories that are entangled with many of the texts in the Western canon are often a motivating factor for theatre-makers who choose to use these plays to '"talk back" to the colonizing culture' (52), and the same is true of the misogynistic overtones and patriarchal structures that are critiqued in feminist appropriations of classic plays. But this is also a complex and ambivalent process which inevitably draws upon – and to an extent perpetuates – the place of such plays in the canon. It's therefore worth considering Laera's warning that

> the act of 'updating', 'recontextualizing' and 'dusting off' old or foreign narratives to make them 'relevant' and easy to digest in the present day can end up consolidating dominant forms, canonical sources, and current power relations. (2014: 9)

Every time theatre-makers return to classic plays, regardless of how irreverent or deconstructive their approach, they risk simply strengthening this limited and exclusionary canon and reinforcing the perceived authority of these plays and their writers. While this question of how – or even if – to approach the dramatic canon moves beyond the scope of this book, some of the politically motivated theatrical experiments discussed in this chapter raise important points about canon creation, preservation, and deconstruction which deserve further exploration elsewhere.

Conclusion

Throughout this chapter, I have explored so-called 'radical' contemporary stagings of the Western dramatic canon and some of the critical responses they have received. This exploration has allowed me to unravel the appeals to text and author that often circulate around these productions and to contest the implicit belief in a stable, unchanging dramatic 'work' that underpins such appeals. Discussing the critical backlash against productions that are perceived to have imposed a 'concept' or directorial interpretation on the play, Aberg makes the crucial point that *all* productions can be understood as elaborating their own concept:

> It's just whether or not you interpret it in a way that is compliant with theatrical tradition. That doesn't make it any less of a concept; it just happens to be a concept that you're familiar with and on some level that you're expecting. (2014)

While the term 'concept' can be freighted with unhelpful associations when used to describe a director's approach to a play, typically indicating a set of ideas that are perceived to have been 'imposed' on the text, this notion of all productions equally being concepts has echoes of my argument that all texts and performances can be understood as non-hierarchical supplements. Seeing texts and performances in this way removes fidelity – either to the play as rendered on the page, or to a vague idea of the 'spirit' or 'essence' of 'the work' – as a benchmark of success in staging the classics, as well as challenging the theoretical coherence of the notion of a 'radical' directorial concept. In the context of a theatre culture which continues to revere the assumed intentions of the writer and the integrity of 'the work', productions that are seen as radical serve to underline the ways in which the perceived authority of text and playwright operate, as well as questioning the theatrical conventions that are viewed as neutrally upholding such authority. In this way, 'radical' revivals can be helpfully distinguished from more (currently) normative approaches. In another sense, though, they simply illuminate a truth about the relationship between text and performance that applies to *all* theatrical productions.

I want to close by considering something that has so far been mostly absent from the discussion in this chapter: the spectatorial pleasure and play that may be found in new versions of canonical dramas. Sanders notes the way in which 'juxtaposed readings' of a text 'are crucial to the cultural operations of adaptation, and the ongoing experiences of pleasure for the reader or spectator in tracing the intertextual relationships', stressing an audience's awareness of similarities and differences between source texts and adaptations (2006: 25). This way of thinking about adaptation is also suggestive for understandings of the playful relationship between text and performance. The inherent possibility of countless iterations of any given playtext is one of the distinct pleasures of theatre as an art form. It's this particular kind of spectatorial enjoyment that induces audience members to see the same play in multiple different productions. While no audience is a monolith, I think it's safe to assume that for many of these spectators it is the promise of a new and different version that brings them back to a play they have seen before. There is an appeal in both the sameness and difference that are characteristic of every individual iteration.

In her review of Filter Theatre's production of *A Midsummer Night's Dream*, Libby Purves asserts that '[i]t is a truth universally acknowledged in 21st-century theatre that you can do what you like with the classics' (2012: 160). In one sense, as seen in this chapter, this is true. Indeed, the potential for countless iterations is a fundamental feature of *all* playtexts – not just the classics. Theatre-makers can, theoretically (and within the legal boundaries of copyright), do what they like with any play. Yet in the discourse perpetuated by directors, critics, and scholars alike, there remains a stubborn attachment to the authoritative intentions of the author and their 'work'. This chapter has identified, analysed, and challenged this attachment. In doing so, my aim is to further liberate new experiments with existing texts and to celebrate the unique pleasure that comes with the mix of familiarity and difference in every fresh production of a decades- or centuries-old play.

Notes

1 Margherita Laera offers a helpful taxonomy of different kinds of adaptation, encompassing these and other forms of transposition (2014: 12–15).
2 It's also worth noting that Dead Centre frames the show as a dialogue with its source material rather than as a new presentation of an existing play, and the company claims ownership of the production as an independent entity.
3 Rebellato also briefly refers to Derrida's theory of the supplement in attempting to account for the inherent ambiguity of plays (2015: 169–170).
4 Examples include Theatre Workshop's productions of Shakespeare's *Richard II* (1954) and Marlowe's *Edward II* (1956), Women's Theatre Group's reclaiming of the role of women in canonical drama, in plays such as *Lear's Daughters* (1987), and the Artaud Company's adaptations of classics by playwrights like Chekhov and Strindberg. There are also some key directorial experiments with the classics that pre-date the period discussed here such as Deborah Warner's work in the 1980s.
5 See, for example, the reviews of Hill-Gibbins' production of *Edward II* in *Theatre Record 27 Aug – 9 Sept 2013* (785–788), Aberg's production of *King John* in *Theatre Record 8 – 21 April 2012* (409–410), and Rice's production of *Twelfth Night* in *Theatre Record 01 – 25 May 2017* (542–545). The latter reviews also comment on the controversy of Rice's brief tenure as artistic director of Shakespeare's Globe, offering an insight into common perceptions of how Shakespeare – and this venue closely associated with his legacy – should be treated.
6 Sanders notes, for example, how 'Shakespeare was undoubtedly deployed as a tool of empire, taught in schools across the world as a means of promoting the English language and the British imperial agenda' (2006: 52).
7 This work began before the period under investigation here: Tara Arts was founded in 1977 and Talawa in 1986.
8 For further discussion of 'Binglish' theatre, see Dominic Hingorani (2010).
9 In her introduction to the term 'auteur' in a theatrical context, Lyn Gardner acknowledges the 'suspicion' attached to this term (2021). Natalie Abrahami has similarly written about the 'derogatory connotation' attached to the word 'auteur' in the UK (2009), responding to an article by Billington titled 'Don't let auteurs take over in theatre' (2009).
10 See *Theatre Record 10 – 23 September 2006* (1054–1055).
11 See reviews of *The Wild Duck* in *Theatre Record 01 – 31 October 2018* (959–962).
12 The idea of the dramatic work is also central to copyright law, though it is loosely defined and can prove problematic in legal disputes. As Luke McDonagh notes, the work concept can 'fail to provide legal certainty in theatre where there is an *iterative* concept of the work at play' (2021: 71, original emphasis). While there's not scope in this chapter to explore the legal perspective introduced by McDonagh, it's worth noting as a further dimension of this discussion.
13 Carlson describes this as 'the theory of performance as fulfillment' and offers an overview of its adherents (1985: 8–9).
14 Although this term calls to mind Roland Barthes' 1971 essay 'From Work to Text', I do not use 'the work' in the same sense as Barthes, for whom 'the work is held in the hand' (1986: 57). While Barthes' assertion that the work 'closes upon a signified' (58) is suggestive of how playtexts have often been understood as originary and authoritative, what Barthes describes as the work is still a bounded literary artefact – indeed, its limits are one of the characteristics that separate it from the text (as defined by Barthes).
15 'Presence', for Derrida, is what is 'at once promised and refused' (1976: 141) in spoken language; it refers to a longed-for immediacy that thinkers such as Jean-Jacques Rousseau saw as being destroyed through writing, but that Derrida argues can be no more found in speech than in the written word. Here, I refer to Derrida's specific use of presence, but presence has a host of other meanings in a theatrical context and is a central, contested term within the field. See Cormac Power (2008) for a detailed

discussion of theatrical presence – including a consideration of Derrida's critique of presence and its implications for understanding live performance.

16 Examples of this kind of performative reconstruction include Stan's Cafe's revival of *The Carrier Frequency* (1999), originally created by Impact Theatre in the 1980s, and Deirdre Heddon's recreation of Mike Pearson's *Bubbling Tom* (2002).

17 There might conceivably be an exception here if a piece is performed just once, but to prevent the future performances that theatre as an art form makes available (the possibility of which would shatter the self-sameness that the ideal of 'the work' suggests), any traces of that performance would have to be destroyed. This seems to be the sort of theatre called for Antonin Artaud (1958), the impossibility of which Derrida has persuasively discussed (2001: 292–316).

18 Laera (2020) discusses some of the complexities of translation in a theatrical context.

4
ON THE PAGE: CHANGING TECHNOLOGIES OF EDITING AND PUBLICATION

When audience members enter the performance space for *Total Immediate Collective Imminent Terrestrial Salvation* (2019), they are each handed a book. This hardback text, penned by Tim Crouch and illustrated by Rachana Jadhav, is an integral part of the show. Whereas some performances claim to faithfully represent and thereby constitute the play as written, here the text is placed directly into the hands of audience members, who turn the pages as the performance proceeds. The book, it gradually emerges, contains the prophecies of Miles, a character who has had a near-death experience and claims he has seen the future. Within the fiction of the play, his followers are not permitted to stray from the words he has written, which foretell a cataclysmic event. Their every encounter follows the text he has set down on the page; reading ahead is not sanctioned.

In *Total Immediate Collective Imminent Terrestrial Salvation*, script becomes scripture. Theatre is framed as a sort of cult, with the playwright as its messianic leader and the playtext as its bible. Performers and audience members obediently read the words they have been given, while the bodies in the performance space arrange themselves to imitate Jadhav's illustrations. And yet. There are moments that go off book – moments that, in the published version of the play, are themselves scripted by Crouch. As the play goes on, word, image, and performance diverge, suggesting different possible realities. And of course audience members have the power, should they choose, to skip ahead, to disobey the leader/playwright's instructions, to stop reading from the script altogether.

In many ways, *Total Immediate Collective Imminent Terrestrial Salvation* continues the pursuit of ideas that have preoccupied Crouch's theatre-making over the last two decades. As demonstrated by the example of *The Author* in Chapter 2, he and his collaborators are interested in exploring authorship, representation, and the relationship between performance and audience. But I turn to this specific example because of the way in which it foregrounds the materiality of the text – the text as an object in performance, as a specific assemblage of printed words (and, in this case, images). For a chapter concerned with the distinct textual identities of plays and the ways in which these might interact with performance, *Total Immediate Collective Imminent Terrestrial Salvation* is a fascinating place to start. Its published text is a curious, composite artefact, representing both the illustrated book that was handed out to audience members during the show and the script used in the creation of the performance, bound together in a way that attempts to convey the theatrical experience – or, at least, its rough outlines – to readers who may or may not have attended a performance.

I am writing these words in a word processor, within a constantly changing draft of the book you now hold in your hands (or, perhaps, that you read on a screen). At the time of writing – or, more accurately, at one of the many times of (re)writing – this document is open alongside another document of research notes and a web browser with tabs open to various reviews of Crouch's show. The windows overlap messily on the screen of my laptop, and as I mould and remould these opening paragraphs I toggle back and forth between them. Beside me on my desk are other relevant documents: a notebook with handwritten notes, a printed copy of *Total Immediate Collective Imminent Terrestrial Salvation*, a pile of other playtexts and academic books, a binder containing printed and annotated drafts of earlier chapters. My own embodied practices of reading and writing are affected by the different digital, print, and handwritten formats that I move between in the process of composing this chapter. Encountering a playtext on the page is a distinct experience that differs from scrolling through it on my screen. The text that I'm creating, meanwhile, might also be thought of as a composite, mutable thing, contained in notebooks and drafts as well as in the finished version that you, the absent reader of the future, are looking at now (a now yet to come, which I imagine from the now of my writing).

I begin by drawing attention to the materiality of text in *Total Immediate Collective Imminent Terrestrial Salvation* and to the processes of my own writing as a way of highlighting what has so far been mostly absent or implicit in my analysis: the text as a tangible object or series of objects, consisting of specific linguistic, bibliographic, and/or digital codes that are subject to change from version to version. To better understand the relationship between text and performance, it's necessary to look more closely at the pages and screens in which plays live out one aspect of their existence. When scholars or practitioners discuss theatre texts, these tend to be conceived in a rather abstract way. We are thinking, often, about a collection of words that we imagine as consistent from edition to edition, rather than considering specific page layouts, uses of spacing, font choices, punctuation conventions, and so on. There's also a tendency to elide or forget the technologies, institutions, and conventions in which printed (or, more recently, digital) plays are embedded. These contexts include everything from the economics of play publishing to the conventions for the formatting of drama on the page to the technical possibilities and limitations of digital publishing. While a single chapter cannot hope to comprehensively address all these aspects of play publication, my aim is to further explore the interplay of text and performance by turning to the specifics of the page itself.

In previous chapters, I have analysed some of the ways in which playwrights, directors, and theatre-makers have abandoned, deconstructed, or subverted conventions of writing and staging, exploring the dynamic interplay between text and performance. But one important element of this experimentation that I have not yet considered in any detail is the way in which writers have used the space and accessories of the page. The identity of the play in print and/or in digital formats, including the various conditions that contribute towards determining that identity, is a crucial but often overlooked component in the relationship between text and performance. This chapter therefore investigates the changing shape and status of the play on the page (or screen), briefly surveying the historical entanglement of performed drama and print culture before looking at more recent developments in play publishing and editing and at innovations in the formatting of theatre texts. I also consider the different lives of theatre texts, across various typescripts, printed editions, and digital versions, and how these differing incarnations of plays might inflect understandings of their relation to performance. In his study of the material forms of drama on the page – upon which several of my ideas in this chapter are building – W. B. Worthen poses the question: 'How much does it matter *what* we read?' (2005: 10, original emphasis). This is the question that this final chapter addresses.

Print and performance

While performance predates print as a technology, the institutions of theatre and publishing are closely connected in British cultural history. The establishment of playhouses in early modern England coincided with the proliferation of print; though print was by no means the only or even the main way in which written plays circulated at this time, the printed book was quickly established as one of the ways in which dramatic writing might be captured and disseminated. It's helpful, then, to pause and briefly consider the development of this print culture. To understand how plays have taken shape on the page over time, this section draws on histories of print and the book, though it's worth noting that theatre texts have formed a relatively marginal part of this history to date. Across the seven volumes of *The Cambridge History of the Book in Britain*, for example, little space is given to dramatic publishing, and much of this space is dedicated solely to the editing and printing of Shakespeare. Theatre histories, meanwhile, have tended to consider play publishing as just one small part of the network of institutions involved in the production and reception of drama. This, again, might be seen as a symptom of the in-between-ness of plays, whose disciplinary identity is divided between literature and theatre.

Julie Stone Peters – one of the few scholars to focus specifically on the history of play printing and publication – argues that we can understand the relationship between theatre and printing as 'the paradigmatic instance of the interaction between text and performance' (2000: 2). Peters' wide-ranging study of the intertwined development of theatre and print in Western Europe from the early modern period through to the late 19th century offers a useful overview of the historical transformations of the printed play, as well as the ways in which the institutions of the stage have defined themselves both through and in resistance to print. Rejecting a straightforward linear historical narrative, Peters suggests instead that 'the significant transformations in the relationship between print and theatre are not best seen as steadily evolutionary or revolutionary, but as something more kaleidoscopic' (4). Worthen concurs that '[i]n the English-speaking world, the absorption of drama to literature and of the ontology of theatre to the iterative logic of print develops slowly and inconsistently' (2005: 6). Rather than falsely imposing a progressive narrative on this history, my aim here is to bring together a collection of observations that reveal some of the assumptions and contradictions that contemporary British theatre culture has inherited. While the following is only a limited look at the long history of the printed play, this selection of examples starts to build a picture of the huge material variety of playtexts, both within and between different historical periods.

First, it's notable that the purposes and printed appearances of playtexts have varied widely. Early printed plays had multiple possible uses, in ways that challenge a modern understanding of the supposedly stable relationship between playwright, play, and performance. They were not conceived primarily as instructions for staging; they could also serve as documentation or souvenirs of the live event of performance, as texts to be read like any other form of literature, or as a tribute to the play's patron. Peters also stresses the mutual influence between page and stage in the early modern period, insisting that the growing professional theatre 'unquestionably exerted a powerful influence on the shape of plays on the page, intensifying the drive towards the conventionalization of dramatic form that print had already set in motion' (2000: 24–26). It was not, then, a simple case of print logic determining the development of drama, or vice versa. John Pitcher similarly notes that in the early 17th century 'the literary scene in England was made out of many contradictory and competing mental and social energies – in print, in manuscript, and on the stage' (2002: 366). It's also worth observing the variety of purposes and transmission routes characteristic of early modern printed drama. Although our knowledge of how and why plays got printed in this period is limited, the evidence points to a mixture of literary and commercial motivations driving early play publishing. While some writers were keen to see their words in print, it appears that it was often actors who brought plays to publishers. They may have had incomplete manuscripts of the plays or could even have transcribed them from memory, entailing a rather messy transmission of the play from the stage into print (Peters 2000). And as Grace Ioppolo (2006) has found, a play's path from writer to playhouse was already circuitous, often involving collaboration and revision at various points. There are also reports of audience members copying down plays to sell them, though Peters warns that it is hard to substantiate these claims. Regardless, it's clear that the journey from playwright's initial manuscript to printed play was often indirect, contradicting the idea that what we receive on the page is a transparent representation of authorial intentions.

In Chapter 1, I observed that the printed play can only be identified as a dramatic text with reference to the external institution of the theatre. While there are genre conventions associated with playtexts, such as speech prefixes and stage directions, these are not universal characteristics and they rely for their meaning on some understanding of live performance. Given this formal contingency, which appears to be characteristic of drama as a genre, it's interesting to note that the earliest printed plays resembled other printed works, with little or no indication of their dramatic form. As Peters observes, '[l]ate fifteenth- and early sixteenth-century drama could be conceptually indistinguishable from other genres' (2000: 21–22). She takes the careful explanations that preface many medieval and early modern dramatic texts as evidence that there was not yet a common understanding of the play as a distinct literary genre. For example, before stage directions, dramatis personae and speech prefixes became formalised as accessories of the dramatic page, the action of the play was often laid out as narrative description. Conventions for indicating speech in printed plays, meanwhile, varied considerably; it was only in the late 16th century that play printing conventions became more fixed (24). But even as the printed play started to assume an identifiable form, it remained a hybrid object with a complicated relationship to performance. Through close attention to various documents associated with early modern theatrical performance, Tiffany Stern has shown that plays in this period were understood as a series of different patched-together elements, some of which have been preserved in print and some of which have not. As she puts it, the play 'was not a single whole entity' (2009: 1).

Moreover, it's important to remember that, although printed plays were becoming more common, there was still widespread circulation of manuscripts during the early modern period (Ioppolo 2006) – and, of course, many plays were never published in print. Even throughout the 17th and into the 18th century, manuscripts continued to be disseminated alongside printed texts. Plays thus appeared in multiple different material forms. It was also accepted that different printers had different typographic styles, and variation between texts – including between different editions of the same play – was common (Peters 2000: 39). The insistence of some scholars and commentators, despite these variations, that materially distinct editions 'transmit the same *substantial* work, clothed in the merely *accidental* differences of punctuation, capitalization, type style, layout, words on the page' can be seen as evidence of what Worthen calls 'the deeply ideological working of print in print culture' (2005: 7, original emphasis). This, though, is a more recent development. Significantly, Peters' assessment of the available evidence suggests that early modern printed plays were not understood as authoritative blueprints or records of performance. As she puts it, 'the point was to capture readers looking for *a* text of a popular play' (2000: 38, original emphasis) – as opposed to *the* definitive text. Even much later, at the end of the 19th century, plays continued to be disseminated in a variety of different forms. For example, playwrights including George Bernard Shaw, Alfred Tennyson, W. S. Gilbert, Arthur Wing Pinero, and Henry Arthur Jones developed a practice of privately printing their plays prior to rehearsals (Stephens 1992: 134). While these texts would sometimes later form the basis for published editions, they existed as separate versions of the plays, much like the circulating manuscripts of earlier centuries. While there have been subsequent efforts to smooth out the differences between these multiple texts and to make claims about the enduring, transcendent quality of *the* authorised (and authorial) text, we may learn more about the shifting relationships between institutions of publishing and performance by paying attention to the '*accidental* differences' between versions of plays.[1]

One key print format that had an important influence on developing understandings of dramatic texts and authorship, laying the groundwork for modern conceptions of text and performance, was the author collection.[2] These volumes had become fairly standard by the mid-17th century and the folio format in particular 'allowed a clear *mise-en-page* and good, legible typography, helping to dignify and canonize the contents' (Hammond 2002: 402). Through this form of publication, playwrights were 'paying closer attention to how their plays were printed: to the preliminary material; to the quality of texts and the look of the page' (Peters 2000: 56). One noteworthy 17th-century development was the use of typography to 'highlight the differences between performance text and author's text' (Peters 2000: 59), suggesting a desire to distinguish the playwright's work from what had appeared on stage and thus implying a certain value attached to the concept of authorial intentions. Increasingly, 'editors and dramatists came to produce editions inspired by the claims to authorial "correctness" and "accuracy" that were so central to the institution of print' (Peters 2000: 137). The text became a place to represent the author's intentions, whether or not these intentions had been followed in performance. Indeed, some playwrights themselves understood print publication as a way to restore elements of their plays that may have been changed in production, or as an opportunity to make revisions that were impossible within the institutions of the theatre.[3] Peters also notes that claims to 'correctness' in these volumes were often seeking to scrape away the accretions of previous editors as much as the accretions of performance. This process reveals the inherent instability of dramatic texts:

> Corrections themselves seemed to breed errors. Texts contradicted one another, refusing to obey unequivocal rules of authenticity. Editions took on their own unstable theatricalism. In the end, the true dramatic author stood alone against the illiterate 'Publishers of his works' – as against the illiterate actors – the dramatist's 'original' the model of 'accuracy' towards which the editor must strive. (2000: 143)

This tendency seems to have increased in the 18th century, when editing practices displayed 'a growing insistence on textual accuracy and the formulation of text-editorial methodologies' (Walsh 2009: 698), particularly in the scholarly editing of Shakespeare.[4] Commenting on the Shakespearean editor's desire to access the 'authentic' intentions of the Bard, Worthen argues that print 'creates the possibility of a dramatic *author* in the modern sense', but it requires us to 'read through the seductive veils of the printed page to see the signs of the evanescent authorial writing embodied there' (2005, 21: original emphasis). In this imagining of dramatic writing, unreliable individual texts – much like flighty, ephemeral performances – become an impediment to accessing *the* authorial text. But the practice of playwrights revising their plays for publication could also, on the other hand, demonstrate the fluid quality of theatre texts and the interplay between text and performance. Oscar Wilde, for example, took the opportunity when correcting proofs for *The Importance of Being Earnest* 'to make some small textual revisions, many of which were based on the improvements (those that he could remember) which had been arrived at during rehearsal' (Stephens 1992: 139). With all these instances of revision – whether to incorporate the collaborative inventions of theatrical production, to restore the 'pure' text of the dramatic author, or to make later additions and improvements to the play – there is the complication of any concept of *the* text, even if using authorial intention as a benchmark. Which of the playwright's various intentions across different versions should be considered definitive?

The history of the printed play thus presents sporadic evidence of both a developing literary understanding of plays and, in the other direction, assertions of the theatricality of drama. One area in which this tussle between two competing understandings of theatre can be most strikingly witnessed is in an element of the text often thought of as marginal: the stage directions. As discussed above, printed plays initially looked similar on the page to other kinds of writing, with conventions such as stage directions only gradually and patchily being established over the course of the 16th and 17th centuries. In the 18th century, there was a crucial shift in the use of stage directions, which began to adopt the present tense format familiar to readers of plays today. Previously, printed drama had tended to use either 'the future tense (instructions for how to perform a piece in the future) or the past tense (descriptions of events now past)' (Peters 2000: 62). The attempt to 'bring the performance to the reader' (ibid.) using the present tense implies two things: a readership seeking to engage with drama as literature, separate from the stage, and an emerging concept of the playtext not as simply a working set of instructions or a document of a specific live event, but as an authoritative 'work' capable of containing both these functions. In the 19th century, meanwhile, printed editions containing 'detailed scenic descriptions, acting indications, and illustrations' (Peters 2000: 70) became common, providing readers with instructions for performance based on specific productions. Peters highlights material evidence of an increasingly visual theatrical culture at this time, such as illustrations of actors and published collections of stage designs. This suggests a certain resistance to literary understandings of the printed play, at the same time as the text sought to represent more and more of the visual world of the stage in book form. While acknowledging the existence of dramatic texts that sought to distinguish themselves from the perceived populism of theatre, Peters suggests that the spectacles of stage and page in the 19th century worked hand in hand: 'dramatists could use the elaborate scenic specifications [...] at once to provide a more novelistic dramatic text and to shape the theatrical scene' (271). There is an inherent tension here, between catering for the reader and celebrating the visual spectacle of the stage; between the dramatist shaping the action of performance and giving way to the other theatrical arts of costume, set design, music, and so on. John Russell Stephens, meanwhile, observes another important shift in the use of stage directions at the end of the 19th century, away from the acting edition and its 'technical language peculiar to the stage' and towards 'readable, well-printed texts with meaningful stage directions' (1992: 132). The main point to take from this is that plays were finding a readership away from the theatre and that playwrights and publishers appeared to be increasingly conscious of these non-specialist readers. But Stephens' description of the stage directions in these editions as 'meaningful' – on which he does not elaborate – raises a series of questions. For whom are these stage directions 'meaningful'? Primarily for readers, presumably, but that then prompts the question of how they 'mean' in relation to the stage. As stage directions become increasingly descriptive, fitting within a frame of meaning-making that is familiar to readers of novels, how does this affect the theatrical status of the play? The more technical, stage-focused directions of acting editions certainly seem to have been out of favour with those who had literary ambitions for drama at the end of the 19th century. William Archer, for instance, commented that the acting edition was 'a negation at all attempt of literary effect' (quoted in Eliot and Nash 2009: 432), while writers such as Shaw paid careful attention to the printed page in an attempt to make their plays more visibly literary.[5]

Finally, it's important to briefly consider the different formats in which printed plays have appeared. This has already been alluded to with the mention of author collections and acting editions. Since first appearing in print, plays have been published in a variety of book forms, including single plays, collections of plays by the same author(s), collected editions of dramatic and non-dramatic literary works, and anthologies of plays. The latter can be traced back to the 18th century and *Bell's British Theatre*: a series of volumes published from 1776, containing a mixture of old and contemporary plays (Stephens 1992: 124). This publishing practice persisted into the 19th century, with series such as *The British Theatre*, edited by novelist and playwright Elizabeth Inchbald, and *Dicks's British Drama*. Penguin's influential *New English Dramatists* series in the 1960s followed a similar but updated format, now with an exclusive focus on new plays, and other play anthologies have continued to be published in the late 20th and early 21st centuries. Such formats potentially have a legitimising and even canonising effect; the process of curation carries with it an implicit value judgement, while the placement of the plays side by side (often accompanied by commentaries) may alter how they are received by readers. It's also worth noting the framing of many of these collected volumes as containing *British* or *English* plays, thus suggesting a national dramatic tradition that implicitly cleaves to the idea of British theatre as – to once again borrow Jen Harvie's phrase – 'fundamentally literary' (2005: 114–115). In the 1980s, meanwhile, publisher Methuen and the Royal Court Theatre pioneered another publication format: the modern playtext programme. Unlike the collected editions, which are more aligned with literary conventions, these versions clearly place the play within the context of its live performance. Like a programme, these books usually contain biographies of the company, as well as details like the dates of the original run, tying the drama to this specific enactment. Andrew Nash and Jane Potter suggest that the introduction of these editions, which have since become widespread at new play producing theatres, 'brought print and performance even closer together' (2019: 315) by linking the published play to its production. However, there's also the danger that these texts position the premiere production – the details of which they preserve – as the definitive performance of the play, while the drive to print the play before the production run can lead to the creation of texts that reflect an earlier stage in rehearsals (hence the common note that the text may differ from what is being performed).

Returning to the present, it's worth asking whether 21st-century British theatre has now moved beyond the print culture that has had such an impact on the textual identity of plays. Peters dates the height of both theatre and print to the mid-19th century, arguing that the birth of cinema marked the end of 'the era of a theatre formed in opposition to the page and understood in relation to the written text' (2000: 311). Since then, she suggests, mass culture and recording technologies have become more significant than print in their relation to theatre. Similar arguments have been made by other scholars. In *Postdramatic Theatre*, for example, Hans-Thies Lehmann begins by asserting that '[w]ith the end of the "Gutenberg galaxy" and the advent of new technologies the written text and the book are being called into question' (2006: 16). Beyond theatre, meanwhile, several thinkers have referred to the early 21st century as the 'late age of print'.[6] While this might seem to imply that a continued focus on the interplay between printed plays and performances is outdated, I'd argue that a print-inflected understanding of theatre still looms large, as seen in notions of textual fidelity that view performances much like new printed editions of a stable literary 'work'. Moreover, while print is arguably waning, text retains a prominent – if transformed – place in our current digital age, as I address towards the end of this chapter. It remains vital, therefore, to interrogate the different forms that theatre texts have taken over the period discussed in this book – whether on the printed page or on the screen.

Texts as material

To further explore some of the questions prompted by the changing historical relationship between print and performance, I want to focus more closely now on the playtext as a material object. As discussed in Chapter 3, part of the issue with how the relationship between text and performance has typically been understood within British theatrical contexts has to do with 'reductive assumptions of the formal consistency of published texts, of texts as material objects that house the work of the author' (Worthen 1997: 7). Within print culture, Worthen suggests, there's a common belief that 'the *work itself* is finally unaltered by the material conditions of its emergence in history, its materialization in a specific printform' (2005: 7, original emphasis). If layout, punctuation, or even the words themselves change between editions, this is not understood as affecting the integrity of the work. I have already begun to address this belief by dismantling the notion of the transcendent, stable 'work' of the dramatic author. To build upon this analysis, I am borrowing insights from textual studies, which over the last few decades has brought increased attention to the history, contexts, and material trappings of the book. As noted in the introduction to *Performance Research*'s special edition on editing, 'while textual studies and performance studies have much to say to each other, they are rarely brought into dialogue' (MacDonald and Sherman 2002: 1). Elizabeth Dyrud Lyman (2002) likewise remarks that theatrical texts have been largely overlooked in the scholarly turn towards the materiality of texts. Although there have been occasional meeting points between the two disciplines in the work of scholars such as Worthen and Peters, this remains a relatively under-explored intersection that is ripe for consideration.

My exploration of some of the textual identities of contemporary British theatre is – like my brief foray into the history of the printed play – unavoidably limited. D. F. McKenzie, who influentially argued for the integration of biblio-graphic, textual, historical, and social investigation in the study of books, stresses the difficulty of ever fully knowing the many interconnecting contexts surrounding the creation of a specific text. He suggests that '[a]t best perhaps we can acknowledge the intricacies of such a textual world and the almost insuperable problems of describing it adequately – and yet still travel imaginatively and responsibly within it' (1999: 4). I take this as a caveat for my own interrogations of theatre texts. My hope, though, is that my provisional investigations might indicate a new direction for the study of playtexts and, in the process, sketch a more complex and nuanced conceptualisation of these texts than in most existing accounts. While citing a number of examples from plays in his lectures on the sociology of texts, McKenzie does not fully address the unique problems posed by dramatic texts. As he acknowledges, the 'relation of textual criticism to the realities of theatrical production has always been one of embarrassed impotence' (50). This, he suggests, is because the 'dramatic text is not only notoriously unstable, but, whatever the script, it is [...] never more than a pre-text for the theatrical occasion, and only a constituent part of it' (ibid.). Although the instability of theatre texts may have discouraged textual criticism from engaging with drama, it is this defining characteristic of plays that might be most illuminated by such a perspective. By which I mean that close attention to the specific, material details of different editions of theatre texts might clarify the precise nature of their instability both as textual objects and as documents used in performance. Playtexts are indeed a 'constituent part' of theatrical performance, but they also exist as books that readers encounter as separate, self-contained objects, and so it's worth considering how the distinctive formats of plays influence their relationships both with the stage and with readers.

Alongside McKenzie, another of the leading figures in the turn to the printed page is Jerome McGann, who asks readers to consider the precise sociohistorical and material conditions in which we encounter texts. He studies 'a much more extensive textual field' than previous scholars, looking at

> the most material (and apparently least 'signifying' or significant) levels of the text: in the case of scripted texts, the physical form of books and manuscripts (paper, ink, typefaces, layouts) or their prices, advertising mechanisms, and distribution venues. (1990: 12)

For McGann, 'the text' is not merely a linguistic entity, but 'a laced network of linguistic and bibliographical codes' (13). Moreover, he argues that texts are constantly changing over time and that they also 'vary from themselves (as it were) immediately, as soon as they engage with the readers they anticipate' (9–10). To study texts, he therefore insists, 'we have to study these complex (and open-ended) histories of textual change and variance' (9). Arguing along similar lines, Johanna Drucker even suggests that we should understand the printing process – including '[g]raphic layout, typographic composition, proofing, trimming, and binding' – as a form of editing which has the power to change how we encounter a text, because 'we read everything according to those many instructions that are graphically encoded in a text' (2002: 101).

These perspectives have significant implications for our understanding of playtexts, which have historically been preserved and transmitted in many different textual forms. This holds even where there might initially seem to be great consistency between versions of a play. While the stability of a given literary product is usually judged by the degree of linguistic variation between editions, McGann argues that texts can be highly unstable while containing relatively few or even no linguistic differences. He proposes that scholars need to pay attention not just to linguistic codes, but also to bibliographical codes – including a vast array of different elements, such as typographical choices, placement of notes and glosses, tables of contents, as well as the processes and contexts of publication – which may significantly alter understandings of the text. Many of these elements are collaboratively created, are out of the playwright's control, or are determined by the typographical conventions of drama as a genre. As readers, we are familiar with certain features, such as cast lists, speech prefixes and scene titles, which are broadly consistent from playtext to playtext. These are often taken for granted, but choices made about the layout of the page – even where these choices are determined by convention – have an impact on the textual identity of the play. While it may seem as though editors and printers are simply vehicles carrying the text to its readers, their decisions, mistakes, and interventions can change the received understanding of a play on the page. As Lyman warns, '[o]nce marks are on a page, approved by the "author", printed and copyright protected they *are* "the" (or at least "a") text' (2002: 98, original emphasis). The process of publication confers an impression of authorial power, even where the playwright has had limited control over the details of that process. As discussed above, moreover, a playtext may invite different meanings depending on whether we encounter it as an individual edition, as part of a playwright's collected works, in an anthology of plays, or as a playtext programme purchased at the live performance event. And just as I have insisted that no single performance can be considered *the* definitive performance of 'the work', 'no single editorial procedure – no single "text" of a particular work – can be imagined or hypothesized as the "correct" one' (McGann 1990: 62).

Of the various formats in which plays are published, the distinction between acting editions and editions published primarily for readers is one that bears further consideration. The practice of publishing versions of plays explicitly identified as acting editions underlines the uncomfortable duality of plays as simultaneously literary and theatrical documents. Although the acting edition was challenged by playwrights with literary aspirations at the end of the 19th century, the format retained a significant place in the 20th-century play publishing market and has persevered to the present day.[7] It's a fascinating exercise to compare acting editions of contemporary plays with the versions published for readers, either as playtext programmes (now often the main or only form of publication for new plays)[8] or as editions published after the first production. My analysis here is partly inspired by the approach of Worthen, who has directly compared the treatment of pauses in acting and trade editions of Harold Pinter's plays (2005: 78–80). Two brief examples illustrate how even very recent plays have often varied and unstable textual identities. First, contrasting the openings of the playtext programme and acting edition of Nick Payne's play *Incognito* (2014) shows how the text of plays continues to evolve after initial publication, creating competing versions of the play that cannot be smoothly collated into a single 'work'. The first scene in the acting edition, which was published in 2020, has been rewritten since the publication of the playtext programme in 2014. While it includes dialogue between the same two characters, Michael and Evelyn, the context of their conversation and the way in which information is revealed is completely different. In the earlier version, it is Evelyn who reveals to Michael the secret identity of her father, which she has discovered via an offstage character named Brian Schulman (Payne 2014); in the later edition, it is Michael who breaks this news to Evelyn (Payne 2020). These two versions establish the relationship between the characters in contrasting ways, with implications for how we understand them both in subsequent scenes. The 2020 text gives no indication of the timing or context of the rewrite; it could have been changed during rehearsals for the premiere production, or it might be the product of later revisions made by Payne. One presumes, as this is the acting edition, that this is the version now intended for performance in new productions of the play, but the earlier edition persists, bearing the authorial imprint of Payne's name.[9]

My second example, *Escaped Alone* (2016) by Caryl Churchill, offers a much subtler distinction between acting edition and playtext programme. Unlike in *Incognito*, there have been no major scene rewrites; plot, characters, and dialogue are all consistent across the two editions. However, the spacing of the text in the acting edition has been changed in ways that affect how the play is read and how it signals certain performance possibilities. The playtext programme opens with the following lines:

MRS J: I'm walking down the street and there's a door in the fence open and inside are three women I've seen before.
VI: Don't look now but there's someone watching us.
LENA: Is it that woman?
SALLY: Is that you, Mrs Jarrett?
MRS J: So I go in.

SALLY: Rosie locked out in the rain (2016: 5)

Here, the additional line break between Mrs Jarrett's 'So I go in' and the next line from Sally suggests a pause or a transition – some change of state, perhaps, or a sense of time passing. In the acting edition, however, this gap is eliminated, running the first part of the scene straight into the dialogue that follows (Churchill 2020). More noticeably, meanwhile, Mrs Jarrett's apocalyptic monologues, which come at the end of the numbered scenes and punctuate the dialogue of the four characters, are laid out differently in the two editions. While in both versions these speeches remain implicitly part of the scene that precedes them, as they are not separated by scene numbers, in the playtext programme they are each given a page to themselves,[10] whereas the acting version has the monologues placed immediately after their respective scenes, with no additional page or line breaks. Though this may seem like a small and relatively insignificant detail, the distinctive uses of spacing have the potential to lend weight to different aspects of the scenes, both for the reader encountering the play on the page and for the director and actors approaching it for performance. It also raises questions about the editorial practices at work here and their relationship to Churchill's intentions. Was the text in the acting edition condensed simply to occupy fewer printed pages?[11] Did Churchill agree to these changes? For that matter, how much influence did the playwright have over the layout of the earlier playtext programme? Again, the problem with making decisions based on perceived authorial intentions becomes apparent.

As these differences demonstrate, it often remains unclear how much of the contents of the printed play readers are to consider as part of the drama. As Worthen observes, 'plays are notable in the history of print precisely because so much of the writing that appears on the page seems at best ambiguously related to a sense of the work's identity, its inherent, even authorized, *meaning*' (2005: 11, original emphasis). These ambiguous elements, including stage directions and speech prefixes, are what Worthen calls the 'accessories of the page'. This recalls earlier discussions of the marginal text of the stage direction, which recurs as a problematic element in printed plays. These 'accessories' in one sense help to define the playtext as a text for performance, indicating the external space of the stage, yet their incompleteness also points towards the ways in which performance exceeds the text. In the various ways in which they challenge, gesture towards and fail to fully account for performance, stage directions signal the incommensurability of script and staging. Moreover, they represent the contested boundaries of the text's authority, as they are in many cases considered optional by directors, and yet in other circumstances are fiercely policed – the close guarding of Samuel Beckett's stage directions by his Estate being the most famous example of the latter. Another much-discussed example which demonstrates the troublesome status of such 'accessories' in printed drama is the Pinteresque pause. Pauses in Pinter's plays have accrued an unusual authority, becoming treated as sacrosanct by directors and actors in a way that is not typical of other plays. Paying attention to the page, Worthen argues that it's not only the frequent inclusion of pauses in Pinter's plays but their emphatic placement within the printed text 'that transforms their status for all modern readers, rendering them not only definitively Authorial, but as part of that part of the text that [...] tends to be regarded as the legitimate sphere of the playwright's work' (2005: 81).

I am intrigued by this question of what in the text is considered as integral to the play and as belonging to the playwright, as it again engages debates about theatrical authorship and intentions in relation to performance. One area where this ambiguity can be observed is in the use of punctuation, capitalisation, and other forms of textual emphasis, such as italics, underlining, and bold text. Over the last few decades, playwrights have increasingly made specific uses of these devices in the printed versions of their plays.[12] It's now common practice for playwrights to include a 'note on the text' in which they explain the intentions behind their use of punctuation, spacing, capitalisation, and so on. A couple of examples will serve to illustrate what I mean. At the start of *[BLANK]* (2018), for instance, Alice Birch includes the following:

> /Denotes the overlapping of speech. Words in square brackets [] are not spoken. The absence of a full stop at the end of a line denotes a kind of interruption – the lines should run at speed. The use of a full stop on a line on its own suggests a pause – whether this is a single beat or ten minutes depends on what feels right.
>
> The spacing of dialogue, the use of upper and lower case letters and the punctuation is all there to help the actor in terms of pacing and the weight of their words. (2018)

Similarly, Alistair McDowall's play *X* (2016) opens with this note:

> A question without a question mark denotes a flatness of tone.
>
> – Indicates an interruption of speech or train of thought.
>
> … Indicates either a trailing off, a breather, a shift, or a transition.
>
> /Indicates where the next line of dialogue interrupts or overlaps. (2016: 2)

The use of dashes as interruptions and forward slashes for overlapping dialogue, meanwhile, is now fairly standard and is noted at the start of many of the plays I've cited throughout this book. In some cases, these instructions primarily serve to clarify meaning. Others, like McDowall's note about questions without question marks, seek to shape aspects of the actors' performances. Similar efforts to guide the actors can be seen in Birch's instructions, though this is ambiguously combined with a recognition of the mutability of live performance. Unlike in Pinter, the treatment of pauses is to be decided based 'on what feels right', and while spacing and capitalisation has been designed with the actor's speech in mind, Birch does not offer any further elaboration of the intentions behind these choices, instead handing them over to the interpretation of directors and performers. Here, then, there is a simultaneous movement of extending and relinquishing control by the playwright, in ways that speak to the discussion in Chapter 2. As I discuss further, this seeming contradiction is even more apparent in examples where playwrights and publishers have played with the space of the printed page, upending conventions and acknowledging the materiality of the play as book.

Innovating on the page

Throughout this book, I have looked at a variety of ways in which contemporary British theatre-makers are experimenting with text. Here, I return to some of these examples and introduce others in order to look more closely at the design of the page, considering how this innovation extends to the formatting of the texts themselves. Before going on, though, it's worth acknowledging that these innovations are by no means unique to British practitioners. The pioneering work of playwrights such as Suzan-Lori Parks, Mac Wellman, and Elfriede Jelinek, as well as the earlier choreo-poetry of Ntozake Shange and the fragmentary writing of Heiner Müller, are all important reference points. In many cases, the textual experiments of British playwrights and theatre-makers are in creative dialogue with innovations elsewhere. For example, debbie tucker green, whose work I discuss below, has named Shange as a significant influence on her writing. But in the specific context of British theatre culture and its attachment to author and script, these experiments continue a complex dialogue between page and stage, challenging models of performance that assume any straightforward transmission from text to staging.

One striking way in which some British playwrights have reinvented the conventions of the dramatic page is through the use of spacing and typography more associated with printed poetry. The most famous example of this can be found in Sarah Kane's *4.48 Psychosis* (2000), which is barely even recognisable as a play. There is no indication of speakers or assigning of lines, with the exception of the use of dashes in sections that appear to be a dialogue between a patient and a doctor or therapist, and no delineation of scenes beyond the use of occasional dividing lines across the page. As well as eschewing these conventional features of the printed play, many sequences in the text use spacing, line breaks and punctuation in a way that appears at first glance to have little to do with performance, but is immediately reminiscent of the poetic page. Take, for example, the following lines:

>My love, my love, why have you forsaken me?
>
>She is the couching place where I never shall lie
>and there's no meaning to life in the light of my loss
>
>>Built to be lonely
>>to love the absent
>
>>Find me
>>Free me
>>>from this
>
>>>>corrosive doubt
>>>>futile despair
>
>>>>horror in repose
>
>>I can fill my space
>>fill my time
>>but nothing can fill this void in my heart
>
>>The vital need for which I would die
>
>>>>>>>>Breakdown (2001: 219)[13]

Here, the text is dispersed across the page, starting at the left-hand margin and ending with the word 'Breakdown' stranded in empty space on the right-hand side of the page, followed by three more line breaks and then a dividing line to (perhaps) indicate the start of a new sequence. When reading, this has the effect of isolating the final word, lending it extra weight. What this means for performance, though, is ambiguous. While contemporary theatrical conventions have typically taken spaces and line breaks in the script to indicate pauses in dialogue, or to give the actor a guide to the rhythm of the speech, this approach cannot wholly account for the use of the page in *4.48 Psychosis*. Trying to interpret the page by understanding its arrangement as a representation of speech raises numerous questions. Should there be a pause at the end of each short line? Does each additional line break signify a longer pause? And how do the varying indentations of the lines of text translate into performance? That's not to mention the uncertainty over how many speakers might voice these words in performance.

In sequences like this, the specificity of the page – the placement of words and punctuation marks, the gaps between them, what Liz Mills aptly calls 'the particular spatializing of language' (2009: 389) – is made inescapably evident to the reader. To borrow McGann's phrasing, poetic texts 'put the resources of the medium on full display' (1990: 14). One effect of this is to resist the perceived absorption of text into performance. The typographical features of modern poetry – which the page of *4.48 Psychosis* often resembles – were designed 'to slow reading, to isolate and materialize "language" as an object, to trouble the transparency of the page, even to prevent the direct assimilation of written language to performance' (Worthen 2005: 61). When reading a sequence like the one above, the expanse of white space and the movement of lines away from and towards the left-hand margin prompts one to become aware of the words as marks distributed across the spatial field of the page, rather than encountering these linguistic signs as a seemingly transparent guide to action, speech, and character. The distinct identity of these words *as text* becomes apparent, thus revealing the incommensurability of the contents of the page and any performance that might use those contents. If the playtext is understood as nothing but a series of words to be spoken by actors, a production could just vocalise the lines shown above and be considered a 'faithful' representation of the script. But it seems clear to me that there is more to Kane's page – and, indeed, to the page of any playtext – than just written dialogue. This particular patterning of language on the page invites multiple readings in performance, both linguistic and visual/spatial; it makes visible the specific texture of the written script, which is never simply assimilable to performance.

Another writer whose plays often read as poetic on the page is debbie tucker green.[14] tucker green's texts combine hyper-realistic vernacular speech with elements of poetry, crafting a distinctive dramatic language. This meeting of textual registers can be seen in the following extract from *random* (2008), in which Mum is narrating the presence of police officers in her home:

> Dark boots
> an' heavy shoes –
> on my clean carpet
> in my good room –
> in my front room –
> my visitor room –
> my room fe best –
> fe formal –
> not even fe fambily.
> Dark boots and heavy shoes –
> beatin down my
> for best carpet
> without a second thought …
> from them. (2008: 26)

While certain non-standard spellings (such as 'fe' in place of 'for') clearly convey accent and dialect, conforming to established conventions of dramatic dialogue, the short, broken lines and the use of repetition (the 'dark boots' and 'heavy shoes') are more redolent of poetry. This approach both materialises the language of the text, as discussed above, and simultaneously suggests an attempted extension of the text into the embodied interpretations of performance. As can be seen in this example, tucker green's writing places 'an emphasis on rhyme, rhythm, repetition, silence, fragmented and incomplete sentences [...] producing a musical language that heightens emotive meaning' (Goddard 2015: 72). Her texts are frequently spoken of as 'scores', an analogy that underlines the musicality of the plays while also implying that the script acts as a form of notation for the rhythms as well as the spoken words of performance.[15] As Worthen notes, the 'score' metaphor suggests 'the capacity of writing not merely to encode the semantic content of performance but the dynamic nuances of its embodiment as well' (2010: 8). Anthony Welsh, who acted in the premiere production of tucker green's play *nut* (2013), reinforces this sense that the script prescribes the spoken patterns of the play's utterances in performance: 'Everything in the script is there for a reason. There isn't a dash or a dot or a comma or anything that is not supposed to be executed' (quoted in Khan 2013). He compares tucker green's writing to jazz, explaining that 'there is structure but you're allowed to play' (ibid.). Here, again, it's possible to see how experimental approaches to language and layout can bring performance and text into dialogue, at once resisting and in some ways perpetuating a literary, print-driven understanding of the written play.

The sparse opening to the second scene of *stoning mary* (2005) illustrates another aspect of tucker green's innovation: her play with minimalism.

Mum: Umm.
        Umm …
Dad: Er.
Mum: Umm.
Dad   *coughs*.
          Yes?
Dad: Er …
Mum: Yes?
Dad: Um … you? (2005: 10)

The text of this scene is composed from mostly non-linguistic utterances – the 'umm's and 'er's that are more typically excised from dramatic dialogue. The result is both prosaic and poetic. For the reader, the sea of white space on the page speaks volumes about the struggle to communicate, while the isolation of these mundane sounds down the left-hand margin elevates them to a sort of avant-garde poetic status, reminiscent in some ways of the nonsensical soundscapes of Dada.[16] As well as this use of minimal lines and transcribed sounds, examples of which can be found across tucker green's plays, the playwright has become known for what she calls 'active silences'. In the texts, these are indicated by speech prefixes that appear without any dialogue. Sometimes, an entire exchange between characters will be indicated on the page in this way.[17] This, again, prioritises the almost sculptural use of empty space on the page, as well as generating a challenge for directors and actors, who must decide how to indicate these 'active silences' in performance. What does it mean for a silence to be 'active'? Moreover, this is yet another instance of the ambivalent mix of determinacy and indeterminacy, control and abdication, that I have previously observed in theatre texts. tucker green's insertion of 'active silences' intervenes in an area of performance often thought of as beyond the writer's control, but these devices offer little indication of how they might translate from page to stage.

There is, then, a contradiction or tension apparent in tucker green's poetic use of the page. Drawing on Charles Olson's theory of 'projective' poetry, which he argues is akin to the printed poetics of much modern drama, Worthen suggests that the layout of the page in a way that suggests orality – such as the use of line breaks and spacing to imply pauses, rhythms, emphasis – actually reproduces a literary, print-oriented model of the dramatic text. The page sets out a series of speech patterns to which the performer is implicitly expected to adhere: 'the rhetoric of the projective line both transmits the poem and claims to govern its proper performance' (2005: 117). Thus, while plays like tucker green's 'resist the "literarization" of the drama by drawing the signals of the stage into the page', this can equally be read as 'a continuation of print culture's efforts to imprint the stage, to locate the signs and signals of appropriate, authorial performance within the text itself' (85). In earlier chapters, I've noted this tension between the ability of theatricality to puncture the apparent literariness of the text and the counter-possibility that these supposed disruptions act as a way of extending the authority of the text. However, the framework for understanding the relationship between text and performance that I have been developing over the course of this book allows for such a tension to be held in suspense, forever unresolved. If we perceive theatre texts as simultaneously complete and incomplete iterations of a never-definitive, ever-absent 'work', the interventions of writers like Kane and tucker green may simply be seen as playful invitations to readers and theatre-makers alike. Moreover, by resisting any frictionless equivalence between text and performance, these plays serve as active reminders of the complexity and contingency that I am arguing is constitutive of the relationship between the two.

Several other writers have similarly played with the placement of words, space, and punctuation on the page in ways that disrupt or complicate the perceived assimilability of text and performance. Examples include the irruption of the eponymous letter into the dialogue of Alistair McDowall's *X*, to the point where X's fill almost four full pages of the printed play (2016: 126–130); the landscape page orientation of Alice Birch's *Anatomy of a Suicide* (2017), which strikingly spatialises the play's three concurrent narratives; the poetic interludes in *Human Animals* (2016) by Stef Smith, which are separated from the surrounding dialogue by being italicised and using varying degrees of indentation from the margin, like the quoted passage from *4.48 Psychosis*. But several recent texts have pushed this remaking of the dramatic page even further. *Total Immediate Collective Imminent Terrestrial Salvation*, with which I opened the chapter, is a prime example. Large chunks of the storytelling in the text both as read and as performed in the premiere production are communicated through Jadhav's illustrations, which depict key events and interactions between the characters, as well as more abstract celestial visions. Text itself sometimes becomes material for these images, such as when the repeated words 'I'm ready' are arranged to depict a planet being consumed by a black hole (2019: 41), or when lines from the preceding scenes are densely overlapped across two pages, surrounding the words 'DARK' and 'MATTER' (54–55). There's a sense here that words are just marks on the page, like any of the other marks in the text, with all these marks given equal weight regardless of whether they convey meaning linguistically or pictorially. Other theatre texts that have made imaginative use of non-linguistic visual content include *seven methods of killing kylie jenner*, which (as discussed in Chapter 2) includes emojis, memes and gifs, and the script of RashDash's *Two Man Show* (2016), in which the company's distinctive movement sequences are loosely represented by sketches drawn by set designer Oliver Townsend. Explaining the latter in a note on the text, RashDash's Abbi Greenland and Helen Goalen write that these sketches 'are not here to act as a blueprint for future productions or accurately capture the first production, but to give a glimpse of what we feel is important about those scenes' (2017: 11). These abstract images resist either prescribing or documenting, instead finding an entirely different way of communicating an aspect of performance that's often understood to evade capture. While the idea of including illustrations in a printed playtext is far from new, as seen in 19th-century play publishing, the difference in these examples is that the images are utterly integral to the ways in which these texts convey meaning on the page. They do not represent scenes from a specific production or offer the reader one possible visual construction of a written sequence; they are a central element of the play in their own right.

To think further about these imaginative uses of the page as a space that might combine different kinds of text and image, I want to look at *Action Plans* (2015), Action Hero's volume of 'selected performance pieces'.[18] This book collects together textual versions of six shows: *A Western* (2005), *Watch Me Fall* (2009), *Frontman* (2010), *Hoke's Bluff* (2013), *Slap Talk* (2013), and *Extraordinary Rendition* (2015). Each is presented in a distinct way on the page, using different layouts, fonts and text sizes, page and text colours, and other visual elements. The company describes them as 'an attempt at re-presenting the live moment on the page', adding the disclaimer that 'some of the texts […] don't include all the words we actually speak on stage' (2015: xxv). What's notable about this collection is the way in which each piece develops its own unique textual idiom in response to not only the documented words of the show but also its form and tone, its conditions of production, and its use of genre. For example, *A Western* evoked the cinematic genre of its title on a shoestring budget; the company exploited an audience's familiarity with the form in place of any sort of mimetic backdrop, with 'our collective imaginations filling in the gaps' (4). The sparseness of the production is reflected in a similarly spare text. The pages are empty save for a couple of lines in the centre, which provide the barest outline of the scene in a way that allows a reader's cinematic memory to complete the picture: 'This is the scene where/our hero shoots at a bandit's feet/forcing him to dance' (17), or 'This is the scene where/the card table gets turned over' (27). The text of DIY stunt show *Watch Me Fall* uses the equally DIY photography of audience members to capture snapshots of the action (57–68); the verbal assault of *Slap Talk* (discussed in Chapter 2) is represented by pages densely filled with small, lower-case text, printed with no line breaks, no margins, and minimal punctuation (29–66). In every instance, the page responds to the specific textures of the piece, rather than being confined by the typographical conventions of printed drama.

The text for *Hoke's Bluff* offers a particularly fascinating hybrid of different linguistic, pictorial, and bibliographic signs. This show is an affectionate parody of American high school sports movies which was staged within the framework of an unspecified sporting event, with the audience seated on bleachers and a mascot handing out popcorn. The page reiterates some of the distinctive visual iconography of the show, using the red and yellow colour scheme of its fictional high school sports team. Each double page of the text, meanwhile, combines several distinct elements. On the right-hand page is (some of) the text spoken in the show, laid out in a range of different formats (two columns, one block of text, just a couple of lines in the centre of the page) without any speech prefixes. On the left-hand page is a scene title, such as 'Pep Rally' (93), and a grid containing three different sections: a diagram of shapes and arrows, suggestive of sporting manoeuvres; a list of references, including movies, songs, television shows, articles, books, and websites; and evocative reflections and notes from the company.[19] These notes sometimes offer insights into the company's process and inspirations, alongside descriptions of sports events, quotations, lists, and more abstract musings. This format remains consistent throughout the text, with the exception of the narrative climax, when the commentary on the big game spills out across a full double page (123–124). Often, the relationship between the various elements of the page is oblique. Occasionally, the notes on the left-hand page clarify an artistic decision, or identify the sources from which the company has lifted lines, but in many instances the connection is left ambiguous. It's unclear, meanwhile, whether the diagrams are to be read as a guide to the movement of bodies across the stage, as some sort of visual representation of the relationships depicted in the scene printed opposite, or as something else entirely. While for the most part the text printed on the right-hand pages appears to straightforwardly represent the spoken content of the show, there are places where this section also exploits the spatial and illustrative possibilities of the page. The first encounter between protagonists Tyler and Connie, for example, is presented as just two lines of dialogue – 'Hey Tyler'/'Hey Connie' (114) – in the centre of the page, separated by one of the yellow lines that dissect the pages of the text in patterns reminiscent of sporting pitches. The show up to this point has established the pair as a caricature of the teen movie golden couple without ever depicting them together. All the empty space on this page, then, functions similarly to the empty space in the text of *A Western*, allowing the gaps to be filled by the imagined clichés of the cinematic genre that *Hoke's Bluff* is evoking.

For those – like me – who have seen *Hoke's Bluff* performed, the published text is an interesting document of some elements of the show and its inspirations. It performs the role of what Carl Lavery calls a 'postscript': a 'relic of/for an event that has passed' which is 'essentially spectral' – 'an architecture for conjuring ghosts' (2009: 37). Lavery emphasises the gaps in this 'postscript', which he imagines as 'a building blasted by holes' (ibid.). But the question remains of how this text, with all its ambiguities, functions in relation to other possible performances – if, indeed, it functions in this way at all. Discussing Suzan-Lori Parks' writing, Lyman poses a question that is pertinent to ask of the sorts of texts discussed in this section:

> The indeterminacy inherent in new forms of graphic notation raises the question of what happens when language doesn't speak clearly. In the case of scripts and scores, particularly, how do those responsible for realizing such works – through printed texts and live performances – make interpretative decisions? And how do the decisions of print interpreters (editor-publishers) affect those of stage interpreters? (2002: 91)

Although I'm arguing that indeterminacy is characteristic of *all* theatre texts, the greater degree of textual indeterminacy in some of the plays explored here does present particular challenges for editors, readers, and theatre-makers alike. While the question of how directors and performers make interpretive decisions is not one that can receive a definitive answer, it's one that we should keep asking of such texts, using this as a way of investigating the complex and ever-shifting relationships between texts and performances. To see texts like Action Hero's *only* as postscripts is to underestimate them and their many possible lives. Moreover, while the published text of *Hoke's Bluff* might appear to function more as documentation of Action Hero's practice than as a starting point for other versions, there is already evidence of students using it to reconstruct performance (Acquah 2016).

It's also worth returning to the second part of Lyman's question: 'how do the decisions of print interpreters (editor-publishers) affect those of stage interpreters?' In particular, the role of publishers in facilitating these new experiments with the page requires consideration. As already noted, the decisions made during the process of bringing a text to print impact how it is read and, consequently, how it might be interpreted in performance. During the period under investigation, play publishing has expanded significantly, as captured in David Edgar's brief history of the sector. Looking at the combined outputs of the four main play publishing houses – Methuen, Faber, Nick Hern Books and Oberon Books – Edgar notes a marked increase from 122 full-length single plays published in 1999 to 255 published two decades later in 2019. The greater share of this growth seems to have occurred in the 2010s; in 2009, for example, the four publishing houses produced 140 playtexts between them (2021: 235). This recent expansion of play publishing has been enabled by technological developments, as digital printing allows for much shorter print-runs than previous lithographic printing. This then opens a publication route for more niche and experimental texts and for plays being produced for short runs at small theatres. Edgar explains that in the 1980s 'the lowest optimum run for a play was in the low thousands, now it is economical to publish 400 (or sometimes fewer) copies of a single play' (234). The recent increase in experimental texts like *Action Plans*, therefore, is as much a consequence of developments in the technologies and economics of publishing as it is a reflection of textual innovation by British theatre-makers.

To date, the publisher that has been at the forefront of the sorts of innovation discussed above is Oberon Books, an independent drama publisher that was acquired by Bloomsbury at the end of 2019. Oberon published *Action Plans*, as well as many other typographically experimental texts by playwrights and artists including Alice Birch, Jasmine Lee-Jones, Breach Theatre, RashDash, Tim Crouch, and Mojisola Adebayo. George Spender, former editorial director at Oberon, has explained that texts like *Action Plans* arose from a desire to 'do something a bit different [...] something that the reader engages with as literature in a way and also as a performance in itself' (2015). Spender's reference to literature and performance in the same breath again invokes the inherent duality of the theatre text – but with a key difference. Whereas plays are typically understood as both literary objects and documents that refer to or instigate theatrical performances, the suggestion is that this sort of experimental theatre text can function as 'a performance in itself'; in some sense, it not only represents performance, but it *is* a separate performance on the page. This is an intriguing idea, suggesting how the page can also use and transform a text in ways more typically seen as reserved for the live, embodied realm of performance.

The bespoke publishing process that Spender helped to develop at Oberon and that he's now continuing with his own independent publishing house, Salamander Street, involves close consultation with theatre-makers, who determine the layout of the script. He notes that many of these texts would not be able to make such creative use of the page if they had to meet the demand of being complete in time to coincide with the premiere production, demonstrating how a whole network of economic and practical considerations shapes the printed playtext.[20] These more creative texts typically have print runs of a few hundred – considerably less than the 1,000 or so copies that might be produced for a new play at the Royal Court or the National Theatre (Spender 2021) – and would be economically impossible to produce without the advancements of digital and on-demand printing. Enabled by this new technology and driven by the work of publishers like Oberon and Salamander Street, the transformation of the printed playtext seen in volumes such as *Action Plans* is rippling outwards. Other publishers are now similarly taking a more experimental approach to layout and typography. Nick Hern Books, for example, has published texts like Sam Steiner's landscape-oriented *You Stupid Darkness!* (2019) and Ella Hickson's *The Writer* (2018), which includes a series of images in the formally playful third scene. Intellect Books, meanwhile, is publishing experimental performance texts by artists like Michael Pinchbeck, Point Blank, and Claire MacDonald, whose work might previously have been denied publication and deemed 'non-text-based'.

Both the overall growth of play publishing and the development of this more experimental strand of published texts have implications for conceptions of the play on the page and its relationship with performance. As Edgar points out, in a very practical sense, 'the availability of a play in print makes it much more likely that it will be revived' (2021: 236). Publication thus reinforces the iterability of playtexts; plays that are not published might more readily (if falsely) be seen as receiving their 'definitive' performance when first produced, especially if they are never revived. But Edgar's conclusion that the expansion of play publishing 'provides yet more evidence that single-voice playwriting remains the dominant form of theatre-making on the British stage' (ibid.) ignores the many co-authored and devised texts that have been made available for readers as part of this play publishing boom. If anything, this development has the potential to reshape the dramatic canon in ways that expand it *beyond* 'single-voice playwriting'. Many theatre-makers are themselves conscious of the connections between publication, longevity, and perceived legitimacy. According to Spender, most artists and companies he has approached are eager to document their work in print, having felt 'a little disgruntled about being overlooked in terms of publishing' (2021). Over recent years, the growing interest of publishers in expanding the range of texts they issue has been met with more and more enquiries from theatre-makers who might previously have resisted the idea of capturing their work in print. These are the sorts of texts that have often come under the broad umbrella of 'writing for theatre', as discussed in Chapter 1. While I maintain that boundaries between different sorts of theatre text are fluid and porous, it is nonetheless worth looking in more detail at the ways in which performances that did not begin with pre-written texts have found their way onto the page. This represents another evolution in the textual life of theatre, posing further questions about the relationship between text and performance.

Design or documentation?

One of the reasons that theatre texts are culturally significant – and one of the bones of contention in competing understandings of these texts and their role – is that they document performance and thus lend it longevity. Live artist Bryony Kimmings captured the legitimising force of publication, as well as the friction between the published text and certain forms of performance, in a blog post in which she asked: 'How does a live artist that plays in the Cabaret space at Soho Theatre and just did her very first stand up gig get her work published … does she need to?' (2012). Kimmings questioned what a text of one of her shows might look like – would it just consist of descriptions of the performance, or would there be space for readers to fill in the gaps? – and acknowledged some discomfort with the idea, but she also made the key point that she did not see the sort of art that she makes represented anywhere in book form.[21] Until recently, the same could be said of many other solo theatre-makers, whose work has typically been seen as ephemeral and inextricable from its performer-creator. As John Freeman notes, solo performances exhibit 'a close and at times inseparable connection between the writer and the written, between performer and performance', and thus, he suggests, 'the bespoke nature of the material augurs against recycling and repetition' (2016: 36). Solo autobiographical performances are written and performed (and sometimes also directed) by the same individual, whose self is to some extent constructed through the act of writing and performing. It might therefore seem reasonable to suggest that in such instances the iterability that I have previously argued is integral to theatre texts does not apply in the same way. If dramatic writing is defined by iterability in performance, enabling stagings by different performers in a countless variety of contexts, then a text that is inscribed with the specific physical embodiment of its author-performer has an uncertain status. In response, I would again draw attention to the second part of the word 'iter*ability*'. As discussed in the previous chapter, it is the *possibility* of other iterations that inheres in the theatrical text, whether or not it has actually been performed in more than one version. Moreover, the play publishing boom discussed above has included the publication of several solo, autobiographical texts by artists such as Selina Thompson, Travis Alabanza, Mojisola Adebayo, Caroline Horton, Jamal Gerald, and Scottee, opening the possibility that these plays might be remounted in contexts far removed from those that produced this seemingly 'bespoke' material.[22] As Kimmings identifies, though, these sorts of texts sit somewhat awkwardly between the play as conventionally understood and what might be thought of as performance documentation.

There is, as Matthew Reason (2006) has explored, a tension within performance practice and scholarship between documentation and disappearance, which is latent in Kimmings' discussion. Notions of transience, liveness and ephemerality are prominent and highly valued by theatre-makers and scholars alike, while at the same time some form of documentation is necessary to prevent performance from being forgotten. Sometimes, the debates among these different discourses follow similar contours to oppositions between text and performance. Indeed, values connected to the ephemerality and transience of performance have often been wielded in resistance to the perceived stability and permanence of the text. As Reason notes, disappearance has become 'more than a description, and more even than an ontology, but also a moral, political and attitudinal statement and assertion of the importance and value of performance' (2006: 13). But he persuasively argues that, rather than existing in an antagonistic or irreconcilable relationship, discourses of disappearance and documentation are two sides of the same coin; they are 'inherently interdependent, self-fulfilling and self-perpetuating' (27). Just as the notion of performance disappearing is reliant on the fact that *something* remains, documentation is as much defined by what *cannot* be documented as by what is captured for posterity. Paying attention to documentation is important because, as Reason puts it, 'in the choices of *what* to record, in the manner of *how* to record and indeed in what *can* be recorded, the act of representation defines its subject' (4, original emphasis). Yet the published text as a means of documenting performance practice (rather than as a piece of writing that precedes performance) remains under-explored. Reason's otherwise wide-ranging study, for example, does not – with the exception of a brief discussion of Forced Entertainment's written documentation of *Emanuelle Enchanted* – look at publicly available texts produced by theatre-makers as a form of documentation, focusing instead on archives, academic research, video recordings, photography, and reviewing. This may be partly explained by the relative paucity of such published texts until very recently, but I wonder if it's also a reflection of the anti-text bias of Performance Studies and the polemical position of some theatre-makers who have seen the rejection of text as a form of political and artistic resistance. In the following discussion, I begin addressing this gap by examining the particular status of the published performance text as document.

As seen above, more and more theatre-makers and companies whose processes do not begin with a pre-written text are choosing to represent their work on the page. The value of publication was recognised early by companies like Complicite, who have been publishing their texts since the 1990s. While pointedly eschewing what they perceive to be playtexts, Forced Entertainment have also been assiduous in documenting their work, as I go on to explore.[23] But it's only in the last decade or so that publication has become more common for theatre-makers who – via various processes – devise their shows. As Lyman points out, '[v]irtually all published play texts are […] not only collaborative, but are also simultaneously "post texts" (referencing past performances) and "pre texts" (pointing toward future ones)' (2002: 98). In this sense, the documenting role of these newly published texts is of a piece with more conventional playtexts. Yet the close association between show and company/artist and the fact that the text emerges from rather than preceding performance suggest a distinct textual status for these documents. Examining the case study of Tectonic Theater Project's verbatim show *The Laramie Project*, Worthen suggests that the text of this piece is framed 'less as an instigation of future performance than as the record of past life' (2005: 90), and as such sees this text as more novelistic than dramatic. This then raises the question of whether certain performance texts which have resulted from devising processes and which are only published *after* production can even be understood as playtexts per se, or whether – as suggested by Lavery's designation of the 'postscript' – they are different sorts of document entirely.

There's certainly an ambivalence to be found in many of these texts. By looking at the stage directions in some of these scripts, it's possible to discern their complex mix of practical direction and descriptive reconstruction, gesturing towards the dual role of the page as both instigator and documenter. Take, for instance, this passage from Complicite's *The Street of Crocodiles* (1992):

> **Joseph** *looks behind him. He is surprised to see these people. He looks away. They laugh and form themselves into little groups, as if at tables in an open-air café courtyard. He looks back. These are the groups behind him:* **Agatha, Charles** *and* **Emil** *left,* **Leon, Theodore** *and* **Adela** *right.* **Mother** *and* **Father** *USR.* **Maria** *centre.* (2003: 13)

Some elements of this chunk of description unambiguously direct themselves to the practical business of staging, such as the references to the positioning of the actors, whose placement is expressed in terms of the technical conventions of the stage (left, right, USR) rather than in terms of the fictional world. Certain descriptions, such as those of Joseph's reactions, merge instruction to the actor and reconstruction for the reader, while other sentences participate more clearly in what Worthen calls the 'novelization' of the script. The note about the characters '*form[ing] themselves into little groups, as if at tables in an open-air café courtyard*', while conveying an image that could potentially guide a director and performers, seems more geared towards enabling the reader to create a picture of the scene in their mind. A similar oscillation can be observed in the published texts of Anthony Neilson's recent plays, which have been created with input from the original cast and not published until after their premiere. For example, Neilson describes his 2013 play *Narrative*, which was written during rehearsals in a collaborative process responding to actors' improvisations, as 'essentially a transcript of a live event' (2018: 168). Some lines in the published text are offered merely as guidance, with actors encouraged to improvise in performance, while the stage directions include time-specific links to YouTube clips, which Neilson notes could be replaced for future productions. As well as offering suggestions, the stage directions document elements of the premiere production and its performance contexts, such as the following note that comes after the character Zawe (named for original cast member Zawe Ashton) enters singing '*a bad version of a song*':

> *though you may choose your own song, in the original production,* **Zawe** *sang David Bowie's 'Where Are We Now?' which was appropriate both thematically and because, having just been released, there was much talk of it on social media. Note also that* **Zawe** *got the lyrics wrong, singing 'walking the dog' instead of 'walking the dead'.* (172)

In these examples, as well as in texts published by companies such as Kneehigh, Filter, and Curious Directive and by writer-performers like Kimmings, there appear to be competing desires to, on the one hand, accurately document performance, and on the other hand to create a more novelistic text that guides the reader's imagination with rich, evocative descriptions between sections of dialogue. And, of course, these texts all gesture – more or less explicitly – towards the possibility of other, future performances.

When considering the different possible functions of performance texts in this vein, Forced Entertainment is a fascinating example because of both its resistance to any notion of 'fixing' its work in text and the paradoxically extensive nature of the company's documentation. In an interview with Reason, Tim Etchells identified two parallel approaches that the company has taken towards the documentation of its performance work. There is what Etchells calls 'extreme pragmatism, without ideology', which has motivated the video documentation of shows for use by theatre programmers, teachers, and students; and 'a more nuanced approach that seeks to "proliferate traces of work in a more artistic nature"' (2006: 57). This latter category includes some of the company's written documentations of its work, such as those published in *Certain Fragments* (1999). Here and elsewhere, the texts of Forced Entertainment's shows are framed by Etchells' theoretical writings, which typically seek to work against what he perceives as the stabilising force of publication. The performance texts themselves mostly consist of the written and displayed texts used in the shows, in a presentational format that resists setting out anything resembling instructions. The text of *Speak Bitterness* (1994), for example, is one long block of text containing a selection of the many confessions read out in different orders and combinations in each performance of the show, while the version of *Emanuelle Enchanted* (1992) published in *Certain Fragments* contains the various spoken texts used in the show, as well as a long list of the titles written out on cardboard signs that were held up by the performers at various moments. The tendency, in both the texts themselves and the notes that precede them, is to emphasise the role of these pieces of writing as partial documentation. As Reason notes, the driving logic and aesthetic of Forced Entertainment's self-representation is one of fragmentation, reflecting the often fragmentary and deconstructive nature of the performances themselves. He suggests, though, that through this form of documentation 'ironically, fragmentation becomes the grand narrative, the overarching and stable meaning, at the same time that (ostensibly) such stable meanings are explicitly rejected' (2006: 63). Here, Reason re-iterates the old opposition between performance and documentation. He acknowledges that fragmentation as a theme also dominates Forced Entertainment's shows, but argues that this is mitigated by 'the multiple layers and diversities of performance as a medium' (ibid.), therefore implying that performance possesses a multiplicity and indeterminacy that is denied to the more 'fixed' domain of documentation.

Reason, like Etchells, also retains an investment in differentiating these texts from plays, firmly positioning them as documents rather than scripts. Discussing an earlier version of *Emanuelle Enchanted* published in *Contemporary Theatre Review*, which omitted any explanation of the show's structure and included ambiguous illustrations and photographs without any indication of what these depict in relation to the text (Forced Entertainment 1994), Reason states that 'it would be impossible to re-create *Emanuelle Enchanted*' from this documentation (2006: 60). He thus seems to disqualify this publication as a theatre text in the commonly understood sense. While he's right that the notes and fragments contained in this version of the piece do not offer enough information for other theatre-makers to produce a precise replica of the show as performed by Forced Entertainment, this does not mean that it is not iter*able* in the way that I have argued is characteristic of all theatre texts. It's no more impossible to create a new performance – a new *iteration* of the text – using the fragments in any of Forced Entertainment's published performance texts than it is to create a new production of a play like *4.48 Psychosis*. This point retraces the argument made in Chapter 1, where I suggested that so-called 'writing for theatre' is not fundamentally different from more conventional dramatic writing, despite observable contrasts in its form and approach.

Yet while the iterability that is characteristic of playtexts also extends to these other sorts of theatre text, there is perhaps a distinction that can be made in the *type* or *degree* of doubleness that can be found across different sorts of text for theatre. In an attempt to pin down what distinguishes plays from other forms of theatre-making, Julia Jarcho suggests that a play on the page promises that it's 'all ready to manifest in performance' (2017: 116), while the play in performance correspondingly promises 'that a text was the origin of this performance, and that even as the performance passes by, its possibility will persist, stored up – as it were – between the pages of the script' (ibid.). It is these 'treacherous promises' (ibid.), as Jarcho calls them, that set plays apart from other kinds of text used in theatre. While these promises are ultimately illusory in their projections of a complete performance ready to spring off the page or of a text that endures as a stable repository of meanings, a doubled awareness of performance-in-text and text-in-performance is a central and troublesome characteristic of plays that is not true in quite the same way of all performances using text. My aim in this book is not to erase all distinctions between different types of theatre text, but to scrutinise the often essentialist and reductive categories that have traditionally obscured the complex relationships between texts and performances of all kinds. Though differences remain, looking again at the boundaries perceived to separate supposedly fluid and fragmentary performance documentation from 'fixed' playtexts allows a more nuanced understanding of how text and performance interact. Reason suggests that '[i]f performance neither disappears, nor fully resides in its documentations, then it seems appropriate to think of the continued cultural manifestation of performance as located somewhere in the space and time between' (2006: 232). I'm trying to capture something similar in thinking of theatre as residing not in texts or in performances, but somehow both/between. This thinking is further complicated, however, by another space in which plays now exist: on the screens of our digital devices.

Plays in the digital space

In the late 20th century, McGann presciently observed 'a move into a space of electronically mediated communication where "texts" adopt and require various kinds of simultaneous yet multiple engagements' (1990: 95). Students and researchers with access to the ever-expanding digital resources of university libraries are now as likely to encounter a play on an online platform or as an e-book as they are to read these texts in print. As noted above, several scholars have suggested that we are therefore now departing – or have already departed – the age of print. N. Katherine Hayles proposes the compelling term 'postprint' to describe the current situation, using the prefix 'post' to imply 'both succession and displacement, continuation and rupture' (2021: 2). She argues that the second half of the 20th century 'constitutes a rupture in the genealogy of printed books' (ibid.), applying the term 'postprint' to all books produced in the aftermath of this break. Others, meanwhile, have seen the evolution of digital technology and its influence on print in less disruptive terms. Kiene Brillenburg Wurth, for example, posits a more reciprocal relationship between print and digital technologies, insisting that 'the book and the many metaphors it embodies continues to haunt digital screens' (2012: 8). But however this shift is conceived – whether as a rupture or as something more gradual – and whenever it's placed historically, it's clear that there has been a significant change in how we read texts of all kinds and that this change requires further investigation. In the fields of literary and textual studies, there have been analyses of electronic literature and discussions of the impact of digital texts on bibliography, while theatre scholars have explored the use of digital technologies in performance and the implications for documentation and archiving in the digital age.[24] To date, though, little attention has been given to the digital texts of plays as they appear in e-books, on platforms like Digital Theatre, and in other electronic forms. These new platforms potentially generate opportunities for thinking afresh about playtexts. As observed in this chapter, theatre texts have long contained important elements other than the words that actors speak on stage, from illustrations to punctuation marks to the arrangement of blank space. There's the possibility, though, that digital publishing might make this more readily apparent. While extra-linguistic features are not new to published drama, digital media may, as Daniela Côrtes Maduro suggests, 'seem to reinforce this idea, and to demonstrate that texts are not anchored in verbal language' (2017: 9). This is an intriguing idea, presenting the possibility that the evolution of theatre texts on digital platforms might further break down some of the assumptions about text and performance that I have been unpicking throughout this book. It's therefore worth exploring whether this potential is being realised in practice.

The growth of digital play platforms aimed at students has unquestionably transformed the play publishing landscape in recent years. In particular, Bloomsbury's Drama Online platform, which now holds collections from Methuen, Faber and Faber, Arden Shakespeare, Oberon and Nick Hern Books (alongside collections from North American play publishers), as well as audio and video recordings from companies including the National Theatre and the Royal Shakespeare Company, has had a significant impact on how plays are accessed and experienced. At the time of writing, their library features more than 3,750 playtexts, over 400 audio plays and 400 hours of video (Drama Online 2022). Alongside this, most new plays can now be purchased as e-books, while various forms of performance documentation – including video recordings, texts, images, and commentaries – have been made available through websites such as Digital

Theatre Plus and the Routledge Performance Archive.[25] Users can now rapidly toggle between these different materials, arguably generating a sense of increased porosity between text and performance. In some instances, digitally available video recordings of live performances also have an accompanying transcript, adding another layer of text that overlaps with but is not identical to the text published in the digital and print editions of the script. To take just one example, Tim Crouch's play *I, Malvolio* (2010) can be accessed as a video recording of a performance captured in 2015 on the Routledge Performance Archive, alongside a transcript of this specific live enactment of the show (Crouch 2016), and as a digitally published script on Drama Online (Crouch 2011b). Comparing the two texts side by side, while also watching the recorded performance, viewers may become aware of the slippages between all three, perceiving each as just one mutable element of the ever-changing entity that is *I, Malvolio*.

Initially, the texts available through these digital channels were limited to more conventionally formatted playtexts, though this is beginning to change. As of 2022, Drama Online now hosts several Oberon-published texts containing unconventional typographical and graphical elements, including texts discussed earlier in the book such as RashDash's *Two Man Show* and *Three Sisters*, and Crouch and Jadhav's *Total Immediate Collective Imminent Terrestrial Salvation*. However, the extent to which the digital editions of these plays enable formal innovation and 'demonstrate that texts are not anchored in verbal language' is debateable. In some cases, what is being done on the printed page cannot be adequately assimilated into the digital space, and the process of digitisation reduces rather than multiplies the complexity of the text. For example, the online version of *Total Immediate Collective Imminent Terrestrial Salvation* reproduces Jadhav's illustrations on the screen, but the dynamic tactile experience of turning the page – which is integral to the aesthetic of the piece – is lost. Inserted as images within the long column of scrolling text, meanwhile, the size and visual impact of Jadhav's drawings is diminished and the ratio of illustration to text in the reader's experience of the play is altered. While hovering the cursor over the text does produce page breaks, these are much less apparent in the online version, lending the initial impression of long blocks of dialogue, as opposed to the purposefully spaced pages of the printed book. And whereas in the printed version text and image are made permeable on pages in which linguistic characters become part of the illustrations, this effect is lost on screen. In this instance, the online platform flattens the text and dilutes its visual experimentation.[26] Likewise, it remains unclear whether a digital interface like Drama Online can accommodate the typographical playfulness of books like *Action Plans* – which, at the time of writing, is not available electronically.

Though it's therefore worth being wary of any attempt to identify an inherent link between digital platforms and a more porous, complex, and multifaceted understanding of the relationship between text and performance, digital technologies have enabled experiments with text that pose intriguing possibilities for the future. In recent years, writers and theatre-makers have increasingly experimented with using digital platforms as theatrical mediums in their own right, rather than as just another means for disseminating text. Seda Ilter (2021) has coined the useful term 'mediaturgical plays' for describing such texts, which not only represent or engage with digital media but use these media as an integral part of their dramaturgy. One striking example of this is David Greig's *The Yes/No Plays*: a series of scenes composed on social media site Twitter, revolving around the Scottish Independence Referendum of 2014. These short, loosely connected scenes unfolded over multiple tweets posted using the Twitter handle @YesNoPlays, capturing interactions between the two characters Yes and No (as well as other peripheral figures), each representing one side of the referendum debate. *The Yes/No Plays* were started by Greig in December 2013 and the most recent tweet at the time of writing is dated 18 April 2017. The tweets were also edited by Greig into a script that was performed at the Traverse Theatre on the day of the referendum, and several of the scenes are collected together in a version published online (Greig 2014).[27] While I do not find Ilter's designation of *The Yes/No Plays* as 'no longer dramatic' particularly helpful, for all the reasons discussed in my consideration of postdramatic theatre in the Introduction, she does pose compelling questions about how such texts might reconfigure our understanding of plays and performances. As she notes, 'the line between writing and performance in these works is far from stable, meaning that the definition of "play" is itself made problematic' (2021: 177). Ilter identifies a 'double-layered' structure in mediaturgical plays, which may be 'performed' live for an online audience as well as later receiving a production in a physical theatre space, as was the case with *The Yes/No Plays*. This type of writing provokes a reconsideration of definitions of terms like 'liveness', 'performance', and 'audience', which might now incorporate online spectators.

There's not room to fully explore the implications of such a reconsideration here, but one aspect of mediaturgical plays that is of particular interest in the context of this study is the way in which they expand and multiply the theatrical text. In addition to the 'double-layered' structure that Ilter observes, texts like *The Yes/No Plays* incorporate the marginal annotations of online audiences, who can use the social media platform on which the play is published as a way of adding to the drama in real time. Other Twitter users often commented on @YesNoPlays' tweets, with Greig occasionally tweeting responses 'in character' as Yes and No.[28] To what extent, then, can these replies be considered part of the text of *The Yes/No Plays*? Are they simply audience responses, specific to the initial online iteration of this play? Or does Greig's practice of incorporating these replies into the unfolding dramatic dialogue fold them into the fabric of the playtext? These questions remain unresolved, generating a productive tension that exposes texts and performances to renewed scrutiny in the context of continuing experimentation with digital technologies. While Ilter suggests that the 'double ontology' of mediaturgical plays might offer 'another way of thinking about text and performance in theatre' (2021: 188), she does not expand on this potential. Rather than contrasting the ongoing, interactive evolution of a play on Twitter with 'the ephemerality of performance and the completeness of dramatic writing' (ibid.), thus reinforcing a reductive opposition between text and performance, I contend that the apparent openness and multiplicity of mediaturgical plays enables a broader rethink of how we conceptualise texts for theatre. This is a nascent area that requires further research, building on Ilter's insights and on the ideas briefly outlined here.

Since early 2020, furthermore, the COVID-19 pandemic and the associated shutdown of theatre venues for many months has accelerated theatre-makers' engagement with the possibilities of disseminating their work digitally, promising a continued exploration of the questions I have begun to discuss in this section. While much of the theatre work made available online during the pandemic was attempting to reproduce the in-person theatrical experience as closely as possible, either through live or archive video recordings, there were also many pieces that might be defined as 'mediaturgical' or as 'technotexts', which are 'partly or fully produced, structured and performed through digital-media platforms', with the media technology acting as 'a material and cultural environment that shapes the form and formation of the text' (Ilter 2018: 69). Examples include Forced Entertainment's *End Meeting for All* (2020), which played with the aesthetic and affective structures of video-conferencing platforms; the online version of Javaad Alipoor's *Rich Kids: A History of Shopping Malls in Tehran* (2020), which already incorporated social media (specifically, Instagram) in its previous, in-person iteration; and *You Just Don't Get It – And It Hurts* (2020), a short video performance by Fehinti Balogun which dramatised a conversation about racism as a series of text messages. In the latter piece, which was structured as a nine-minute screen recording of an unfolding exchange of messages between two friends – one white, one Black – text itself was, in a sense, the performer. Shown from the perspective of the unnamed Black protagonist, the digital frame allowed access to this character's messages as they were being composed, conveying meaning through the halting process of typing, editing and erasing. In another intriguing example of digital performance, Crouch extended his explorations of liveness and audience involvement into the online space with a new version of his play *I, Cinna (the Poet)* reimagined for video-conferencing platform Zoom. Using Zoom's comment function, this interactive online performance folded a further layer of textual contributions from audience members into yet another iteration of a play that had previously been staged in multiple productions. Now that COVID-19 restrictions have been lifted and theatre buildings have reopened, it remains to be seen whether these experiments will have a lasting impact on theatrical practice and its interaction with digital spaces and technologies.

Observing the impact of late 20th- and early 21st-century technological developments, Wurth asserts that '[l]iterature no longer has a single material location, and one may wonder if it ever had one' (2012: 1). Of course, one of the troubling things about drama from a literary perspective is the way in which it complicates the idea of a unified location for the literary work. Plays have never had 'a single material location'. In the digital age, as more attention is concentrated on the different material locations of all texts, the ways in which theatre texts – as well as performances – evade the desire for a unified 'work' might become increasingly apparent. Speaking to this sense of non-unity, Maduro stresses the dispersal of digital texts, which 'exist elsewhere, in our devices, or spread across the web' (2017: 9). In this context, '[l]ocating the text – or bringing it to the surface – has become an intrinsic part of the reading act' (ibid.). As Hayles points out, 'in the postprint era hard copy becomes merely one kind of output among many possible displays' (2021: 3) – an observation that might be extended to various forms of printed and digital performance documentation, available on a multiplying array of platforms and devices. The thing that we call, for example, *I, Malvolio* exists as a printed play in different editions, as any one of multiple live performances, as a digitised text on a computer, tablet, or smartphone screen, as an e-book on an e-reader, as a scrolling transcript of a specific performance, as a video recording – the list goes on. When users access so many of these assorted documents on the same device, meanwhile, there's the potential to unsettle hard, hierarchised divisions between different textual and performative iterations. Discussing the proliferation of online texts and performances, which has only accelerated in the years since he made this observation, Worthen notes that 'performance is delivered through the same medium as writing, the screen, and is technically identical to writing, composed of bits of binary code' (2010: 7). Here, then, oppositions between text and performance have the potential to melt away, dispersing into countless 0s and 1s. This promises to be another rich area for future research. While digital versions of playtexts have, to date, largely reproduced the conventions of the printed page, the digital environment multiplies the possibilities for how we encounter written texts, in ways that might well disrupt the perceived authority of the playtext. Now that multiple editions, annotations, and recordings of performance(s) can all exist in the same digital space, it may finally become easier to conceptualise plays as multiple, mutable things.

Conclusion

Throughout this chapter and the book as a whole, I have sought to examine the relationship between text and performance in a way that accounts for its inherent complexity. My investigation of this relationship recognises what Worthen calls 'the drama's two lives' (2010: xii), on the page (or screen) and on the stage, challenging many of the assumptions about playtexts that have shaped British theatre practices, institutions, and discourses. Starting from an acknowledgement of the playtext's paradoxical doubleness, which has proved troubling for many scholars and practitioners alike, I have revisited models of theatrical authorship; unsettled the notion of the complete dramatic 'work'; explored the ongoing mutual exchange between texts, performances and their contexts; and investigated the multiplicity of ways in which playtexts have appeared on pages and screens. In the process, I've explored some of the many and various lives of text in contemporary British theatre, from revivals of the canon to devised performances to dramaturgically innovative new plays. In this chapter, that exploration has been taken further by looking more closely at the play's existence as a series of texts, both in a variety of printed formats and on digital platforms.

The practices analysed in these pages are worthy of attention in their own right as innovations of theatrical form and as meditations on the medium itself. This book has brought together a diverse range of shows and theatre-makers who share a self-reflexive concern with the very nature of the theatre text and its relationship to performance. As I have reiterated throughout the preceding chapters, these examples challenge certain conventions and dominant understandings that are specific to the theatre culture that produced them, while demonstrating the essential characteristics of *all* theatre texts. Both texts and performances are by their nature simultaneously complete and incomplete, while remaining forever incommensurable. Each individual printed/digital text and each individual performance is just one iteration, one supplement for an ever-absent, illusory 'work', which can never fully contain or express the intentions of its creators. These seemingly paradoxical complexities have made the theatre text tricky for literary critics, theatre scholars and artists alike. It is possible that the pressure exerted on the text-performance dynamic by the practices discussed in this book are indicative of a crisis point in this long-problematic relationship, which may in turn lead to a new conception of the interplay between page and stage within a British context. My analysis throughout the book has aimed to be part of this evolution in our shared understanding of the art form.

While some of this book's theoretical investigations may seem abstracted and somewhat detached from the messy realities of practice, shared conceptualisations of texts and performances sit beneath and inform how theatre is funded, programmed, staged, and discussed. In this sense, then, the work that I have undertaken here might have many practical implications for theatre-makers. Armed with an understanding of theatre texts as mutable and iterable things, it may be possible to begin questioning, subverting, and maybe even restructuring the institutional frameworks that have been built upon earlier misrepresentations of the relationship between text and performance. But I also write with an awareness of the hazards of discussing the present and the recent past. The analysis in these pages may soon be overtaken by new developments in practice and new shifts in the organisational structures of the British theatre sector. The ideas that I have put forward here, then, are intended to be flexible and open to future challenges and expansions. It's also worth questioning the very possibility of formulating a critical lexicon that could successfully account for the complex relationship between text and performance and for the multiplicity of ever-evolving theatre practices. At a symposium organised to explore some of the ideas that have since developed into this book, Andy Field suggested that what was really being discussed on a panel about the 'text-based'/'non-text-based' divide was 'the nuances and the contradictions and the complications and the messiness and the personalities of any development process suffering under the weight of institutions' (Love 2015a). His contention was that 'every single creative process ever is going to be too complicated or too nonsensical to be able to be described neatly by the institutions that are attempting to do so' (ibid.). It might be suggested, then, that any vocabulary is as insufficient as the next. However, the attempts of institutions, critics and scholars to describe creative practice have material implications. The inaccuracy of institutional vocabularies becomes a problem when those vocabularies are used as part of the arsenal of justification for supporting, funding or promoting certain practices over others, as seen in my discussion of subsidy in Chapter 1.

The critical terminologies that we as scholars apply to theatre may be always and inevitably flawed, but they have repercussions nonetheless. We should, therefore, remain alert to these repercussions and open to a continual reassessment and reformulation of our vocabularies in response to such impacts on theatre-makers, as well as in response to changing ideological contexts. By dismantling reductive and binarised conceptualisations of text and performance, we may afford ourselves the opportunity of digging deeper, of addressing the ideological underpinnings and implications of individual pieces of theatre, rather than becoming burdened and blinkered by the baggage of inherited terms. Any new conceptual framework for considering texts and performances must thus admit to its own flaws and be alert to shifting contexts, with the flexibility to shift alongside these. By leaving certain questions open or not fully resolved, I have attempted to acknowledge the complexity of the problem that this book addresses and the need for ongoing explorations of the dynamic interaction between text and performance. But while no study can conclusively theorise the theatre text in a way that's futureproof – because, as I've discussed, texts and their contexts are constantly changing – my aim has been to further nuance understandings of the complicated and fascinating relationship between text and performance. By engaging with the 'problem' of the theatre text in this way, it becomes possible to more fully appreciate and analyse the many roles that text plays in contemporary British theatre-making.

Notes

1. Examples of this attempt to determine authoritative texts include editorial practices that have sought to reconstruct the 'original', 'authorial' versions of early modern plays – especially Shakespeare's plays.
2. Important early examples include the collected works of Ben Jonson and Shakespeare, as well as the Beaumont and Fletcher folio published by Moseley and Robinson in 1647, which is accorded particular significance in the accounts of both Peters and Pitcher.
3. There are examples of this from the 17th, 18th and 19th centuries, including prominent figures like Ben Jonson (perhaps the first English playwright to see print as a way of fashioning a literary, authorial persona) and Henry Arthur Jones.
4. An account of some of the editorial practices and debates surrounding Shakespeare's plays can be found in Walsh's chapter on scholarly editing in 18th-century Britain (2009).
5. Worthen has looked in considerable detail at the design of Shaw's printed plays and its implications for how readers understand these plays as both text and performance (2005: 39–57).
6. The phrase was introduced in Jay David Bolter's book *Writing Space: Computers, Hypertext, and the Remediation of Print* (2001) and its implications have been explored at length by Ted Striphas in *The Late Age of Print* (2009), which looks at how the book industry has adapted to changes driven by digital technology.

7 In their account of 20th-century dramatic publishing, Nash and Potter stress the divide between reading and acting editions, highlighting the prominent role of publisher Samuel French (2019: 312), which continues to publish acting editions in the 21st century.
8 David Edgar notes that more than half of the over 500 plays published by Nick Hern Books in the 2010s were playtext programmes (2021: 235).
9 Another contemporary play that has undergone considerable changes during its publishing history is Duncan Macmillan and Robert Icke's adaptation of *1984*, which went through a number of editions as the production changed during its initial run and subsequent tour (Spender 2015). Similarly, Scenario 13 of *Attempts on Her Life* by Martin Crimp is entirely different in the 1997 and 2007 versions of the play. In the earlier published text, this scenario is titled 'JUNGFRAU (WORD ASSOCIATION)' and describes an encounter between a young woman and a married man (Crimp 1997: 58); in the later version, there is a scenario called 'COMMUNICATING WITH ALIENS', which discusses alien technology (Crimp 2007: 64).
10 The one exception to this is the monologue at the end of scene 5, which in the playtext programme version shares a page with the first part of scene 6, which consists of just a stage direction (Churchill 2016).
11 The economics of different forms of publishing plays a role here; the acting edition is priced £1 lower than the playtext programme.
12 This development arguably began before the period under consideration in this book. For example, Caryl Churchill is commonly credited with introducing the forward slash as an indication of overlapping dialogue in the 1980s.
13 I've reproduced the spacing used in both the playtext programme (Kane 2000) and in Kane's *Complete Plays* (2001). Notably, spacing, page layout, and number of pages are all identical across these two published versions of the play; it's only the surrounding textual material (such as the biographies of the company in the playtext programme version) that differs. Perhaps because the play was performed and published posthumously, there appears to be an enhanced investment in formatting the page in precisely the same way across editions, reinforcing the impression of a single, authorised version of the text.
14 Although tucker green's work is frequently positioned within a lineage of (white) British experimental playwrights such as Kane, it's important to acknowledge the ways in which her writing also draws on Afro-Caribbean and African American oral storytelling traditions, the music of pioneering Black female artists, and the politicised poetry of first and second generation British Caribbean writers. Deirdre Osborne cites the influence of poets such as Louise Bennett, John La Rose, Andrew Salkey, James Berry, Linton Kwesi-Johnson, John Agard, Grace Nichols, Valerie Bloom, and Jean Binta Breeze (2020), while tucker green herself has cited the importance of Bennett alongside African American songwriters Jill Scott and Lauryn Hill.
15 David Ian Rabey, for example, describes tucker green's texts as 'dramatic scores' (2020), while director Tinuke Craig suggests that 'she really uses consonants and vowels in the same way that you might think about beats in music' (quoted in Bowie-Sell 2018).
16 A poem like 'Karawane' by Dada artist Hugo Ball (1917) is a particularly interesting comparison, both for its transcription of non-linguistic sound and for the ways in which the printed version attempted to capture Ball's anarchic performance style on the page through the use of a combination of different typefaces.
17 There's a clear similarity here with Suzan-Lori Parks' 'spells': scenes consisting purely of speech prefixes, with no accompanying dialogue.
18 Belgian theatre company Ontroerend Goed's *All Work and No Plays* (2014), also published by Oberon Books, was a key forerunner of the innovative use of the page in *Action Plans*.
19 The contents of these left-hand pages were first created for the *Hoke's Bluff Playbook*, designed by the company in collaboration with Jessie Price and produced to be sold at performances (Action Hero 2013). It was in fact this document that led Oberon Books to approach Action Hero about publishing its work (Spender 2021).

20 One notable exception is the text of *seven methods of killing kylie jenner*, which was published as a standard Royal Court playtext programme to coincide with the production but is far more graphically and typographically creative than most other texts produced in this way.
21 Since instigating this discussion, Kimmings has published texts of her shows *Credible Likeable Superstar Role Model* (2013), *Fake It 'Til You Make It* (2015), *A Pacifist's Guide to the War on Cancer* (2016), and *I'm a Phoenix, Bitch* (2021).
22 Indeed, Thompson's play *salt.* (2017), which was based on the theatre-maker's own experiences of racism and inherited trauma and her journey retracing the route of the transatlantic slave trade, has already been performed by another actor.
23 Other theatre companies who have been publishing the texts of their shows for a longer period include Kneehigh and Filter.
24 See, for example, the work of N. Katherine Hayles (2021) and Jerome McGann (2014) and the edited collection *Digital Media and Textuality* (Maduro 2017). In Performance Studies, examples include *Theatre and Performance in Digital Culture* by Matthew Causey (2006), Steve Dixon's *Digital Performance* (2007), the edited collection *Documenting Performance* (Sant 2017), and Nadja Masura's *Digital Theatre* (2020).
25 It's important to note that many of these platforms are designed primarily for scholars and students and are often rendered inaccessible to audiences beyond those constituencies by prohibitively expensive subscription fees. Their impact, therefore, remains largely confined to academic and training contexts – though these of course feed into the wider theatre sector.
26 A similar effect can be seen in Sh!t Theatre's published performance texts (2017, 2018, 2019). In performance, these pieces are heavily reliant on projected images and video, which add a different texture to the theatrical experience. In the versions of the texts preserved on Drama Online, a small selection of these images become absorbed into the flow of words, which dominate the script.
27 This version of *The Yes/No Plays* only captures tweets published up to 26 January 2014.
28 See, for example, tweets and replies from 7 January 2014 (https://twitter.com/YesNoPlays/status/420570743181549569), 10 January 2014 (https://twitter.com/YesNoPlays/status/421724924579823616), 30 April 2014 (https://twitter.com/YesNoPlays/status/461626983643115520), and 21 April 2014 (https://twitter.com/YesNoPlays/status/458363183666044929).

BIBLIOGRAPHY

Aberg, Maria (2014). Unpublished interview with author.
Abrahami, Natalie (2009). 'Why are we Afraid of Auteurs?' *The Guardian*, 30 April. Available at: https://www.theguardian.com/stage/theatreblog/2009/apr/30/auteur-theatre-director-play [Accessed 14 July 2021].
Acquah, Nikki (2016). 'Reconstruction – Hoke's Bluff Playbook – Action Hero.' Available at: https://jazzhandsandjesus.wordpress.com/2016/11/18/reconstruction-hokes-bluff-playbook-action-hero/ [Accessed 5 July 2021].
Action Hero (2013). *Hoke's Bluff Playbook*. Bristol: Action Hero.
Action Hero (2015). *Action Plans: Selected Performance Pieces*. London: Oberon Books.
Action Hero (2016). *Wrecking Ball*. London: Oberon Books.
Adorno, Theodor W. (2013 [1997]). *Aesthetic Theory*. Translated by Robert Hullot-Kentor. London: Bloomsbury Academic.
Alberge, Dalya (2017). 'David Hare: Classic British drama is 'being infected' by radical European staging.' *The Guardian*, 29 January. Available at: https://www.theguardian.com/stage/2017/jan/29/david-hare-classic-british-drama-infected-radical-european-staging [Accessed 3 March 2021].
Allfree, Claire (2006). 'Review of *The Seagull*.' *Theatre Record 18 June–1 July 2006*. London: Theatre Record Ltd., p. 767.
Alston, Adam (2016). *Beyond Immersive Theatre: Aesthetics, Politics and Productive Participation*. London: Palgrave Macmillan.
Anderson, Benedict (2006). *Imagined Communities: Reflections on the Origin and Spread of Nationalism*. Revised edition. London: Verso.
Andrews, Dennis (1977). 'The Statistics of Subsidy.' *Theatre Quarterly* VII (27), 88–91.
Angelaki, Vicky (Ed.) (2013). *Contemporary British Theatre: Breaking New Ground*. Basingstoke: Palgrave Macmillan.
Ansorge, Peter (1975). *Disrupting the Spectacle: Five Years of Experimental and Fringe Theatre in Britain*. London: Pitman Publishing.
Archer, William (1882). *English Dramatists of Today*. London: Sampson Low, Marston, Searle and Rivington.

Artaud, Antonin (1958). *The Theater and Its Double*. Translated by Mary Caroline Richards. New York: Grove Press.
Arts Council England (ACE) (1996). *Annual Review 1995–1996*.
Arts Council England (ACE) (1998). *Annual Review 1997–1998*.
Arts Council England (ACE) (1999). *Annual Review 1998–1999*.
Arts Council of Great Britain (ACGB) (1951). *Annual Review 1950–1951*.
Arts Council of Great Britain (ACGB) (1952). *Annual Review 1951–1952*.
Arts Council of Great Britain (ACGB) (1953). *Annual Review 1952–1953*.
Arts Council of Great Britain (ACGB) (1954). *Annual Review 1953–1954*.
Arts Council of Great Britain (ACGB) (1957). *Annual Review 1956–1957*.
Arts Council of Great Britain (ACGB) (1959). *Annual Review 1958–1959*.
Arts Council of Great Britain (ACGB) (1966). *Annual Review 1965–1966*.
Arts Council of Great Britain (ACGB) (1967). *Annual Review 1966–1967*.
Arts Council of Great Britain (ACGB) (1969). *Annual Review 1968–1969*.
Arts Council of Great Britain (ACGB) (1974). *Annual Review 1973–1974*.
Arts Council of Great Britain (ACGB) (1975). *Annual Review 1974–1975*.
Arts Council of Great Britain (ACGB) (1976). *Annual Review 1975–1976*.
Arts Council of Great Britain (ACGB) (1977). *Annual Review 1976–1977*.
Arts Council of Great Britain (ACGB) (1979). *Annual Review 1978–1979*.
Arts Council of Great Britain (ACGB) (1986). *Annual Review 1985–1986*.
Arts Council of Great Britain (ACGB) (1990). *Annual Review 1989–1990*.
Arts Council of Northern Ireland (2022). *Drama*. Available at: http://artscouncil-ni.org/the-arts/performing-arts1/drama [Accessed 1 June 2022].
Auerbach, Nina (2004). 'Before the Curtain'. In Kerry Powell (Ed.), *The Cambridge Companion to Victorian and Edwardian Theatre*. Cambridge: Cambridge University Press, pp. 3–14.
Austin, J. L. (1976). *How to Do Things with Words*. London: Oxford University Press.
Ball, Hugo (1917). *Karawane and Dada Kasserole*. Available at: https://library-artstor-org.libproxy.york.ac.uk/asset/ARTSTOR_103_41822001752540 [Accessed 22 September 2021].
Barish, Jonas (1981). *The Antitheatrical Prejudice*. Berkeley: University of California Press.
Barnett, David (2008). 'When Is a Play Not a Drama? Two Examples of Postdramatic Theatre Texts.' *New Theatre Quarterly* 24 (1), 14–23.
Barthes, Roland (1977 [1967]). 'The Death of the Author.' In *Image Music Text*. Translated by Stephen Heath. London: Harper Collins, pp. 142–148.
Barthes, Roland (1986). *The Rustle of Language*. Translated by Richard Howard. Oxford: Basil Blackwell.
Bartlett, Neil (2013). 'Bringing Glamour to the Masses; The Lyric Hammersmith 1994–2004.' In Lois Keidan and C.J. Mitchell (Eds.), *Programme Notes: Case Studies for Locating Experimental Theatre*. London: Oberon Books, pp. 110–118.
Bassett, Kate (2015). 'Review of *Oresteia*'. In *Theatre Record: 27 August–9 September 2015*. London: Theatre Record Ltd., p. 867.
Bassnett, Susan (2014). *Translation*. Abingdon: Routledge.
Bennett, Benjamin (1990). *Theater as Problem: Modern Drama and Its Place in Literature*. Ithaca: Cornell University Press.
Bennett, Benjamin (2005). *All Theater Is Revolutionary Theater*. Ithaca, N.Y.: Cornell University Press.
Billington, Michael (2006). 'Review of *The Seagull*.' *Theatre Record 18 June–1 July 2006*. London: Theatre Record Ltd., p. 763.

Billington, Michael (2007). *State of the Nation: British Theatre since 1945*. London: Faber.
Billington, Michael (2009). 'Don't let auteurs take over in theatre.' *The Guardian*, 14 April. Available at: https://www.theguardian.com/stage/theatreblog/2009/apr/14/auteur-theatre [Accessed 14 July 2021].
Billington, Michael (2012). 'D is for director's theatre.' *The Guardian*, 3 January. Available at: https://www.theguardian.com/stage/2012/jan/03/d-director-s-theatre-modern-drama [Accessed 3 March 2021].
Billington, Michael (2013). 'Is it OK to rewrite classic plays?' *The Guardian*, 2 July. Available at: https://www.theguardian.com/stage/2013/jul/02/is-it-ok-rewrite-classic-plays [Accessed 3 March 2021].
Billington, Michael (2020). 'Review of *The Wild Duck*.' *Theatre Record 01–31 October 2018*. London: Theatre Record Ltd., p. 960.
Birch, Alice (2017). *Anatomy of a Suicide*. London: Oberon Books.
Birch, Alice (2018). *[BLANK]*. London: Oberon Books.
Blythe, Alecky (2014). *Little Revolution*. London: Nick Hern Books.
Boenisch, Peter M. (2010). 'Towards a Theatre of Encounter and Experience: Reflexive Dramaturgies and Classic Texts.' *Contemporary Theatre Review* 20 (2), 162–172.
Boenisch, Peter M. (2015). *Directing Scenes and Senses: The Thinking of Regie*. Manchester: Manchester University Press.
Bolter, Jay David (2001). *Writing Space: Computers, Hypertext, and the Remediation of Print*. Abingdon: Routledge.
Bolton, Jacqueline (2011). *Demarcating Dramaturgy: Mapping Theory onto Practice*. Unpublished: University of Leeds. PhD.
Bolton, Jacqueline (2012). 'Capitalizing (on) New Writing: New Play Development in the 1990s.' *Studies in Theatre and Performance* 32 (2), 209–225.
Bolton, Jacqueline (Ed.) (2014). *Pornography* by Simon Stephens. Student edition. London: Bloomsbury Methuen Drama.
Bottoms, Stephen (2009a). 'Editorial: Performing Literatures.' *Performance Research* 14 (1), 1–5.
Bottoms, Stephen (2009b). 'Authorizing the Audience: The Conceptual Drama of Tim Crouch.' *Performance Research* 14 (1), 65–76.
Bratton, Jacky (2003). *New Readings in Theatre History*. Cambridge: Cambridge University Press.
Breach Theatre (2017). *Tank*. London: Oberon Books.
British Theatre Consortium (BTC) (2009). *Writ Large: New Writing on the British Stage 2003–2009*.
British Theatre Consortium (BTC) (2016). *British Theatre Repertoire 2014*.
Brown, Ian (2011). 'Introduction: A Lively Tradition and Creative Amnesia.' In Ian Brown (Ed.), *The Edinburgh Companion to Scottish Drama*. Edinburgh: Edinburgh University Press, pp. 1–5.
Brown, Ian, Robert Brannen, and Douglas Brown (2000). 'The Arts Council Touring Franchise and English Political Theatre after 1986'. *New Theatre Quarterly* 16 (4.4), 379–387.
Brown, John Russell (Ed.) (1968). *Modern British Dramatists: A Collection of Critical Essays*. Englewood Cliffs, N.J.: Prentice-Hall, Inc.
Bull, John (Ed.) (2016). *British Theatre Companies: 1965–1979*. London: Bloomsbury Methuen Drama.
Bull, John (2018). 'Add-Aptation: Simon Stephens, Carrie Cracknell and Katie Mitchell's 'Dialogues' with the Classic Canon.' *Journal of Contemporary Drama in English* 6 (2), 280–299.

Bullock, Philip Ross. (2017). 'An Antidote to Ibsen? British Responses to Chekhov and the Legacy of Naturalism.' In Geraldine Brodie and Emma Cole (Eds.), *Adapting Translation for the Stage*. London: Routledge, pp. 75–86.
Burke, Gregory (2010). *Black Watch*. London: Faber and Faber.
Byrne, Ophelia (2016). 'Northern Irish Drama.' *Drama Online*. Available at: http://www.dramaonlinelibrary.com/genres/northern-irish-drama-iid-21658 [Accessed 24 October 2016].
Callery, Dymphna (2015). *The Active Text: Unlocking Plays through Physical Theatre*. London: Nick Hern Books.
Carlson, Marvin (1985). 'Illustration, Translation, Fulfillment or Supplement?' *Theatre Journal* 37 (1), 5–11.
Carlson, Marvin (2003). *The Haunted Stage: The Theatre as Memory Machine*. Ann Arbor: The University of Michigan Press.
Carlson, Marvin (2004). *Performance: A Critical Introduction*. Second edition. Abingdon: Routledge.
Casey, Edward S. (1976). *Imagining: A Phenomenological Study*. Bloomington: Indiana University Press.
Cassiers, Edith, Timmy De Laet, and Luk Van den Dries (2019). 'Text: The Director's Notebook.' In Michael Shane Boyle, Matt Cornish, and Brandon Woolf (Eds.), *Postdramatic Theatre and Form*. London: Methuen Drama, pp. 33–47.
Causey, Matthew (2006). *Theatre and Performance in Digital Culture: From Simulation to Embeddedness*. London: Routledge.
Cavendish, Dominic (2006). 'Review of *The Seagull*.' *Theatre Record 18 June–1 July 2006*. London: Theatre Record Ltd., p. 763.
Chambers, Colin (2011). *Black and Asian Theatre in Britain: A History*. Abingdon: Routledge.
Chisholm, Alex (2012). 'The End of "New Writing"?' *Exeunt Magazine*, 11 May. Available at: http://exeuntmagazine.com/features/the-end-of-new-writing/ [Accessed 23 September 2016].
Christine Hamilton Consulting (2012). *Review of the Theatre Sector in Scotland for Creative Scotland*. Creative Scotland.
Churchill, Caryl (2008). *Far Away*. In *Plays: 4*. London: Nick Hern Books, pp. 129–159.
Churchill, Caryl (2012). *Love and Information*. London: Nick Hern Books.
Churchill, Caryl (2016). *Escaped Alone*. London: Nick Hern Books.
Churchill, Caryl (2020). *Escaped Alone*. Acting edition. London: Samuel French.
Clapp, Susannah (2006). 'Review of *The Seagull*.' *Theatre Record 18 June–1 July 2006*. London: Theatre Record Ltd., pp. 765–766.
Clare, Janet (2012). 'Shakespeare and Paradigms of Early Modern Authorship.' *Journal of Early Modern Studies* 1 (1), 137–153.
Clayton, J. Douglas, and Yana Meerzon (Eds.) (2013). *Adapting Chekhov: The Text and Its Mutations*. Abingdon: Routledge.
Cox, John D. and David Scott Kastan (Eds.) (1997). *A New History of Early English Drama*. New York: Columbia University Press.
Craig, Edward Gordon (1957 [1911]). *On the Art of the Theatre*. London: Butler and Tanner Ltd.
Craig, Sandy (1980). *Dreams and Deconstructions: Alternative Theatre in Britain*. Oxford: Amber Lane Press.
Crimp, Martin (1997). *Attempts on Her Life*. London: Faber and Faber.
Crimp, Martin (2007). *Attempts on Her Life*. London: Faber and Faber.

Crouch, Tim (2011a). *The Author.* In *Plays One*. London: Oberon Books, pp. 161–203.
Crouch, Tim (2011b). *I, Shakespeare.* London: Oberon Books.
Crouch, Tim (2011c). '*The Author*: Response and Responsibility.' *Contemporary Theatre Review* 21(4), 416–422.
Crouch, Tim (2016). *I, Malvolio. The Routledge Performance Archive.* Available at: https://www.routledgeperformancearchive.com/video/i-malvolio [Accessed 7 July 2021].
Crouch, Tim (2019). *Total Immediate Collective Imminent Terrestrial Salvation.* London: Oberon Books.
Curious Directive (2012). *Your Last Breath, Olfactory and After the Rainfall.* London: Methuen Drama.
Davies, Nick (2019). 'Welsh Theatre: A Look Back at the Past Decade.' *Welsh Arts Review*, 17 December. Available at: https://www.walesartsreview.org/a-look-back-at-a-decade-in-welsh-theatre/ [Accessed 20 July 2021].
de Jongh, Nicholas (2000). *Politics, Prudery & Perversions: The Censoring of the English Stage 1901–1968.* London: Methuen.
de Jongh, Nicholas (2006). 'Review of *The Seagull*.' *Theatre Record 18 June–1 July 2006.* London: Theatre Record Ltd., pp. 763–764.
Dead Centre (2016). *Chekhov's First Play.* London: Oberon Books.
Delgado, Maria M. and Dan Rebellato (Eds.) (2020). *Contemporary European Theatre Directors.* Second edition. Abingdon: Routledge.
Delgado-García, Cristina (2015). *Rethinking Character in Contemporary British Theatre: Aesthetics, Politics, Subjectivity.* Berlin: De Gruyter.
Dempsey, Noel (2016). *Arts Funding: Statistics.* London: House of Commons Library.
Dennett, Daniel Clement (1993). *Content and Consciousness.* London & New York: Routledge.
Derbyshire, Harry (2008). 'Backpages: The Culture of New Writing.' *Contemporary Theatre Review* 18 (1), 131–134.
Derrida, Jacques (1976). *Of Grammatology.* Translated by Gayatri Chakravorty Spivak. Baltimore & London: Johns Hopkins University Press.
Derrida, Jacques (1988). *Limited Inc.* Translated by Jeffrey Mehlman and Samuel Weber.Evanston, IL: Northwestern University Press.
Derrida, Jacques (2001). *Writing and Difference.* Translated by Alan Bass. London: Routledge.
Dixon, Steve (2007). *Digital Performance: A History of New Media in Theater, Dance, Performance Art, and Installation.* Cambridge, Massachusetts: The MIT Press.
Drain, Richard (Ed.) (1995). *Twentieth-Century Theatre: A Sourcebook.* London: Routledge.
Drama Online (2022). *Drama Online Library.* Available at: https://www.dramaonlinelibrary.com/ [Accessed 26 April 2022].
Drama Panel (1958). *ACGB/43/1–Minutes of the 69th Meeting.* Arts Council of Great Britain Archive.
Drama Panel (1967). *ACGB/43/3–Minutes of the 120th Meeting.* Arts Council of Great Britain Archive.
Drama Panel (1968). *ACGB/43/3–Minutes of the 121st Meeting.* Arts Council of Great Britain Archive.
Drama Panel (1970). *ACGB/43/3–Minutes of the 136th Meeting.* Arts Council of Great Britain Archive.
Drama Panel (1987). *ACGB/43/6–Minutes of the 279th Meeting.* Arts Council of Great Britain Archive.
Drama Panel (1995). *ACGB/43/8–Minutes of the Drama Policy Working Group.* Arts Council of Great Britain Archive.

Drucker, Johanna (2002). 'Lexicon (5).' *Performance Research* 7(1), 101–102.
Dunton, Emma, Roger Nelson, and Hetty Shand (2009). *New Writing in Theatre 2003–2008: An Assessment of New Writing within Smaller Scale Theatre in England*. London: Arts Council England.
Edgar, David (1988). *The Second Time as Farce: Reflections on the Drama of Mean Times*. London: Lawrence and Wishart.
Edgar, David (1999). *State of Play: Playwrights on Playwriting*. London: Faber and Faber.
Edgar, David (2009). 'Shock of the new play.' *The Guardian*, 9 December. Available at: https://www.theguardian.com/commentisfree/2009/dec/09/new-play-text-based-drama [Accessed 29 August 2016].
Edgar, David (2010). *How Plays Work*. London: Nick Hern Books.
Edgar, David and Amanda Whittington (Eds.) (2012a). *The Working Playwright: Agreements and Contracts*. London: The Writers' Guild of Great Britain.
Edgar, David and Amanda Whittington (Eds.) (2012b). *The Working Playwright: Engaging with Theatres*. London: The Writers' Guild of Great Britain.
Edgar, David (2021). 'From Stage to Page: The Irresistible Rise of the Published Play.' *Contemporary Theatre Review* 31 (1–2), 233–236.
Edwardes, Jane (2006). 'Review of *The Seagull*.' *Theatre Record 18 June–1 July 2006*. London: Theatre Record Ltd., p. 767.
Eliot, Simon, and Andrew Nash (2009). 'Mass Markets: Literature.' In David McKitterick (Ed.), *The Cambridge History of the Book in Britain – Volume 6: 1830–1914*. Cambridge: Cambridge University Press, pp. 416–442.
Ellams, Inua (2019). *Three Sisters*. London: Oberon Books.
Elsom, John (1979). *Post-War British Theatre*. London: Routledge and Kegan Paul.
Erne, Lukas (2013). *Shakespeare as Literary Dramatist*. Second edition. Cambridge: Cambridge University Press.
Etchells, Tim (1996). 'Additional Comments from the Contributors for the 1996 Reprint'. In Theodore Shank (Ed.), *Contemporary British Theatre*. London: Macmillan, pp. x–xx.
Etchells, Tim (1999). *Certain Fragments: Contemporary Performance and Forced Entertainment*. London: Routledge.
Evans, Lloyd (2015). 'Review of *Oresteia*'. In *Theatre Record 27 August–9 September 2015*. London: Theatre Record Ltd., pp. 868–869.
Experimental Drama Committee (EDC) (1972a). *ACGB/43/36–Minutes of the 11th Meeting*. Arts Council of Great Britain Archive.
Experimental Drama Committee (EDC) (1972b). *ACGB/43/36–Minutes of the 14th Meeting*. Arts Council of Great Britain Archive.
Experimental Drama Committee (EDC) (1973). *ACGB/43/36–Minutes of the 25th Meeting*. Arts Council of Great Britain Archive.
Experimental Drama Committee (EDC) (1975). *ACGB/43/36–Minutes of the 48th Meeting*. Arts Council of Great Britain Archive.
Experimental Drama Committee (EDC) (1975). *ACGB/43/36–Minutes of the 49th Meeting*. Arts Council of Great Britain Archive.
Field, Andy (2009). 'All Theatre Is Devised and Text-Based.' *The Guardian*, 21 April. Available at: http://www.theguardian.com/stage/theatreblog/2009/apr/21/theatre-devised-text-based [Accessed 7 October 2017].
Field, Andy (2021). 'Made in China.' In Maddy Costa and Andy Field (Eds.), *Performance in an Age of Precarity: 40 Reflections*. London: Methuen Drama, pp. 63–68.
Forced Entertainment (1994). '*Emanuelle Enchanted (Or A Description OF This World As If It Were A Beautiful Place)*: Notes and Documents.' *Contemporary Theatre Review* 2 (2), 9–24.

Foster, Verna A. (2013). 'After Chekhov: The Three Sisters of Beth Henley, Wendy Wasserstein, Timberlake Wertenbaker, and Blake Morrison.' *Comparative Drama* 47 (4), 451–472.

Foucault, Michel (1991). 'What Is an Author?' In Paul Rabinow (Ed.), *The Foucault Reader: An Introduction to Foucault's Thought.* London: Penguin Books, pp. 101–120.

Freeman, John (2007). *New Performance/New Writing.* Basingstoke: Palgrave Macmillan.

Freeman, John (2016). *New Performance/New Writing.* Second edition. London: Palgrave.

Freeman, Sara (2006). 'Towards a Genealogy and Taxonomy of British Alternative Theatre.' *New Theatre Quarterly* 22 (4), 364–378.

Freeman, Sara (2014). 'Gay Sweatshop, Alternative Theatre, and Strategies for New Writing.' *New Theatre Quarterly* 30 (2), 136–153.

Freeman, Sara (2015). 'Gay Sweatshop.' In Graham Saunders (Ed.), *British Theatre Companies 1980–1994.* London: Bloomsbury Methuen Drama, pp. 141–163.

Freshwater, Helen (2002). 'Anti-Theatrical Prejudice and the Persistence of Performance.' *Performance Research* 7 (4), 50–58.

Freshwater, Helen (2008). 'Physical Theatre: Complicite and the Question of Authority.' In Nadine Holdsworth and Mary Luckhurst (Eds.), *A Concise Companion to Contemporary British and Irish Drama.* Oxford: Blackwell Publishing, pp. 171–199.

Frye, Northrop (2020 [1957]). *Anatomy of Criticism: Four Essays.* Princeton: Princeton University Press.

Fuchs, Elinor (1996). *The Death of Character: Perspectives on Theater after Modernism.* Bloomington and Indianapolis: Indiana University Press.

Ganzel, Dewey (1961). 'Patent Wrongs and Patent Theatres: Drama and the Law in the Early Nineteenth Century.' *PMLA* 76 (4), 384–396.

Gardner, Lyn (2009). 'Interview: Sean Holmes's pick'n'mix plans for the Lyric Hammersmith.' *The Guardian*, 3 June. Available at: https://www.theguardian.com/stage/2009/jun/03/sean-holmes-lyric-hammersmith [Accessed 24 September 2021].

Gardner, Lyn (2020). 'Joe Hill-Gibbins: "I find the Little Englander attitude to theatre embarrassing".' *The Stage*, 11 March. Available at: https://www.thestage.co.uk/big-interviews/joe-hill-gibbins [Accessed 3 March 2021].

Gardner, Lyn (2021). 'Auteurs – the Authors of Performance.' *Digital Theatre Plus*. Available at: https://edu-digitaltheatreplus-com.manchester.idm.oclc.org/content/guides/auteurs-the-authors-of-performance [Accessed 14 July 2021].

Geliot, Emma, and Cathy Gomez (2016). 'What Gives Theatre in Wales Its Radical Edge?' British Council. Available at: http://theatreanddance.britishcouncil.org/blog/2016/09/what-gives-theatre-in-wales-its-radical-edge/ [Accessed 26 September 2016].

Goddard, Lynette (2015). *Contemporary Black British Playwrights: Margins to Mainstream.* Basingstoke: Palgrave.

Goode, Chris (2012). 'Series 1: Episode 6.' Podcast. Available at: http://www.chrisgoodeandcompany.co.uk/podcast/ [Accessed 29 June 2016].

Gooch, Steve (1984). *All Together Now: An Alternative View of Theatre and the Community.* London: Methuen.

Goodman, Lizbeth (1991). 'Conference in Cambridge: Theatre under Threat?' *New Theatre Quarterly* 7 (26), 187–190.

Govan, Emma, Helen Nicholson, and Katie Normington (2007). *Making a Performance: Devising Histories and Contemporary Practices.* London: Routledge.

Greenstreet, Hannah (2019). 'Anger, Ambivalence, and Ella Hickson's *The Writer* (2018).' *Contemporary Theatre Review* 29 (3), 348–351.

Greig, David (2010). *San Diego.* London: Faber and Faber.

Greig, David (2014). *The Yes/No Plays*. Available at: http://www.nationalcollective.com/2014/02/02/david-greig-the-yesno-plays/ [Accessed 27 August 2021].

Greig, David (2017). 'The Yes No Plays'. *Twitter*. Available at: https://twitter.com/YesNoPlays [Accessed 27 August 2021].

Grochala, Sarah (2017). *The Contemporary Political Play: Rethinking Dramaturgical Structure*. London: Bloomsbury Methuen Drama.

Hadingue, Amanda (2007). 'Experimental Theatre and the Legacy of the 1990s.' *Stans Cafe*. Available at: http://www.stanscafe.co.uk/helpfulthings/experimentaltheatreessay.html [Accessed 24 August 2016].

Hammond, Paul (2002). 'The Restoration Poetic and Dramatic Canon.' In John Barnard and D. F. McKenzie, with Maureen Bell (Eds.), *The Cambridge History of the Book in Britain – Volume 4: 1557–1695*. Cambridge: Cambridge University Press, pp. 388–409.

Hancher, Michael (1972). 'Three Kinds of Intention.' *MLN* 87 (7), 827–851.

Hare, David (2009). *The Power of Yes*. London: Faber and Faber.

Hart, Christopher (2015). 'Review of *Song From Far Away*.' *Theatre Record 27 August–9 September 2015*. London: Theatre Record Ltd., pp. 861–862.

Harvie, Jen (2005). *Staging the UK*. Manchester: Manchester University Press.

Harvie, Jen, and Andy Lavender (Eds.) (2010). *Making Contemporary Theatre: International Rehearsal Processes*. Manchester: Manchester University Press.

Haydon, Andrew (2013). 'Theatre in the 00s.' In Dan Rebellato (Ed.), *Modern British Playwriting: 2000–2009: Voices, Documents, New Interpretations*. London: Methuen Drama, pp. 40–98.

Haydon, Andrew (2015). 'Song From Far Away – Young Vic.' *Postcards from the Gods*. Available at: https://postcardsgods.blogspot.com/2015/09/song-from-far-away-young-vic.html [Accessed 21 March 2022].

Haydon, Andrew (2016). 'A Brief History of Online Theatre Criticism in England.' In Duška Radosavljević (Ed.), *Theatre Criticism: Changing Landscapes*. London: Bloomsbury Methuen Drama, pp. 135–151.

Hayles, N. Katherine (2021). *Postprint: Books and Becoming Computational*. New York: Columbia University Press.

Heddon, Deirdre (2002). 'Performing the Archive Following in the Footsteps.' *Performance Research* 7 (4), 64–77.

Heddon, Deirdre (2008). *Autobiography in Performance: Performing Selves*. Basingstoke: Palgrave Macmillan.

Heddon, Deirdre, and Jane Milling (2006). *Devising Performance: A Critical History*. Basingstoke: Palgrave Macmillan.

Hickson, Ella (2016). *Oil*. Lonodn: Nick Hern Books.

Hickson, Ella (2018). *The Writer*. Lonodn: Nick Hern Books.

Higgins, Charlotte (2016). 'Katie Mitchell, British theatre's queen in exile.' *The Guardian*, 14 January. Available at: https://www.theguardian.com/stage/2016/jan/14/british-theatre-queen-exile-katie-mitchell [Accessed 3 March 2021].

Hinchcliffe, Arnold P. (1974). *British Theatre 1950–70*. Oxford: Blackwell.

Hingorani, Dominic (2006). 'Tara Arts and Tamasha: Producing Asian Performance – Two Approaches.' In Dimple Godiwala (Ed.), *Alternatives within the Mainstream: British Black and Asian Theatres*. Newcastle: Cambridge Scholars Publishing, pp. 174–200.

Hingorani, Dominic (2010). *British Asian Theatre: Dramaturgy, Process and Performance*. New York: Palgrave Macmillan.

Hirsch, E. D. (2001). 'Objective Interpretation.' In William E Cain, Laurie A. Finke, Barbara E. Johnson, John McGowan and Jeffrey J. Williams (Eds.), *The Norton Anthology*

of Theory and Criticism. New York & London: W. W. Norton & Company, pp. 1684–1709.
Hirschfield, Heather (2001). 'Early Modern Collaboration and Theories of Authorship.' *PMLA* 116 (3), 609–622.
Hodgdon, Barbara (2005). 'Introduction: A Kind of History.' In Barbara Hodgdon and W. B. Worthen (Eds.), *A Companion to Shakespeare and Performance*. Oxford: Blackwell Publishing, pp. 1–9.
Hoffman, Beth (2009). 'Radicalism and the Theatre in Genealogies of Live Art.' *Performance Research* 14 (1), 95–105.
Hurley, Kieran (2018). *Mouthpiece*. London: Oberon Books.
Hutcheon, Linda (2013). *A Theory of Adaptation*. Second edition. Abingdon: Routledge.
Icke, Robert and Andrew Scott (2017). '*Hamlet*: Andrew Scott & Robert Icke in Conversation.' *YouTube*. Available at: https://www.youtube.com/watch?v=kIzwvg9isCg [Accessed 3 March 2021].
Icke, Robert (2020). *Works One*. London: Oberon Books.
Ilter, Seda (2015). 'Rethinking Play Texts in the Age of Mediatization: Simon Stephens's *Pornography*.' *Modern Drama* 58 (2), 238–262.
Ilter, Seda (2018). 'Blast Theory's *Karen*: Exploring the Ontology of Technotexts.' *Performance Research* 23 (2), 69–74.
Ilter, Seda (2021). *Mediatized Dramaturgy: The Evolution of Plays in the Media Age*. London: Methuen Drama.
Inchley, Maggie (2015). *Voice and New Writing, 1997–2007: Articulating the Demos*. Basingstoke: Palgrave Macmillan.
Ioppolo, Grace (2006). *Dramatists and their Manuscripts in the Age of Shakespeare, Jonson, Middleton and Heywood: Authorship, Authority and the Playhouse*. Abingdon: Routledge.
Itzin, Catherine (1980). *Stages in the Revolution: Political Theatre in Britain since 1968*. London: Eyre Methuen.
Jarcho, Julia (2017). *Writing and the Modern Stage: Theater Beyond Drama*. Cambridge: Cambridge University Press.
Jenkins, Anthony (1991). *The Making of Victorian Drama*. Cambridge: Cambridge University Press.
Jestrovic, Silvija (2020). *Performances of Authorial Presence and Absence: The Author Dies Hard*. Cham, Switzerland: Palgrave Macmillan.
Johnston, John (1990). *The Lord Chamberlain's Blue Pencil*. London and Sydney: Hodder & Stoughton.
Jürs-Munby, Karen (2006). 'Introduction.' In Hans-Thies Lehmann (Ed.), *Postdramatic Theatre*. Abingdon: Routledge, pp. 1–15.
Jürs-Munby, Karen (2010). 'Text Exposed: Displayed Texts as Players Onstage in Contemporary Theatre.' *Studies in Theatre and Performance* 30 (1), 101–114.
Kane, Sarah (2000). *4.48 Psychosis*. London: Methuen Drama.
Kane, Sarah (2001). *Complete Plays*. London: Methuen Drama.
Kendrick, Ellie (2018). *Hole*. London: Oberon Books.
Kene, Arinzé (2018). *Misty*. London: Nick Hern Books.
Khan, Naima (2013). '"The imagination is the place to go": Anthony Welsh on debbie tucker green.' Available at: https://naimakhan.com/2013/12/30/the-imagination-is-the-place-to-go-anthony-welsh-on-debbie-tucker-green/ [Accessed 7 June 2021].
Kimmings, Bryony (2012). 'Oberon and on and on and on.' Available at: https://thebryonykimmings.tumblr.com/post/28491568031/oberon-and-on-and-on-and-on [Accessed 8 July 2021].

Kimmings, Bryony (2013). *Credible Likeable Superstar Role Model.* London: Oberon Books.
Kimmings, Bryony (2021). *I'm a Phoenix, Bitch.* London: Methuen Drama.
Kimmings, Bryony, Brian Lobel and Tom Parkinson (2016). *A Pacifist's Guide to the War on Cancer.* London: Oberon Books.
Kimmings, Bryony, and Tim Grayburn (2015). *Fake It 'Til You Make It.* London: Oberon Books.
Klimenko, Svetlana O. (2001). 'Anton Chekhov and English Nostalgia.' *Orbis Litterarum* 56, 121–137.
Knapp, Jeffrey (2005). 'What Is a Co-Author?' *Representations* 89 (1), 1–29.
Knapp, Steven, and Walter Benn Michaels (1982). 'Against Theory.' *Critical Inquiry* 8 (4), 723–742.
Knowles, Ric (2010). *Theatre & Interculturalism.* Basingstoke: Palgrave Macmillan.
Komporaly, Jozefina (2017). *Radical Revival as Adaptation: Theatre, Politics, Society.* London: Palgrave Macmilan.
Laera, Margherita (Ed.) (2014). *Theatre and Adaptation: Return, Rewrite, Repeat.* London: Bloomsbury Methuen Drama.
Laera, Margherita (2020). *Theatre & Translation.* London: Red Globe Press.
Lamb, Charles and Mary Lamb (1811). *Works in Prose and Verse.* London: Henry Frowde for Oxford University Press.
Lane, David (2010). 'A Dramaturg's Perspective: Looking to the Future of Script Development.' *Studies in Theatre and Performance* 30 (1), 127–141.
Lavender, Andy (1989). 'Theatre in Crisis: Conference Report, December 1988.' *New Theatre Quarterly* 5 (19), 210.
Lavery, Carl (2009). 'Is There a Text in This Performance?' *Performance Research* 14 (1), 37–45.
Lee-Jones, Jasmine (2019). *Seven Methods of Killing Kylie Jenner.* London: Oberon Books.
Lehmann, Hans-Thies (2006). *Postdramatic Theatre.* Translated by Karen Jürs-Munby. Abingdon: Routledge.
Leigh, Eve (2019). *Midnight Movie.* London: Oberon Books.
Lewis, Helen (2020). 'Introduction.' In Robert Icke (Ed.), *Works One.* London: Oberon Books, pp. vii–xxvi.
Lilley, Heather (2017). 'Kneehigh's Retellings.' In Kara Reilly (Ed.), *Contemporary Approaches to Adaptation in Theatre.* London: Palgrave Macmillan, pp. 5–24.
Livingston, Paisley (2005). *Art and Intention: A Philosophical Study.* Oxford: Clarendon Press.
Love, Catherine (2015a). 'Symposium: Are We on the Same Page? Approaches to Text and Performance.' *Royal Holloway.* University of London, 26 September 2015. Author's transcript.
Love, Catherine (2015b). 'Song From Far Away, Young Vic.' Available at: https://catherinelove.co.uk/2015/09/16/song-from-far-away-young-vic/ [Accessed 21 March 2022].
Love, Catherine (2015c). *'Tonight I'm Gonna Be The New Me,* or Who's in charge of this story?' Available at: https://catherinelove.co.uk/2015/09/19/tonight-im-gonna-be-the-new-me/ [Accessed 10 May 2021].
Love, Catherine (2016). 'New Perspectives on Home: Simon Stephens and Authorship in British Theatre.' *Contemporary Theatre Review* 26 (3), 319–327.
Love, Catherine (2017). *Tim Crouch's An Oak Tree.* Abingdon: Routledge.
Love, Catherine (2018). *Are We on the Same Page? A Critical Analysis of the 'Text-Based'/ 'Non-Text-Based' Divide in Contemporary English Theatre.* Unpublished: Royal Holloway, University of London. PhD.

Love, Catherine (2020). 'Prelude: The (play)text is the Set.' In Michael Pinchbeck (Ed.), *Acts of Dramaturgy: The Shakespeare Trilogy*. Bristol: Intellect, pp. 26–40.

Luckhurst, Mary (2006). *Dramaturgy: A Revolution in Theatre*. Cambridge: Cambridge University Press.

Lyas, Colin (1995). 'Wittgensteinian Intentions.' In Gary Iseminger (Ed.), *Intention and Interpretation*. Philadelphia: Temple University Press, pp. 132–151.

Lyman, Elizabeth Dyrud (2002). 'The Page Refigured: The Verbal and Visual Language of Suzan-Lori Parks's *Venus*.' *Performance Research* 7(1), 90–100.

Macaulay, Alastair (2006). 'Review of *The Seagull*.' *Theatre Record 18 June–1 July 2006*. London: Theatre Record Ltd., p. 765.

MacDonald, Claire, and Bill Sherman (2002). 'Enter Editor.' *Performance Research* 7 (1), 1–2.

Mackey, Sally, and Simon Cooper (2000). *Drama and Theatre Studies*. Cheltenham: Stanley Thornes.

Maduro, Daniela Côrtes (Ed.) (2017). *Digital Media and Textuality: From Creation to Archiving*. Bielefeld: Transcript-Verlag.

Marowitz, Charles, Tom Milne and Owen Hale (Eds.) (1965). *New Theatre Voices of the Fifties and Sixties: Selections from Encore Magazine 1956–1963*. London: Methuen.

Marsh, Cynthia (2020). *Translated and Visiting Russian Theatre in Britain, 1945–2015: A 'Russia of the Theatrical Mind'?*. Cham: Palgrave Macmillan.

Masten, Jeffrey (1997). *Textual Intercourse: Collaboration, Authorship, and Sexualities in Renaissance Drama*. Cambridge: Cambridge University Press.

Masura, Nadja (2020). *Digital Theatre: The Making and Meaning of Live Mediated Performance, US & UK 1990-2020*. Cham: Palgrave Macmillan.

McDonagh, Luke (2021). *Performing Copyright: Law, Theatre and Authorship*. Oxford: Hart Publishing.

McDowall, Alistair (2016). *X*. London: Bloomsbury Methuen Drama.

McDowall, Wallace (2013). 'Overcoming Working-Class Ulster Loyalism's Resistance to Theatricality after the Peace Process.' *Contemporary Theatre Review* 23 (3), 323–333.

McGann, Jerome (1990). *The Textual Condition*. Princeton: Princeton University Press.

McGann, Jerome (2014). *A New Republic of Letters: Memory and Scholarship in the Age of Digital Reproduction*. Cambridge, Massachusetts: Harvard University Press.

McGinn, Colin (2004). *Mindsight: Image, Dream, Meaning*. Cambridge, Mass.: Harvard University Press.

McKenzie, D. F. (1999). *Bibliography and the Sociology of Texts*. Cambridge: Cambridge University Press.

Megson, Chris (Ed.) (2012). *Modern British Playwriting – The 1970s: Voices, Documents, New Interpretations*. London: Methuen Drama.

Mele, Alfred R., and Paisley Livingston (1992). 'Intentions and Interpretations.' *MLN* 207 (5), 931–949.

Mermikides, Alex, and Jackie Smart, (Eds.) (2010). *Devising in Process*. Basingstoke: Palgrave Macmillan.

Merrifield, Nicola (2013). 'Edgar Criticises Universities' "Ideological Hostility" Towards Playwrights'. *The Stage*, 17 September. Available at: https://www.thestage.co.uk/news/edgar-criticises-universities-ideological-hostility-towards-playwrights [Accessed 24 May 2022].

Middeke, Martin, Peter Paul Schnierer, and Aleks Sierz (Eds.) (2011). *The Methuen Drama Guide to Contemporary British Playwrights*. London: Methuen Drama.

Milling, Jane (Ed.) (2012). *Modern British Playwriting – The 1980s: Voices, Documents, New Interpretations*. London: Methuen Drama.

Millman, Anne, and Jodi Myers (2009). *Theatre Assessment 2009*. London: Arts Council England.
Mills, Liz (2009). 'When the Voice Itself Is Image.' *Modern Drama* 52 (4), 389–404.
Mitchell, Kaye (2008). *Intention and Text: Towards an Intentionality of Literary Form*. London: Continuum.
Mitchell, Katie (2009). *The Director's Craft*. Abingdon: Routledge.
Mitchell, Katie, and Robert Icke (2016). 'On Chekhov: Katie Mitchell and Robert Icke in Conversation, Almeida Theatre, London.' *YouTube*. Available at: https://www.youtube.com/watch?v=FaeAgWMYu8w&t=5s [Accessed 3 March 2021].
Mitra, Royona (2015). *Akram Khan: Dancing New Interculturalism*. Basingstoke: Palgrave Macmillan.
Moody, Jane (2000). 'The State of the Abyss: Nineteenth Century Performance and Theatre Historiography in 1999.' *Journal of Victorian Culture* 5 (1), 112–128.
Morin, Emilie (2011). '"Look Again": Indeterminacy and Contemporary British Drama', *New Theatre Quarterly* 27 (1), 71–85.
Mullarkey, Rory (2014). *Each Slow Dusk*. London: Methuen Drama.
Mullarkey, Rory (2014). *The Wolf from the Door*. London: Methuen Drama.
Murray, Simon David, and John Keefe (2016). *Physical Theatres: A Critical Introduction*. London: Routledge.
Nash, Andrew, and Jane Potter (2019). 'Literature.' In Andrew Nash, Claire Squires, and I. R. Wilson (Eds.), *The Cambridge History of the Book in Britain – Volume 7: The Twentieth Century and Beyond*. Cambridge: Cambridge University Press, pp. 279–318.
Neilson, Anthony (2018). *Plays: 3*. London: Methuen Drama.
Nicholson, Steve (2003). *The Censorship of British Drama 1900–1968: 1900–1932*. Exeter: University of Exeter Press.
Nicholson, Steve (2005). *The Censorship of British Drama 1900–1968: 1933–1952*. Exeter: University of Exeter Press.
Nicholson, Steve (2011). *The Censorship of British Drama 1900–1968: The Fifties*. Exeter: University of Exeter Press.
Nicholson, Steve (Ed.) (2012). *Modern British Playwriting – The 1960s: Voices, Documents, New Interpretations*. London: Methuen Drama.
Nicholson, Steve (2015). *The Censorship of British Drama 1900–1968: The Sixties*. Exeter: University of Exeter Press.
Osborne, Deirdre (2020). '"Hearing Voices" and Performing the Mind in Debbie Tucker Green's Dramatic-Poetics.' In Siân Adiseshiah and Jacqueline Bolton (Eds.), *debbie tucker green: Critical Perspectives*. Cham: Palgrave Macmillan, pp. 233–255.
Overend, David (2011). *Underneath the Arches: Developing a Relational Theatre Practice in Response to a Specific Cultural Site*. Unpublished: University of Glasgow. PhD.
Oxford English Dictionary (OED) (2017). "supplement, n.1." Available at: www.oed.com/view/Entry/194624 [Accessed 13 October 2017].
Page, Adrian (Ed.) (1992). *The Death of the Playwright? Modern British Drama and Literary Theory*. London: Palgrave Macmillan.
Panjwani, Varsha (2017). 'Not Minding the Gap: Intercultural Shakespeare in Britain.' *Multicultural Shakespeare: Translation, Appropriation and Performance*, 15 (30), 43–57
Pattie, David (Ed.) (2012). *Modern British Playwriting – The 1950s: Voices, Documents, New Interpretations*. London: Methuen Drama.
Pavis, Patrice (2005 [1992]). *Theatre at the Crossroads of Culture*. London: Routledge.
Payne, Ben (1998). 'In the Beginning Was the Word.' In John Deeney (Ed.), *Writing Live*. London: New Playwrights Trust, pp. 9–50.

Payne, Nick (2014). *Incognito*. London: Faber and Faber.
Payne, Nick (2020). *Incognito*. Acting edition. London: Samuel French.
Peacock, D. Keith (1999). *Thatcher's Theatre: British Theatre and Drama in the Eighties*. London: Greenwood Press.
Pearson, Deborah (2015). *The Future Show*. London: Oberon Books.
Pearson, Deborah (2016). *The Shape of a Thought: A Made-up Game – Narrative Preoccupations in Contemporary Performance*. Unpublished: Royal Holloway, University of London. PhD.
Peters, Julie Stone (2000). *Theatre of the Book 1480–1880: Print, Text, and Performance in Europe*. Oxford: Oxford University Press.
Phelan, Mark (2004). 'The Critical "Gap of the North": Nationalism, National Theatre, and the North.' *Modern Drama* 47 (4), 594–606.
Phelan, Mark (2016). 'From Troubles to Post-Conflict Theatre in Northern Ireland'. In Nicholas Grene and Chris Morash (Eds.), *The Oxford Handbook of Modern Irish Theatre*. Oxford: Oxford University Press, pp. 372–388.
Pinchbeck, Michael (Ed.) (2020). *Acts of Dramaturgy: The Shakespeare Trilogy*. Bristol: Intellect.
Pitcher, John (2002). 'Literature, the Playhouse and the Public.' In John Barnard and D. F. McKenzie, with Maureen Bell (Eds.), *The Cambridge History of the Book in Britain – Volume 4: 1557–1695*. Cambridge: Cambridge University Press, pp. 351–375.
Power, Cormac (2008). *Presence in Play: A Critique of Theories of Presence in the Theatre*. Amsterdam: Rodopi.
Price, Tim (2021). *Teh Internet is Serious Business*. London: Methuen Drama.
Projects Committee (1985). *ACGB/43/6 – Minutes of the 32nd Meeting*. Arts Council of Great Britain Archive.
Puchner, Martin (2002). *Stage Fright: Modernism, Anti-Theatricality, and Drama*. Baltimore: Johns Hopkins University Press.
Puchner, Martin (2011). 'Drama and Performance: Toward a Theory of Adaptation.' *Common Knowledge* 17 (2), 292–305.
Purves, Libby (2012). 'Review of *A Midsummer Night's Dream*.' *Theatre Record 12–25 February 2012*. London: Theatre Record Ltd., p. 160.
Quigley, Karen (2020). *Performing the Unstageable: Success, Imagination, Failure*. London: Bloomsbury.
Rabkin, Gerald (1985). 'Is There a Text on This Stage? Theatre/Authorship/Interpretation.' *Performing Arts Journal* 9 (2/3), 142–159.
Raczka, Lulu (2014). *Nothing*. London Oberon Books.
Radosavljević, Duška (2013a). *Theatre-Making: Interplay Between Text and Performance in the 21st Century*. Basingstoke: Palgrave Macmillan.
Radosavljević, Duška (Ed.) (2013b). *The Contemporary Ensemble: Interviews with Theatre-Makers*. Abingdon: Routledge.
RashDash (2017). *Two Man Show*. London: Oberon Books.
RashDash (2018). *Three Sisters*. London: Oberon Books.
Ravenhill, Mark (2004). 'A Tear in the Fabric: The James Bulger Murder and New Theatre Writing in the 'Nineties.' *New Theatre Quarterly* 20 (4), 305–314.
Reason, Matthew (2006). *Documentation, Disappearance and the Representation of Live Performance*. Basingstoke: Palgrave Macmillan.
Rebellato, Dan (1999). *1956 and All That*. London: Routledge.
Rebellato, Dan (2009). 'When We Talk of Horses: Or, What Do We See when We See a Play?' *Performance Research* 14 (1), 17–28.

Rebellato, Dan (2013). 'Exit the Author.' In Vicky Angelaki (Ed.), *Contemporary British Theatre: Breaking New Ground*. Basingstoke: Palgrave Macmillan, pp. 9–31.
Rebellato, Dan (Ed.) (2013). *Modern British Playwriting: 2000–2009: Voices, Documents, New Interpretations*. London: Methuen Drama.
Rebellato, Dan (2014). 'Doing the Impossible: Katie Mitchell in Conversation with Dan Rebellato.' In Margherita Laera (Ed.), *Theatre and Adaptation: Return, Rewrite, Repeat*. London: Bloomsbury Methuen Drama, pp. 158–166.
Rebellato, Dan (2015). 'Writing Writing: British Playwriting in the Twenty-First Century.' In Zhen Zhaotao (Ed.), *The Confrontation: Read the New Text*. Hong Kong: International Association of Theatre Critics (Hong Kong), pp. 128–178.
Reid, Trish (2012). *Theatre and Scotland*. Basingstoke: Palgrave Macmillan.
Roberts, Matthew (2015). 'Vanishing Acts: Sarah Kane's Texts for Performance and Postdramatic Theatre.' *Modern Drama* 58 (1), 94–110.
Sanders, Julie (2006). *Adaptation and Appropriation*. Abingdon: Routledge.
Sant, Toni (Ed.) (2017). *Documenting Performance: The Context and Processes of Digital Curation and Archiving*. London: Bloomsbury Methuen Drama.
Saunders, Graham (2003). '"Just a Word on a Page and There Is the Drama." Sarah Kane's Theatrical Legacy.' *Contemporary Theatre Review* 13 (1), 97–110.
Saunders, Graham (Ed.) (2015). *British Theatre Companies 1980–1994*. London: Bloomsbury Methuen Drama.
Schechner, Richard (1992). 'A New Paradigm for Theatre in the Academy.' *TDR: The Drama Review* 36 (4), 7–10.
Scott, Charlotte (2007). *Shakespeare and the Idea of the Book*. Oxford: Oxford University Press.
Sh!t Theatre (2017). *Letters to Windsor House*. London: Oberon Books.
Sh!t Theatre (2018). *Dollywould*. London: Oberon Books.
Sh!t Theatre (2019). *Sh!t Theatre Drink Rum with Expats*. London: Oberon Books.
Shellard, Dominic and Steve Nicholson, with Miriam Handley (2004). *The Lord Chamberlain Regrets … a History of British Theatre Censorship*. London: The British Library.
Shepherd, Simon and Peter Womack (1996). *English Drama: A Cultural History*. Oxford: Blackwell.
Shuttleworth, Ian (2015). 'Review of *Song From Far Away*.' *Theatre Record 27 August–9 September 2015*. London: Theatre Record Ltd., p. 860.
Sierz, Aleks (2001). *In-Yer-Face Theatre: British Drama Today*. London: Faber.
Sierz, Aleks (2011). *Rewriting the Nation: British Theatre Today*. London: Methuen Drama.
Sierz, Aleks (Ed.) (2012). *Modern British Playwriting – The 90s: Voices, Documents, New Interpretations*. London: Methuen Drama.
Sigal, Sarah (2017). *Writing in Collaborative Theatre-Making*. London: Palgrave.
Sinclair, Andrew (1995). *Arts and Cultures: The History of the 50 Years of the Arts Council of Great Britain*. London: Sinclair-Stevenson.
Smith, Mark (2013). *Processes and Rhetorics of Writing in Contemporary British Devising: Frantic Assembly and Forced Entertainment*. Unpublished: University of York. PhD.
Smith, Stef (2016). *Human Animals*. London: Nick Hern Books.
Spencer, Charles (2012). 'Review of *A Midsummer Night's Dream.*' *Theatre Record 12–25 February 2012* London: Theatre Record Ltd., p. 159.
Spender, George (2015). Unpublished interview with author.
Spender, George (2021). Unpublished interview with author.
Steiner, Sam (2019). *You Stupid Darkness!*. London: Nick Hern Books.

Stephens, John Russell (1992). *The Profession of the Playwright: British Theatre 1800–1900*. Cambridge: Cambridge University Press.
Stephens, Simon (2008a). *Pornography*. London: Methuen Drama.
Stephens, Simon (2008b). *Pornography: Rehearsal Version 25th July 2008*. British Library Modern Playscripts Collection.
Stephens, Simon (2009). *Plays: 2*. London: Methuen Drama.
Stephens, Simon, and Mark Eitzel (2015). *Song From Far Away*. London: Bloomsbury Methuen Drama
Stern, Tiffany (2009). *Documents of Performance in Early Modern England*. Cambridge: Cambridge University Press.
Storey, Taryn (2012). 'Devine Intervention: Collaboration and Conspiracy in the History of the Royal Court.' *New Theatre Quarterly* 28 (4.4), 363–378.
Stowell, Sheila (1992). 'Rehabilitating Realism.' *Journal of Dramatic Theory and Criticism* 6 (2), 81–88.
Striphas, Ted (2009). *The Late Age of Print: Everyday Book Culture from Consumerism to Control*. New York: Columbia University Press.
Sugiera, Małgorzata (2004). 'Beyond Drama: Writing for Postdramatic Theatre.' *Theatre Research International* 9 (1), 16–28.
Svendsen, Zoe (2013a). 'The Structure of What Changes.' *Exeunt Magazine*, 15 February. Available at: http://exeuntmagazine.com/features/the-structure-of-what-changes/ [Accessed 3 March 2021].
Svendsen, Zoe. (2013b). 'Dark, Then Light, Then Dark Again.' *Exeunt Magazine*, 15 October. Available at: http://exeuntmagazine.com/features/dark-then-light-then-dark-again/ [Accessed 3 March 2021].
Swain, Rob (2011). *Directing – A Handbook for Emerging Theatre Directors*. London: Methuen Drama.
Taylor, John Russell (1963). *Anger and After: A Guide to the New British Drama*. Revised edition. Harmondsworth: Penguin.
Taylor, Paul (2012). 'Review of *King John*.' *Theatre Record 8–21 April 2012*. London: Theatre Record Ltd., p. 410.
Theatre Writers' Union (TWU) (1987). *Playwrights: A Species Still Endangered?*
Theatre Writing Committee (TWC) (1952). *ACGB/40/126 – Minutes of the 1st Meeting*. Arts Council of Great Britain Archive.
Theatre Writing Committee (TWC) (1960). *ACGB/40/126 – Minutes of the 40th Meeting*. Arts Council of Great Britain Archive.
Theatre Writing Committee (TWC) (1967). *ACGB/40/126 – Minutes of the 74th Meeting*. Arts Council of Great Britain Archive.
Theatre Writing Committee (TWC) (1969). *ACGB/40/126 – Minutes of the 84th Meeting*. Arts Council of Great Britain Archive.
Theatre Writing Committee (TWC) (1975). *ACGB/40/126 – Discussion Paper: The Promotion of New Drama: A Scheme to Help the Authors of Plays in 1975/6*. Arts Council of Great Britain Archive.
Thomas, David, David Carlton and Anne Etienne (2007). *Theatre Censorship: From Walpole to Wilson*. Oxford: Oxford University Press.
Thompson, Selina (2018). *Salt*. London: Faber and Faber.
Tomlin, Liz (2009). '"And Their Stories Fell Apart Even as I Was Telling them": Poststructuralist Performance and the No-Longer-Dramatic Text.' *Performance Research* 14 (1), 57–64.

Tomlin, Liz (2013). *Acts and Apparitions: Discourses on the Real in Performance Practice and Theory, 1990–2010.* Manchester: Manchester University Press.
Tomlin, Liz (Ed.) (2015). *British Theatre Companies 1995–2014.* London: Bloomsbury Methuen Drama.
Tripney, Natasha (2008). 'Katie Mitchell – director or destroyer?' *The Guardian*, 30 July. Available at: https://www.theguardian.com/stage/theatreblog/2008/jul/30/katiemitchelldirectorordes [Accessed 5 March 2021].
Trueman, Matt (2015). '*Song From Far Away* (Young Vic).' *WhatsOnStage*, 7 September. Available at: https://www.whatsonstage.com/london-theatre/reviews/song-from-far-away-young-vic_38668.html [Accessed 21 March 2022].
tucker green, debbie (2005). *Stoning Mary.* London: Nick Hern Books.
tucker green, debbie (2008). *Random.* London: Nick Hern Books.
Turner, Cathy (2008). 'Writing Space: The First Project.'Academia. Available at:http://www.academia.edu/660106/Writing_Space_The_First_Project[Accessed 30 June 2020].
Turner, Cathy (2010). 'Writing for the Contemporary Theatre: Towards a Radically Inclusive Dramaturgy.' *Studies in Theatre and Performance* 30 (1), 75–90.
Turner, Cathy, and Synne K. Behrndt (2008). *Dramaturgy and Performance.* Basingstoke: Palgrave Macmillan.
Tynan, Kenneth (1975). *A View of the English Stage.* London: Methuen.
Ukaegbu, Victor (2013). 'Intercultural to Cross-Cultural Theatre: Tara Arts and the Development of British Asian Theatre.' In Patrick Duggan and Victor Ukaegbu (Eds.), *Reverberations across Small-Scale British Theatre: Politics, Aesthetics and Forms.* Bristol: Intellect, pp. 117–136.
Unwin, Stephen (2004). *So You Want to Be a Theatre Director?* London: Nick Hern Books.
Various (2006). 'Reviews of *Cymbeline*.' *Theatre Record 10–23 September 2006.* London: Theatre Record Ltd., pp. 1054–1055.
Various (2012). 'Reviews of *King John*.' *Theatre Record 8–21 April 2012.* London: Theatre Record Ltd., pp. 409–410.
Various (2013). 'Reviews of *Edward II*.' *Theatre Record 27 Aug–9 Sept 2013.* London: Theatre Record Ltd., pp. 785–788.
Various (2017). 'Reviews of *Twelfth Night*.' *Theatre Record 01–25 May 2017.* London: Theatre Record Ltd., pp. 542–545.
Various (2018). 'Reviews of *The Wild Duck*.' *Theatre Record 01–31 October 2018.* London: Theatre Record Ltd., pp. 959–962.
Verma, Jatinder (1998). 'Binglishing the Stage: A generation of Asian Theatre in Britain.' In Richard Boon and Jane Plastow (Eds.), *Theatre Matters: Politics and Culture on the World Stage.* Cambridge: Cambridge University Press, pp. 126–134.
Verma, Jatinder (2008). 'What the migrant saw.' *The Guardian*, 10 January. Available at: https://www.theguardian.com/stage/2008/jan/10/theatre1 [Accessed 8 March 2021].
Vickers, Brian (2007). 'Incomplete Shakespeare: Or, Denying Coauthorship in *1 Henvry VI*.' *Shakespeare Quarterly* 58 (3), 311–352.
Walsh, Marcus (2009). 'Scholarly Editing: Patristics, Classical Literature and Shakespeare.' In Michael F. Suarez and Michael L. Turner (Eds.), *The Cambridge History of the Book in Britain – Volume 5: 1695–1830.* Cambridge: Cambridge University Press, pp. 684–698.
Waters, Steve (2011). *The Secret Life of Plays.* London: Nick Hern Books.
Wayne, Valerie (2007). 'Kneehigh's Dream of *Cymbeline*.' *Shakespeare Quarterly* 58 (3), 228–237.

Weimann, Robert (2010). 'Performance in Shakespeare's Theatre: Ministerial and/or Magisterial?'. In Graham Bradshaw and Tom Bishop (Eds.), *The Shakespeare International Yearbook: Volume 10*. London: Routledge, pp. 3–30.

Wiles, David (2000). *Greek Theatre Performance: An Introduction*. Cambridge: Cambridge University Press.

Williams, Nora J. (2018). 'Multivalence: The Young Vic and a Postmodern *Changeling*, 2012.' In Kara Reilly (Ed.), *Contemporary Approaches to Adaptation in Theatre*. London: Palgrave Macmillan, pp. 317–330.

Wimsatt Jr., W. K., and M. C. Beardsley (1946). 'The Intentional Fallacy.' *The Sewanee Review* 54 (3), 468–488.

Wittgenstein, Ludwig (2009). *Philosophical Investigations*. Translated by G. E. M. Anscombe, P. M. S. Hacker and Joachim Schulte. Fourth edition. Chichester: Wiley-Blackwell.

Woddis, Jane (2005). *Spear-Carriers or Speaking Parts? Arts Practitioners in the Cultural Policy Process*. Unpublished: University of Warwick. PhD.

Worthen, W. B. (1997). *Shakespeare and the Authority of Performance*. Cambridge: Cambridge University Press.

Worthen, W. B. (2003). *Shakespeare and the Force of Modern Performance*. Cambridge: Cambridge University Press.

Worthen. W. B. (2005). *Print and the Poetics of Modern Drama*. Cambridge: Cambridge University Press.

Worthen, W. B. (2010). *Drama: Between Poetry and Performance*. Chichester: Wiley-Blackwell.

Worthen, W. B. (2011). 'Intoxicating Rhythms: Or, Shakespeare, Literary Drama, and Performance (Studies).' *Shakespeare Quarterly* 62 (3): 309–339.

Worthen, W. B. (2014). *Shakespeare Performance Studies*. Cambridge: Cambridge University Press.

Wu, Duncan (Ed.) (2000). *Making plays: Interviews with Contemporary British Dramatists and Their Directors*. Basingstoke: Macmillan.

Wurth, Kiene Brillenburg (Ed.) (2012). *Between Page and Screen: Remaking Literature through Cinema and Cyberspace*. New York: Fordham University Press.

INDEX

Aberg, Maria 92, 93, 110, 112n5
Abrahami, Natalie 92, 112n9
Action Hero 2, 133–135; *Hoke's Bluff* 134–135; *Slap Talk* 70, 134; *Wrecking Ball* 53–54, 69–70
adaptation 4, 27, 86–87, 89–90, 92–93, 101, 102, 105, 108–112
Adebayo, Mojisola 136, 138
Adorno, Theodor 12–13, 82
Alabanza, Travis 138
Almeida Theatre 1, 84n14
alternative theatre 18, 36, 37, 40–44, 51n17, 51n19, 51n20, 51n21, 51n22, 62, 92
Angelaki, Vicky 4
anti-theatrical prejudice 26, 34–35, 39
Archer, William 33, 34, 121
Artaud, Antonin 25, 113n17
Arts Council England 17, 52n26, 52n29
Arts Council of Great Britain 5, 37–46, 51n9, 51n14, 51n16, 51n20, 51n21, 51n25, 51n27
Arts Council of Northern Ireland 19
Arts Council Wales 17
authorship 2, 4–7, 11, 13–15, 20, 28, 30–36, 39, 53–85, 86–88, 91, 92, 94, 96, 98–100, 102–103, 107–108, 110, 111, 121–128, 132, 147

Balogun, Fehinti; *You Just Don't Get It – And It Hurts* 146
Barish, Jonas 25, 26, 32
Barnett, David 8–10, 75

Barrel Organ Theatre; *Nothing* 75
Barthes, Roland 13–14, 20, 54–56, 58, 62, 66, 83n1, 112n14
Beckett, Samuel 12, 16, 127
Bennett, Benjamin 24, 26, 48–49, 103–104
Billington, Michael 19, 66, 87–88, 99, 103, 112n9
Birch, Alice 136; *Anatomy of a Suicide* 132; *[BLANK]* 75, 77, 127–128
Bloomsbury 136, 143
Blythe, Alecky; *Little Revolution* 67–68, 69
Boenisch, Peter M. 8, 88
Bolton, Jacqueline 5, 26, 37, 45, 47, 58, 76
Bottoms, Stephen 7–8, 21n3, 26–27
Bratton, Jacky 31, 33
Breach Theatre 68, 136
British Theatre Consortium 17, 45–46
Bull, John 43, 51n9, 51n10, 51n19, 89, 107
Bush Theatre 48

Callery, Dymphna 6
Carlson, Marvin 14, 90–91, 103, 104, 112n13
censorship 32, 34–36, 38–39, 41, 51n13, 51n14
Chekhov, Anton 62, 86–87, 89, 99–100, 106–110, 112n4
Chisholm, Alex 48, 58
Churchill, Caryl 51n18, 75, 80; *Escaped Alone* 125–126, 150n10, 150n12
Complicite 6, 48, 56, 139; *The Street of Crocodiles* 139–140
copyright 30, 32, 34, 36, 50n7, 56–57, 83n2, 111, 112n12, 124

Cracknell, Carrie 89, 92
Craig, Edward Gordon 25, 35
Craig, Sandy 40–41, 51n19
Creative Scotland 17
Crimp, Martin 9–10, 15, 54, 99; *Attempts on Her Life* 74, 77, 150n9
Crouch, Tim 6–7, 21n3, 54, 136, 146; *The Author* 62–64, 65, 68–69; *I, Malvolio* 144; *Total Immediate Collective Imminent Terrestrial Salvation* 114–115
Curious Directive 140

Dead Centre 16, 92, 106; *Chekhov's First Play* 62, 86–87, 112n2
Derrida, Jacques 13–14, 21, 54, 90–91, 96–97, 104, 112n3, 112n15, 113n17
devising 4, 6–7, 15, 28, 37, 43, 45–47, 49–50, 52n28, 55–58, 62, 74, 105–106, 93, 139
digital texts 3, 15, 21, 115–116, 122, 142–148
director's theatre 58, 88, 99, 103
documentation 15, 21, 105, 117, 135, 137–142, 143, 147
dreamthinkspeak; *The Rest Is Silence* 93

Edgar, David 43, 46, 50n4, 51n18, 52n24, 52n30, 83n2, 135–137, 150n8
Ellams, Inua 16; his version of *Three Sisters* 108–109
Etchells, Tim 52n27, 56, 141

Field, Andy 2, 47–48, 52n32, 148–149
Filter Theatre 93, 101, 111, 140, 151n23
Forced Entertainment 6, 44, 52n27, 56, 93, 139, 140–142, 146; *Emanuelle Enchanted* 141–142
Foucault, Michel 13–14, 54, 57–58, 59, 68–69
Frantic Assembly 6, 18, 56
Freeman, John 6, 28, 138
Freeman, Sara 44, 51n17, 52n25
Freshwater, Helen 6, 34, 35, 39, 44, 56
Fuchs, Elinor 35, 69
funding 3, 5, 17, 36–39, 41–46, 149

Gerald, Jamal 138
Goold, Rupert 92
Greig, David 18, 21n5, 62; *The Yes/No Plays* 145

Hare, David 44, 51n18, 68, 83n5, 88
Harvie, Jen 4, 15–16, 19, 29, 36, 121
Hayles, N. Katherine 143, 147, 151n24

Heddon, Deirdre 4, 55, 56, 113n16
Hickson, Ella; *Oil* 80; *The Writer* 63–65, 68–69, 80, 136–137
Hill-Gibbins, Joe 88, 89, 92, 101, 112n5
Hoffman, Beth 36, 40–41, 47, 52n31
Holmes, Sean 76, 92, 101
Horton, Caroline 138
Hurley, Kieran; *Mouthpiece* 71–72
Hutcheon, Linda 86–87, 90

Ibsen, Henrik 89, 102–103, 106–107
Icke, Robert 92, 100, 150n9; his production of *Hamlet* 100–101, 105; his production of *Oresteia* 1–2, 21n1; his production of *The Wild Duck* 102–103
Ilter, Seda 145–146
intention 3, 5, 13, 20, 26, 27, 53–55, 58–61, 63–69, 70, 72–77, 78, 81, 83–84, 94, 96–97, 99–103, 105–106, 111, 118–120, 126–128, 148
iterability 14, 21, 90, 95–97, 106, 109, 111, 137, 138, 142, 148

Jarcho, Julia 12–13, 82, 142
Jelinek, Elfriede 9, 19, 128
Jestrovic, Silvija 30, 55
Jürs-Munby, Karen 8–9, 69, 72, 75

Kane, Sarah 9–10, 15, 54, 77, 80; *4.48 Psychosis* 74, 59, 128–130, 132, 150n13, 150n14
Kendrick, Ellie; *Hole* 79
Kene, Arinzé 68; *Misty* 65
Kidd, Ben 92
Kimmings, Bryony 137–138, 140, 151n21
Kneehigh 93–94, 98, 140, 151n23; its production of *Cymbeline* 101–102, 105
Komporaly, Jozefina 89, 92

Laera, Margherita 89, 110, 112n1, 113n18
Lamb, Charles 24–25
Lavery, Bryony 56
Lavery, Carl 135, 139
Lee-Jones, Jasmine; *seven methods of killing kylie jenner* 78–79, 133, 151n20
Lehmann, Hans-Thies 8–12, 122
Leigh, Eve; *Midnight Movie* 79
liveness 12, 25–26, 35, 39, 70, 80, 82, 112n15, 138, 145–146
Livingston, Paisley 60, 84n7, 84n9
Lyman, Elizabeth Dyrud 123, 124, 135, 139

Made in China 1–2, 48, 53, 62
Maduro, Daniela Côrtes 143, 147, 151n24

Index

McDonagh, Luke 30–31, 32, 56–57, 83n3, 83n4, 112n12
McDougall, Ellen 92
McDowall, Alistair; *X* 80, 127–128, 132
McGann, Jerome 124–125, 129, 142, 151n24
McKenzie, D. F. 123–124
Mele, Alfred R. 60, 84n7, 84n9
Methuen 121, 135, 143
Milling, Jane 4, 51n9, 55, 56
Mitchell, Katie 89, 92; her production of *The Seagull* 99–100, 107
Mitra, Royona 94
Morin, Emilie 21n3, 75
Mullarkey, Rory 1; *Each Slow Dusk* 81, 85n23; *The Wolf from the Door* 80–81

National Theatre of Great Britain 48, 108, 136, 143
National Theatre of Scotland 17, 48
National Theatre Wales 18, 48
Neilson, Anthony 18, 21n5; *Narrative* 140
New Earth 94
new writing 4, 37–48, 51n11, 52n25, 52n28, 58, 65, 76
Nick Hern Books 135, 136, 143, 150n8

Oberon Books 135–136, 143–144, 150n18, 150n19

Parks, Suzan-Lori 12, 19, 128, 135, 150n17
Payne, Ben 28, 29
Payne, Nick; *Incognito* 125
Pearson, Deborah 16; *The Future Show* 70–71, 84n18
Peters, Julie Stone 30, 50n5, 116–120, 122, 123, 149n2
physical theatre 6–7, 15, 18, 42, 44–47
Pinchbeck, Michael 62, 72, 137
Pinter, Harold 125, 127–128
postdramatic 8–11, 14, 122, 145
poststructuralism 5–6, 13–14, 54, 58
Price, Tim; *Teh Internet is Serious Business* 79
print culture 30, 116, 118, 122, 132
publishing 3, 5, 7, 15, 21, 31, 32, 34, 91, 115–122, 125, 135–139, 143–144, 150n7, 150n11
Puchner, Martin 26, 27, 35–36, 56, 78
Punchdrunk 89, 93

Quigley, Karen 65, 77–78, 80, 81, 85n22, 86–87

Raczka, Lulu; *Nothing* 75
Radosavljević, Duška 4–5, 21n3, 93–94, 102
RashDash 2, 136, 144; *Two Man Show* 113; its version of *Three Sisters* 108–109
Reason, Matthew 138–139, 141, 142
Rebellato, Dan 13–14, 19, 37, 40, 49, 51n9, 54–55, 58, 59, 62, 82, 84n8, 84n16, 112n3, 93, 96, 106
Rice, Emma 92, 93–94, 101, 112n5
Royal Court Theatre 36, 40–41, 46, 48, 51n16, 63, 121, 136, 151n20

Sanders, Julie 89, 109–110, 111, 112n6
Scottee 138
Sh!t Theatre 2, 52n34, 151n26
Shakespeare, William 3, 10, 11, 24–25, 31–32, 33, 50n3, 91, 93, 95, 98, 99, 100–102, 105, 106, 112n4, 112n5, 112n6, 116, 119, 149n2
Shaw, George Bernard 16, 33, 34, 118, 121, 149n5
Shepherd, Simon 26, 29, 30, 32, 34, 40
Sierz, Aleks 4, 19, 51n9, 84n13
Sigal, Sarah 6
Smith, Mark 6, 56
Smith, Stef; *Human Animals* 132; *Swallow* 75
Spender, George 136–137, 150n9, 150n19
stage directions 22, 39, 63, 65, 71, 75, 77, 78–79, 80–81, 85n22, 118, 120–121, 126–127, 139–140
Stephens, John Russell 32–33, 50n7, 119, 120, 121
Stephens, Simon 58, 85n21, 89; *Pornography* 74–75, 76–77, 80; *Song from Far Away* 22–23
supplement 9, 14, 21, 25, 61, 90–91, 104–106, 112n3, 148
Svendsen, Zoë 89, 101

Talawa 94, 112n7
Tara Arts 94–95, 112n7; its production of *Macbeth* 95, 98
textual studies 123–124, 143
Thompson, Selina 138, 151n22
Tomlin, Liz 6, 8, 10–11, 14, 44, 47, 51n9, 51n10, 82
Tribe Arts 94
tucker green, debbie 128, 150n14, 150n15; *random* 130–131; *stoning mary* 131–132
Turner, Cathy 7, 48, 51n9

Ukaegbu, Victor 94
unstageable 25, 61, 65, 76, 77–82

van Hove, Ivo 22–23, 50n2, 88
verbatim theatre 4, 67–68, 139
Verma, Jatinder 94–95

Wilde, Oscar 16, 33, 50n8, 120
Wittgenstein, Ludwig 73, 84n16

Womack, Peter 26, 29, 30, 32, 34, 40
Wooster Group, The 19, 62, 84n12, 92
Worthen, W. B. 11–12, 23, 31, 50n3, 66, 90, 91, 97–98, 99, 104, 116–119, 122–123, 125–127, 130–132, 139, 140, 147, 149n5
Wurth, Kiene Brillenburg 143, 146

ZU-UK 93

For Product Safety Concerns and Information please contact our EU
representative GPSR@taylorandfrancis.com
Taylor & Francis Verlag GmbH, Kaufingerstraße 24, 80331 München, Germany

www.ingramcontent.com/pod-product-compliance
Lightning Source LLC
Chambersburg PA
CBHW051400290426
44108CB00015B/2092